THE
COMPLETE
BOOK
OF
CARD GAMES

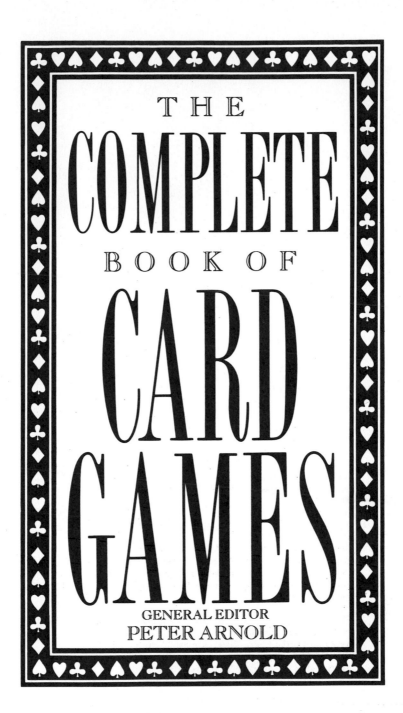

THE
COMPLETE
BOOK OF
CARD
GAMES

GENERAL EDITOR
PETER ARNOLD

OCTOPUS BOOKS

First published in 1989 by
Octopus Books Limited
Michelin House
81 Fulham Road
London SW3 6RB

Some of the material in this book first appeared in *The Hamlyn
Illustrated Book of Card Games* (Hamlyn 1973) and was reprinted in
The Complete Book of Indoor Games (Hamlyn 1981). Other material first
appeared in *The Book of Games* (Newnes Books 1985). Full details are
given in the Introduction

ISBN 0 7064 3893 0

Typeset by MS Filmsetting Limited, Frome, Somerset
Printed in Portugal

CONTENTS

INTRODUCTION

The card games selected for inclusion in this book include games which have stood the test of time and have so caught public fancy as to have earned the right to be included and others which, while they have not become so widespread, nevertheless have their followers and will repay those who make the effort to learn them.

The bulk of the descriptions were written by the late George F. Hervey, and appeared originally in a book entitled *The Hamlyn Illustrated Book of Card Games* (Hamlyn 1973). Later many were incorporated into a book which embraced other types of indoor games entitled *The Complete Book of Indoor Games* (Hamlyn 1981). They are reprinted with minor changes of style and presentation.

Mr Hervey's introduction to the former book outlined his intention and paragraphs from it which are relevant to this volume are reprinted here:

Card games do not admit of a precise arrangement. In this book they have been arranged according to the number of players who may take part at one table. As, however, most card games can be played, in one form or another, by a varying number of players, it is more correct to say that the games have been arranged according to the number of players for which they are best suited. But party games and banking games are grouped separately, and among the party games some will be found suitable for members of the younger generation who may find that playing a game of cards is a less noisy pastime than playing an electric guitar. It is not an ideal arrangement, but it has the merit of convenience, and is less arbitrary than arranging the games in alphabetical order, and more practical than arranging them by their family resemblances. Most card games have a number of variations. Only the more popular ones have been given a place in this book, and, with some rare and inevitable exceptions, descriptions of them follow the description of the parent game.

The aim of the present writer is nothing higher than to explain how the various games are played; and when no authoritative organization has laid down the scoring, rules of play and appropriate penalties for breaking them, the practice that he recommends is that of the majority of experienced players. If here and there he has broken form and given a few hints on skilful play, it is not to compete with the text books, but because without them the bare bones would be unreadable. When the play of a deal is summarized, the standard practice of underlining the card that wins the trick (the player leading to the next trick) is followed.

George Harvey was one of the best writers on card games and, although he points out that his aim was 'nothing higher than to explain how the various games are played', his descriptions of sample games nevertheless convey the elements of good play.

Other games have been added to those originally described by George Hervey. Some first appeared in a book entitled *The Book of Games* (general editor Peter Arnold, Newnes Books 1985). These were written by Peter Arnold (Gin Rummy) and by Matthew Macfadyen (Skat, Canasta, Miss Milligan, Terrace and Three Blind Mice). Some descriptions were specially written for this book by Peter Arnold: Eights, *Le Truc*, Russian Bank, Calabrasella, Five Hundred, 500 Rum, Oklahoma, Schafkopf, Cinch, Quinto, Crazy Eights, Lift Smoke, Panguingue, Beleaguered Castle and Golf.

The descriptions of these games follow the principles set out by George Hervey. It is hoped that readers will try games with which they are at present unfamiliar, and that they will find them satisfying.

ALL FOURS

*A*LL FOURS *was mentioned in Charles Cotton's* Compleat Gamester *in 1674 as being 'much played in Kent'. It became popular in the United States, where it acquired other names such as Seven-up, High-low Jack or Old Sledge.*

NUMBER OF PLAYERS

All Fours is a game for two players, but it can be adapted for four as described later.

CARDS

The full pack of 52 cards is used, the cards ranking from Ace (high) to 2 (low).

Six cards are dealt in lots of three to both players, and the 13th card is turned up to determine the trump suit.

The deal passes in rotation.

THE PLAY

The game is won by he who first scores seven points. The points are scored as follows:

High. The player who is dealt the highest trump in play scores one point.

Low. The player who is dealt the lowest trump in play scores one point.

Jack. The player who wins the Jack of trumps (if it is in play) scores one point.

Game. Each player counts the honours among the tricks he has won, and, counting the Ace as four, the King as three, the Queen as two, the Jack as one and the 10 as ten, the player with the highest total scores one point. If there is equality the non-dealer scores the point.

The points are not counted until the end of the deal, but they should be understood from the start because they illustrate the object of the game.

The non-dealer now declares whether he will stand or beg. If he says 'I stand' he accepts the turned-up card as the trump suit and play begins. If he says 'I beg' he rejects the turned-up card as the trump suit, and the dealer must either accept or refuse the proposal to make another suit trumps. To refuse he says 'Take one'. The non-dealer then scores one point for gift and play begins. To accept he says 'I run the cards'. He deals three more cards to his opponent and three to himself, and turns up the next card to determine the trump suit. If this is the same suit as the original trump suit, he runs the cards again, and continues to run them until a different trump suit is turned up. In the rare, but not impossible, event of the pack being exhausted without a different trump suit being turned up, there is a redeal by the same player. If the turned-up card is a Jack, the dealer scores one point, and if, when the cards are run, the turned-up card is again a Jack, the dealer again scores one point.

Play begins when the trump suit has been determined, and if the cards have been run, the players first discard from their hands enough cards to reduce the number held to six. The non-dealer leads to the first trick. His opponent must follow suit or trump. Unlike at most games, however, a player may trump even though he is able to follow suit, but he must not discard if he holds either a card of the suit led or a trump. If he does he has revoked and his opponent scores one point.

The winner of a trick leads to the next, and so on until all six tricks have been played. The players then turn up their tricks and score for High, Low, Jack and Game.

These four scoring features are fundamental to the game and are counted whenever it is possible to do so. If, for example, there is only one trump in play it counts two points, because it is both High and Low.

ALL FOURS FOR FOUR PLAYERS

This version is played with two players playing in partnership against the other two in partnership.

The method of play is the same as in the parent game, except that only the dealer and the opponent on his left (eldest hand) look at their cards to determine the trump suit. When they have done this, but not before, the other two players look at their cards and come into the game for play.

If a player exposes a card it is liable to be called by an opponent i.e. the player must play it at the first legitimate opportunity.

SEVEN-UP

This is a variation of the parent game that takes its name from the method of scoring.

Both players (or both sides if four are playing) begin with seven counters each. Every time that a point is scored the player (or side) that wins it puts a counter aside, and the player (or side) who first gets rid of his counters wins the game. If both go out in the same deal, the winner is he who first counts out when the points are scored for High, Low, Jack and Game.

ALL FIVES

This variation of the parent game is played for 61 points up. For convenience the score is best kept on a cribbage board.

The mechanics of the game are the same as those of the parent game, and points are pegged when the following trumps are won in a trick: Ace four points, King three points, Queen two points, Jack one point, 10 ten points and 5 five points. After the hand has been played, the honours are counted as in the parent game, to determine the point for Game, with the addition that the player who has won the 5 of trumps scores five points for it.

BEZIQUE

*B*EZIQUE *was popular in France and came to England in the late 19th century, where the Prince of Wales helped popularize it before he succeeded to the throne. Americans generally prefer the development from it called Pinocle.*

NUMBER OF PLAYERS

Bezique is for two players, but can be adapted for three or four as described later.

CARDS

Bezique is played with two packs of cards from which the 6s, 5s, 4s, 3s and 2s have been removed, but can be played with three, four, six or eight packs as described later. The cards rank in the order: Ace, 10, King, Queen, Jack, 9, 8, 7.

Eight cards are dealt to each player — three, two and three at a time. The remaining 48 (the stock) are placed face downwards on the table, and the top card exposed alongside to denote the trump suit; if it is a 7 dealer scores 10 points.

THE PLAY

The non-dealer leads to the first trick. As in most games the winner of a trick leads to the next, but it is a feature of bezique that a player is under no obligation to follow suit to the card led. The object of the game is to score points for declaring certain cards and combinations of cards. The declarations, and the points that may be scored for them, are as follows:

Double bezique Two ♠Q and two ◇J (or ♣Q and ♡J if spades or diamonds are trumps) 500

Sequence in trumps A, 10, K, Q,
J of the trump suit   250
Any 4 Aces   100
Any 4 Kings   80
Any 4 Queens   60
Any 4 Jacks   40
Bezique ♠Q (or ♣Q if spades
or diamonds are trumps) and
◇J (or ♡J if spades or
diamonds are trumps)   40
Royal marriage K and Q of
trump suit   40
Common marriage K and Q of
same plain suit   20

A player scores 10 points if he holds a 7 of the trump suit and exchanges it for the turn-up card; and 10 points are scored for playing a 7 of the trump suit.

When a player has won a trick he may declare by placing the appropriate cards face upwards on the table. He may make as many declarations as he chooses, always provided that the declarations do not involve the same cards. If the exposed cards show more than one declaration the player must announce which declaration he intends to score, and leave the other to be scored when he wins another trick. A card that has once scored cannot again be used to form part of a similar declaration. As an example, a player may expose ♠K, ♠Q, ◇J score 40 for bezique and announce 'Twenty to come' meaning that the next time he wins a trick he will score 20 points for the common marriage of the ♠K and ♠Q. He may not expose a second ◇J and score bezique with the ♠Q. The cards that have been declared, and so

exposed on the table, remain a part of the player's hand and he may play them to later tricks.

Tricks should be gathered and kept by the player who wins them, because at the end of a deal a player scores ten points for every Ace and every 10 that he has won. They are known as brisques.

When both players have played to a trick they replenish their hands from the stock: winner takes the top card, loser the next.

When the stock is exhausted the last eight tricks are played, and the game takes on a rather different character. Now, if a player has a card of the suit that has been led he must play it, and he must win a trick if he is able to. No further declarations may be made, and the aim of the player is to win brisques and the last trick, for which 10 points are scored.

The deal passes to the other player, and so alternately, until one of them has reached an agreed number of points, usually 2,000.

The score cannot be kept satisfactorily with pencil on paper. It is best to use the special bezique markers that take the form of indicators marked as clocks on thin cardboard.

The following deal, played by two experienced players, illustrates many of the finer points of good play.

South dealt, and the hands were as in the illustration opposite.

Clubs were trumps, the ♣10 having been turned up.

The turn-up card is important because it is a sequence card, and a high

North   South

one at that since it ranks immediately below the Ace.

The main features of North's hand are that he holds two sequence cards (the ♣Q and ♣J), a 7 of trumps to exchange for the valuable 10, and three Queens, which put him well on the way to a declaration of four Queens.

The main features of South's hand are a bezique Queen (the ♠Q) and three low trumps, including the 7; but, of course, as yet South does not know that North holds both the Queens of trumps, so that a sequence for him is impossible. It is South's lead, and it is necessary for him to win a trick to exchange the ♣7 for the ♣10. An inexperienced player might be tempted to lead an indifferent card, such as the ♥7, hoping that North will have nothing to declare and will refuse to win the trick. This, however, is very artless play, and the better play is for South to lead his highest trump because it compels North to use a sequence card if he wants to take the trick and make a declaration. So...

Trick 1 South led the ♣9. North, who appreciated the importance of the turn-up card, won with the ♣Q. This was North's best play, although it suffers from the defect that it reduces

North's best chance of declaring four Queens, and it informs South that he has virtually no hope of a sequence because North would hardly play a sequence card if he lacked a duplicate. North exchanged the ♣7 for the turn-up card, and scored 10 points. He drew the ♣K (giving him no fewer than four of the five sequence cards), and South the ♥9.

Trick 2 North led the ◇9, and South played the ♥7. North declared the royal marriage and scored 40 points, making his total 50 points. North drew the ♥K, and South the ♥A.

Trick 3 North led the ♥7, and South played the ◇9. North declared the common marriage in hearts and scored 20 points, making his total 70 points. North drew the ♣A, and South the ♥J.

Trick 4 North now held a sequence, but, in order to declare it, he had first to win a trick. A heart must be led, and he chose the Queen. Undoubtedly it was the best lead. The ♥A is not a good lead, because, if trumped, it will cost North a brisque; and it is better for North to save for four Kings, instead of for four Queens, because not only does it gain 20 more points, but North

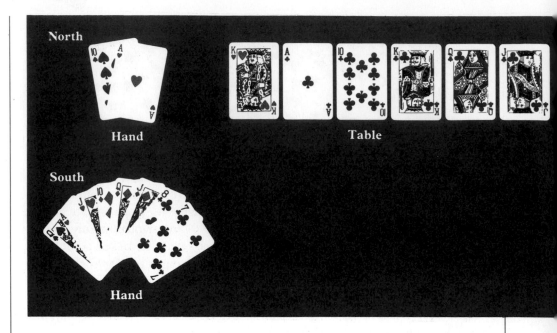

North

Hand

Table

South

Hand

had already played a Queen so the chance of drawing a Queen was slightly less than that of drawing a King. South played the ♡9. North declared his ♧A,10,J, and scored 250 points for the sequence, giving him a total of 320 points. South had not yet scored. North drew the ♤10, and South the ◇J.

At this point the hands were as in the illustration above.

Trick 5 North's trumps were no longer of vital importance to him, and could be played if desired. The two Kings were important because North had made up his mind to save for Kings, and it is an error of tactics to change one's mind during the game. The Aces and 10s were important, because they furnish brisques. So North led the ♧J. South had a bezique in his hand, but unfortunately he could

not win the trick and declare it. The best he could do was to play the ♡J. North drew the ◇8, and South the ◇Q.

Trick 6 North led the ◇8. South won with the ◇10, putting away a brisque for himself, and declared bezique. South's 40 points for bezique was his first score, and he was a long way behind North's 320 points. South drew the ♡10, and North the ♧A.

Trick 7 South now had the lead. He chose the ♧7 and scored 10 points, making his total 50. It was the best lead, because the lead of either heart would probably be trumped and a brisque lost. He had to save for four Queens, and the ◇J was out of the question since there was always the possibility of declaring double bezique. North was more or less compelled to win with the ♧Q. North drew the ♢8, and South the ♧Q.

Trick 8 North led the ♢8, and South won with the ♧8 and declared four Queens (60 points) giving him a total of 110. North, with a total of 320 points, was still well ahead, but he noted with some concern that South would be able to declare double bezique if he was lucky enough to draw the other ♢J. South drew the ♧9, and North the ♧8.

Trick 9 South led the ♧9, and North won with the ♧10. North drew the ♧J, and South the ♧8.

Trick 10 North led the ♧8, and South played the other ♧8. North drew the ♡8, and South the ♡J.

Trick 11 North led the ♡8, and South won with the ♡10. South drew the ♢K, and North the ♡8.

At this point the hands were as in the illustration below.

The score was North 320 points, South 110 points.

Trick 12 South led the ♡J, and North played the ♡8. It would not have been good play for North to win with the ♡A because, though this would have given him a brisque, it is better for North to save for four Aces now that he held three. South laid down his ♢K and scored a common marriage (20 points), giving him a total of 130 points. South drew the ♧7, and North the ♧A.

Trick 13 South led the ♧7. North won with the ♧J, and declared four Aces (100 points). This raised his total to 420, and he had a good lead on South, whose score was only 130 points. North drew the ♧J, and South the ♧9.

The hands were now as in the illustration overleaf.

South's hand with its three bezique cards was not without possibilities.

Trick 14 North led the ♧J, and South played the ♧9. North drew the ♧J, and South the ♡9.

Trick 15 North led the ♧J, and

15

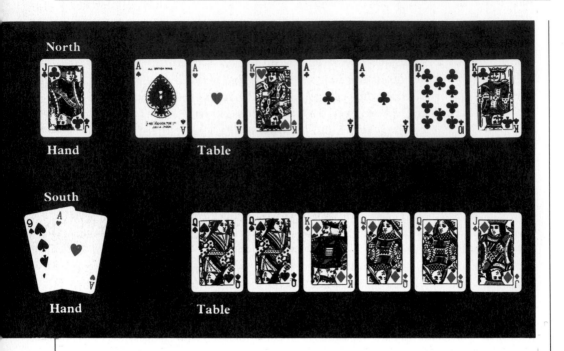

South played the ♡9. North drew the ♣K, and South the ◇J.

Trick 16 Now, of course, the whole game changed, because South held a double bezique, though he had to win a trick before he could declare it. If the stock is nearly exhausted it is proper for North to lead trumps in an attempt to prevent South from winning a trick. It was, however, too early in the game for these tactics, so North led the ♠A, hoping that it would not be trumped, and South, who had no trump in his hand, discarded the married ◇Q. North drew the ◇10, and South the ♣10, a vital card.

Trick 17 North, who by this time suspected that South held double bezique, led the ♡A, hoping that South would still not be able to trump. This time, however, he was doomed to disappointment, because, of course, South was able to win with the ♣10 and declare double bezique. The score of 500 points for double bezique raised South's total to 630 and gave him a lead of 210 points because North's score was only 420 points. South drew the ♠A, and North the ♠K.

Trick 18 South, who had no further use for his bezique Jacks, led a ◇J. North won with the ◇10 and declared four Kings (80 points), raising his score to 500 points. North drew the ♣9, and South the ◇A.

Trick 19 North led the ♣9, and South played the ◇J. North drew the ♣8, and South the ◇A.

The hands were now as at the top of the opposite page.

Trick 20 North now suspected that South was on the point of declaring

North

Hand

Table

South

Hand

Table

four Aces. His tactics, therefore, had to be aggressive, and, since the other ♣10 had been played, his trumps were all winners, and he played them to prevent South from declaring. North led the ♣A, and South played the ♠Q. North drew one ◇7 and South the other.

Trick 21 North led the ♣A, and South played the ◇7. North drew the ♡Q, and South the ♡10.

Trick 22 North led the ♣10, and South played the ♠Q. North declared the common marriage in hearts (20 points) raising his total to 520 points. North drew the ♠K, and South the ♠7.

Trick 23 North led the ♣K, and South played the ♠7. North drew the ◇K, and South the ♡10.

Trick 24 (last trick) North led the ♣K, and South played the ◇Q. North scored 10 points for the last trick, bringing his total to 530 points. South's score was 630 points, and from the time that he had declared double bezique North had little chance to overtake him. He did well, however, to prevent South from declaring four Aces and so adding another 100 points to his score. North drew the ♡K, and South picked up the ♣7 exposed on the table.

After picking up their cards from the table, the hands of the two players were as below.

North   **South**

The play to the last eight tricks was:

North	South
♡K	♡A
◇7	◇A
◇K	◇A
♤K	♤A
♡Q	♡10
♤K	♤10
♣8	◇K
♡K	♣7

South was lucky to win all his brisques, giving him a score of 100 points; North won six brisques for a total of 60 points. The final score, therefore, was South 730 points, North 590 points.

Altogether a fine deal, and one worth studying, because it illustrates the importance of playing for double bezique. For the first half of the deal North was well ahead, but after South had won the highest prize that the game has to offer, it was practically impossible for North to win the deal, and all his efforts had to be directed towards preventing South from gaining an even bigger lead. North played well to reduce South's lead of 210 points (gained at the 17th trick) to 140.

RUBICON BEZIQUE

This version of the game has the advantage over the parent game that, as long ago as 1887, a committee of the Portland Club drew up a code of laws under which it should be played.

It is very similar to the parent game, and, like it, is a game for two players, but four packs of cards, not two, are used, and there are some differences in the preliminaries, the scoring and the routine of the game.

In the preliminaries, nine cards (not eight) are dealt to each player, either singly or in threes, and there is no turn-up of the top card of the stock, so that the peculiar value of the 7 of trumps is lost.

The scoring is the same as in the parent game, with the following additions:

Carte blanche a hand without a court card	50

Both players are entitled to score it. Before a player can score, however, he must show his hand to his opponent. Thereafter, each time that he draws a card from the stock he may show it to his opponent and score 50 points if it is not a court card.

Ordinary sequence A, 10, K, Q, J of any suit other than the trump suit	150
Triple bezique Three ♤Q and three ◇J (or ♣Q and ♡J if either spades or diamonds are trumps)	1,500
Quadruple bezique Four ♤Q and four ◇J (or ♣Q and ♡J if either spades or diamonds are trumps)	4,500
Last trick	50

The routine differs from that of the parent game in the following essentials:

A game is complete in one deal.

Trumps are determined by the first marriage or sequence declared by either player.

The tricks are left exposed on the

table until such time as a brisque is played. After this the tricks are gathered and turned as usual.

If a card is played from a declared combination, subsequently the combination may be filled by adding an appropriate card and the declaration scored again.

If a player has declared two marriages in the same suit, he may rearrange the Kings and Queens on the table and declare two more.

Brisques are disregarded for scoring except to break a tie or to save a player from being rubiconed.

If a player fails to score 1,000 points he is rubiconed. His score is added to (not subtracted from) that of his opponent, who adds a further 1,300 points (not 500) for the game. Further, if a player fails to score 100 points, the winner adds an extra 100 points to his score.

BEZIQUE FOR THREE PLAYERS

This is played with three packs of cards, and the players all compete against each other. The play is the same as in the parent game with the addition of a score of 1,500 points for triple bezique.

BEZIQUE FOR FOUR PLAYERS

This is played with six packs of cards, or 192 cards in all. Two play in partnership against the other two.

The dealer places 24 cards face downwards in a pile on the table, and on this he places a marker so that the players will be warned when the stock is nearing exhaustion. He deals nine cards to each of the four players and places the remainder of the pack (132 cards in all) face downwards on top of the marker.

In general, the play follows that described under rubicon bezique but there are some differences in the scoring and in declaring.

Carte blanche   100

Double carte blanche Both partners being dealt hands without a court card   50

Quintuple bezique Five ♠Q and ◇J (or ♣Q and ♡J if either spades or diamonds are trumps)   13,500

Sextuple bezique is so unlikely that no score has been allotted to it. Should it occur, the correct score is   40,500

Any 4 Aces   1,000

Any 4 Tens   900

Any 4 Kings   800

Any 4 Queens   600

Any 4 Jacks   400

The game bonus is 1,000 points, the rubicon 2,500 points and brisques are disregarded.

In all other essentials the scoring is the same as in rubicon bezique. The partnership principle, however, introduces two new features in the methods of declaring combinations. First, after winning a trick, a player may either declare or leave it to his partner to do so. Secondly, a player may declare a combination either with his own cards (including those on the table already declared by him) or with one or more of his own cards and one or more of his partner's declared cards. Indeed, since a player holds only nine cards, quintuple bezique (and sextuple bezique if it occurs) can only be declared with the help of partner.

The player on the left of the dealer leads to the first trick.

Beyond these additions, the play follows that of rubicon bezique.

SIX-PACK BEZIQUE

This version, sometimes, but rarely, known as Chinese bezique, is a game for two players, and generally considered the most popular variation of the family. Sir Winston Churchill was a keen player and an able exponent of the game.

Six packs are shuffled together and both players lift a part of the pack and show the bottom cards to determine choice of seat and deal. The one who shows the higher card has the choice, and would be advised to pass the deal to his opponent because there is a slight disadvantage in dealing. If equal cards are shown the players cut again.

The dealer takes a number of cards at random off the top of the pack, and the non-dealer estimates how many have been taken. If his estimate proves correct he scores 150 points. The dealer deals 12 cards, one by one, to his opponent and himself, and scores 250

points if he has taken exactly 24 cards from the top of the pack.

There is no turn-up to determine the trump suit. It is determined, as in rubicon bezique, by the first declared marriage or sequence by either player.

The declarations are scored for as follows:

Sequence in trumps	250
Sequence in plain suit	150
Royal marriage	40
Common marriage	20
Bezique	40
Double bezique	500
Triple bezique	1,500
Quadruple bezique	4,500

If spades are trumps bezique is ♠Q and ♦J; if diamonds are trumps ♦Q and ♠J; if hearts are trumps ♡Q and ♣J; and if clubs are trumps ♣Q and ♡J.

Four aces in trumps	1,000
4 10s in trumps	900
4 Kings in trumps	800
4 Queens in trumps	600
4 Jacks in trumps	400
Any 4 Aces	100
Any 4 Kings	80
Any 4 Queens	60
Any 4 Jacks	40
Carte blanche	250

The non-dealer leads to the first trick. It is not compulsory to follow suit, and the card that is led holds the trick unless a higher card of the same suit is played or a trump is played to the lead of a plain suit. As points are not scored for brisques, nor for winning tricks, the tricks are not gathered and turned but left face upwards on the table in a pile. The winner of a trick may score for a declaration. He takes the top card of the stock (the loser takes the next card of the stock) and leads to the next trick.

A declaration is made by placing the appropriate cards face upwards on the table. They are left there and are available for play as though in the hand of the player. Declarations are scored when made, and the same card may be counted in a declaration more than once.

No declaration may be made after the last two cards of the stock have been drawn. The players then pick up any cards they have on the table and play off the last 12 tricks. As in the parent game, a player must now follow suit to the card led, and must win a trick if he is able to.

Every deal constitutes a game, and the player with the higher score wins. He adds 1,000 points to his score, and rubicons his opponent if he has failed to score 3,000 points.

EIGHT-PACK BEZIQUE

This game is identical Six-Pack Bezique except for the increased number of cards and the following differences in the routine and scoring:

1. Each player is dealt 15 cards.
2. The scores for beziques are:

Bezique	50
Double bezique	500
Triple bezique	1,500
Quadruple bezique	4,500
Quintuple bezique	9,000

3. In the trump suit the scores are:

5 Aces	2,000
5 Tens	1,800
5 Kings	1,600
5 Queens	1,200
5 Jacks	800

4. A player who fails to score 5,000 points is rubiconed.

CALIFORNIA JACK

CALIFORNIA JACK is a game arising from All Fours, but it uses the full pack rather than the shortened pack, and is more complex and skilful. It is thought by most to be better than the original game.

A good California Jack hand. There are two good cards for trick-winning and three for losing.

NUMBER OF PLAYERS

California Jack can only be played satisfactorily by two players.

CARDS

California Jack is played with the full pack of 52 cards, the Ace ranking high, the 2 low.

The non-dealer cuts the pack and exposes the bottom card to decide the trump suit. The dealer deals six cards, one at a time, to each player, and places the remainder of the pack face upwards on the table, taking the precaution to square it up so that only the top card can be seen.

THE PLAY

The non-dealer leads to the first trick. The winner of a trick takes the top card of the stock, the loser the next card. A player must follow suit if he can, and he loses one point if he revokes.

When the stock is exhausted and the last six cards have been played, the tricks won by each player are examined, and one point is scored for winning High (Ace of trumps), Low (2 of trumps), Jack (Jack of trumps) and Game (majority of points, counting each Ace won as four points, each King as three points, each Queen as two points, each Jack as one point and each 10 as ten points).

The game is won by the player who first scores ten points.

The player should aim to keep both winning and losing cards in his hand because if the exposed card of the stock is valuable he will wish to win it, but if it is not, he will wish to lose the trick on the chance of the next card of the stock being a more valuable one. The 10s, of course, are the cards to go for.

SHASTA SAM

This is a variation of the game in which the stock is placed face downwards on the table instead of face upwards. It is a less skilful game as, of course, the winner of a trick does not know what card he will draw.

CASINO

*C*ASINO *is a game of Italian origin, sometimes spelt as Cass-ino, but this is believed to be an early printing error which was per-petuated. The game possibly takes its name from the casino — where gambling takes place.*

NUMBER OF PLAYERS

Although Casino is essentially a game for two, it may be played by three or four. The only difference is that if three players take part they all play against each other, and if four take part two play in partnership against the other two.

CARDS

The full pack of 52 cards is used.

The numeral cards count at their pip values. The Ace counts as 1, and the court cards are used only for pairing: they have no pip value.

The dealer deals two cards face downwards to his opponent, then two face upwards to the table, and then two face downwards to himself. This is repeated, so that both players end with four cards each, and there are four exposed cards (the layout) on the table.

The remaining 40 cards (the stock) are placed face downwards on the table.

The object of the game is to take in cards which score as follows:

◇ 10 (great casino)	2
♠ 2 (little casino)	1
Majority of cards (27 or more)	3
Majority of spades (7 or more)	1
Aces	1
All cards in layout (the sweep)	1

THE PLAY

Each player in turn, beginning with the non-dealer, plays a card until both players have exhausted their four cards. When this occurs, the same dealer deals four more cards to his opponent and four to himself, but none to the layout. Play continues in this way until the stock has been exhausted. In all, therefore, there are six deals to complete the game, and before making the final deal the dealer must announce it. If he does not, his opponent has a right to cancel the deal.

When a player plays a card from his hand he has the choice of several plays.

He may *Pair*. If, for example, there are one or more 5s in the layout, he may play a 5 from his hand and take it up as a trick with all the other 5s in the layout. A court card, however, may be paired with only one card of the same rank at a time.

He may *Combine*. It is an extension of pairing that allows a player to pick up cards from the layout of the total pip value of a card in his hand. Thus a player playing a 9 may take up a 7 and a 2, or a 6 and a 3 from the layout, or all four cards if they are in the layout.

He may *Build*. He may play a card to a card in the layout to make up a total that he is in a position to take with another card in his hand. If, for example, a player holds a 9 and a 2, and there is a 7 in the layout, he may build the 2 on the 7, so that the next time he plays (provided his opponent has not

forestalled him) he may play the 9 and take all three cards as a trick. The build may be continued by either player up to a maximum of five cards, but a build can be taken only as a unit. The player who has built must take up the combination when next it is his turn to play, unless he prefers to win something else, or he decides to make another build.

He may *Call*. It is an extension of building that allows a player to earmark one or more combinations for subsequent capture. Suppose, for example, a player holds in his hand two 8s and that there is a 5 and a 3 in the layout (see illustration). He could, of course, combine one of his 8s with the 5 and 3 in the layout, but this would

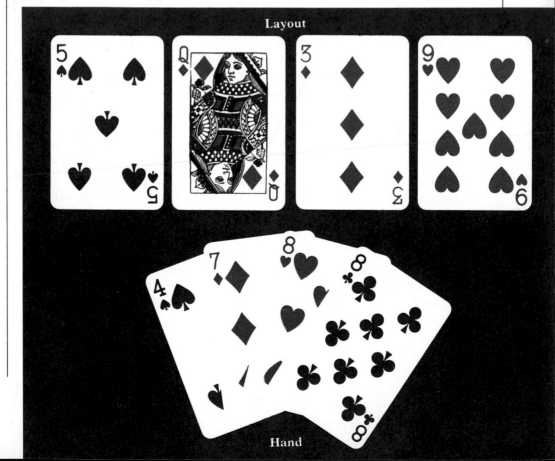

Layout

Hand

only give him three cards in the trick. The better play, therefore, is for him to play one of his 8s to the layout and announce 'Eight'. Then, when next it is his turn to play, provided his opponent has not forestalled him, he may play his other 8 and pick up all four cards in the trick.

When a player cannot pair, combine, build or call, he must play one of his cards to the layout. It is known as trailing. It is advisable to play a low card, but not an Ace, little casino or a spade.

When the last eight cards have been played any left in the layout are the property of the winner of the final trick, but it does not count as a sweep.

This ends the game, except for the formality of the players examining their tricks and counting their scores.

There is no penalty for making a build incorrectly, or for capturing cards to which a player is not entitled, because his opponent has the opportunity to see the error and demand that it is corrected. If, however, a player makes a build when he has no card in his hand to capture it or trails when he has a build in the layout, he automatically forfeits the game. If a card is faced in the pack, or if the dealer when dealing exposes a card, other than when dealing cards to the layout, the exposed card is played to the layout and the dealer plays the hand with fewer than four cards.

Casino is sometimes considered a game for children. It is, however, very far from being so. Among card players it is widely spoken of as one of the best

of all two-handed games and it is often played for high stakes. To be successful a player needs an elephantine memory, and the capacity to deduce from the card played by an opponent what cards he is most likely to be holding in his hand.

ROYAL CASINO

This is an improvement on the parent game because the court cards play a more important part. The Aces count 1 or 14 (at the option of the player), the Kings 13, the Queens 12 and the Jacks 11, and they may be used for combining and building. Thus an 8 and a 4 may be taken with a Queen, a 6, a 4 and a 3 with a King, and so on.

Twenty-one points constitute the game.

DRAW CASINO

In this version of the game, after the first round of a deal, the 40 undealt cards are placed face downwards on the table to form a stock. Then each player, after playing, draws a card from the stock to bring the number of cards in his hand up to four. When the stock is exhausted the hands are played out and the count made as in the parent game.

SPADE CASINO

This version may be played either as royal casino or as the parent game, with the addition that the Ace, Jack and ♠2 count two points each, and all the other spades one point each.

Game is 61 points, and it is convenient and customary to keep the score on a cribbage board.

COLONEL

COLONEL *is a version of Coon Can (see page 164), adapted for fewer players and with fewer cards.*

NUMBER OF PLAYERS

Colonel is for two players only.

CARDS

The full standard pack of 52 cards is used, cards ranking from Ace (high) to 2 (low).

The players cut for deal, and the higher deals. Each player is dealt ten cards, one at a time. The rest of the pack is placed face downwards on the table, between the players, and the top card (known as the optional card) is turned face upwards and placed alongside the stock.

THE PLAY

The object of the game is to make sequences of the same suit, or threes or fours of a kind, and declare them by placing them face upwards on the table. The hand ends when one of the players has declared all his cards. A sequence must be of at least three cards, but once it has been declared either player, in his turn, may add to it. In the same way, if three of a kind has been declared, either player in his turn may add the fourth card to it.

The non-dealer plays first. He takes into his hand either the optional card or the top card of the stock. He declares any sequences, or threes or fours of a kind that he holds, and discards a card from his hand. The discard is placed on top of the optional card, or in its place if the optional card has been taken up. The dealer plays next. He has the choice of taking the card that the non-dealer has discarded or the top card of the stock.

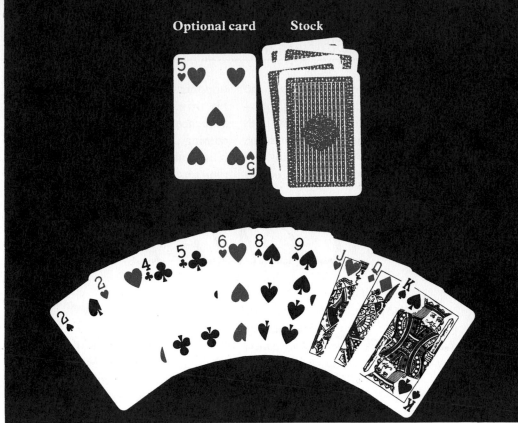

It would be good play to take the ♡5 as it gives chances of a set of 5s or a sequence in hearts. The ♧K might be discarded.

It will be seen, therefore, that the routine of the play is very simple. Each player in turn takes into his hand either the top card of the stock or the card his opponent has discarded, he then declares any sequences, threes or fours that he holds, or adds to those already declared either by himself or his opponent, and then discards a card from his hand. In a sequence the Ace is high. A player is not under compulsion to declare: indeed it is good play to refuse to declare for as long as possible in an attempt to declare one's hand all at once. This way one's opponent has less chance to declare all his cards, but it is to be borne in mind that a player who fails to declare when he can runs the risk that his opponent will go out before him.

When a player has declared all his cards, his opponent loses points for every card remaining in his hand, the Ace, King, Queen and Jack counting as 10 points each, the remaining cards their pip values.

If the stock is exhausted before either player has declared all his cards, both players show the cards remaining in their hands and the player with the lower total wins the hand. He adds to the score the total of his opponent's hand less that of his own.

A refinement of the game is that before the stock is exhausted either player may challenge. If the challenge is rejected by the opponent, the hand continues to be played out. If, however, the challenge is accepted, both players expose their hands and the player with the lower total wins. He adds to his score the total of his opponent's hand without deducting his own. If the right cards to make sequences and threes of a kind are not coming to a player, it is good play for him to fill his hand with low cards and then challenge.

COMET

OMET was probably invented around 1759 (when Halley's Comet reappeared and caused great excitement).

NUMBER OF PLAYERS

Comet is for two players, but a variation called Commit (no doubt a mistake by an early printer, but nevertheless useful) can be played by up to five players, and is described later.

CARDS

Two 52-card packs, with the same design on their backs, are used alternately. The packs must be prepared by rejecting all the Aces, putting all the red cards into one pack and all the black cards into another, and interchanging a red and a black 9.

Eighteen cards are dealt to each player, one at a time, and the remaining 12 cards are put aside; they play no part in the game.

THE PLAY

The non-dealer begins the game by playing one of his cards, face upwards, to the centre of the table. The players then, alternately, build up on it by rank only. Suits are disregarded. Any number of cards, provided they are of the proper rank, may be played in one turn. The four 8s, for example, may be built on a 7, the four Jacks on a 10, and so on. When a player is unable to build it is a stop, and his opponent begins a new sequence by playing any card he chooses. Obviously a King is always a stop.

The 9 of the opposite colour is called the comet. It may represent any card that the holder chooses, but may be played only in turn. It is a stop, and the player who plays it begins a new sequence.

The player who is first to get rid of all the cards in his hand is the winner. He scores the total of pips left in his opponent's hand, the court cards counting as 10 each. If both players are stopped and both are left with cards in their hands, both hands are counted. The lower hand wins and scores the value of his opponent's hand less the value of his own. If a player wins the hand while the comet is in the hand of his opponent he scores double. If a player wins by playing the comet, he doubles his score, and if he wins the hand by playing the comet as a 9 he quadruples his score.

COMMIT

This is a variation of the parent game that is suitable for more than two players. It is played with the standard pack of 52 cards from which the ◇8 has been removed, and as many other 8s and 7s as may be necessary for the players to be dealt an equal number of cards.

The players place an equal number of units into a pool.

The player on the left of the dealer begins by playing any card to the centre of the table. The others play cards on it as able, and not necessarily in rotation. The cards played must follow in sequence. Only the ♠6 may be played on the ♠5, the ♣8 on the ♣7, and so on.

The ◇9 is the comet and may be played either when all the players are stopped or when the holder of it has played regularly and is unable to continue the sequence. After it has been played, any player in rotation may either continue by playing the ◇10 on it, or the card next above that for which the comet has been substituted.

The player who plays the comet receives two units from each of the other players, and any player who plays a King receives one unit from each of the other players. The player who is first to get rid of his cards wins the pool, and receives two units from a player who has been left with the comet in his hand, and one unit for each King.

CRIBBAGE

*C*RIBBAGE *is believed to have been developed out of the older card game of Noddy, by Sir John Suckling in the reign of Charles I. In the manner of scoring it is unique, and the play calls for no effort of memory. Good judgement and concentration are the chief qualities that lead to success.*

NUMBER OF PLAYERS

Originally cribbage was a two-handed game as described first, but variations for three and four players are now played and are described later.

The two-handed game is the most popular, and of it there are three variations: five-, six- and seven-card.

CARDS

The full pack of 52 cards is used, and they rank from King (high) to Ace (low). The King Queen and Jack! count as ten each, and the other cards their pip values.

Five-card Cribbage for two players, which is the original game, is generally considered the most scientific of the variations.

The players cut for deal; the lower deals first. Five cards are dealt to each player, and the non-dealer pegs three holes (Three for Last) as compensation against the advantage of the first deal of a game.

A cribbage or noddy board.

THE PLAY

Points won are marked with a peg on what is known as a noddy board (see illustration). It is oblong in shape, has a double row of holes, 30 in each row, and is divided, for convenience in scoring, into groups of five holes. The board is placed between the two players; both start from the same end

of the board and peg their scores first along the outer row of holes and then along the inner row – once round the board at the five-card game, twice round at the six-card game and three times round at the seven-card game. In each case the game ends when one player reaches the hole from which he started. Thus, at five-card cribbage the game is 61 holes, at six-card 121 holes, and at seven-card 181 holes.

The players look at their cards, and then place two of them face downwards on the right of the dealer. These four cards are known as the crib. The non-dealer then cuts the pack, and the dealer turns up the top card of the cut and places it on top of the pack. The card is known as the start, and if it is a Jack the dealer pegs two holes (Two for his Heels).

Scores are made partly in play and partly by the scoring values of the cards in hand. The latter, however, are not pegged until the play ends.

During the play of the hand, scores are made as follows:

If a player plays a card of the same rank as the previous one played, he pegs two for a pair, but court cards pair only rank with rank – that is to say King with King, Queen with Queen and Jack with Jack.

If a player plays a third card of the same rank as a pair he pegs 6 for pair-royal.

If a player plays a fourth card of the same rank as a pair-royal he pegs 12 for a double pair-royal.

A sequence (or run) is pegged at one for each card with a minimum of three cards and a maximum of seven. The cards need not be of the same suit, nor need they be played in sequential order, but, as the Ace is low, A, K, Q is not a sequence, and a sequence is destroyed by a pair or an intervening card. If the dealer plays a 7 and the non-dealer a 5, the dealer may now play a 6 and peg three, and the non-dealer may continue either with a 4 or an 8 and peg four.

If a player plays a card which, with those already played, adds up to 15 he pegs two, and, again, if they total 31 he pegs two.

Out of this an important point arises. If, when the player whose turn it is to play cannot do so without exceeding 31, he says 'Go'. His opponent then plays a card or cards up to the limit. If the cards that he plays bring the total up to exactly 31 he pegs two; if not he pegs one (One for Last).

This ends the play, and the players, beginning with the non-dealer, count their scores by combining their own cards with the start. The dealer then exposes the crib (it is his exclusive property) and any values that he finds in it (making full use of the start) he pegs to his score. Should either player hold the Jack of the same suit as the start he pegs one (One for his Nob). If a player holds in his hand three cards all of the same suit he pegs three for a flush, and four if the start is of the same suit. In the crib, however, nothing is scored for a flush unless, with the start, it is a flush of five; if it is the dealer pegs five.

Two other features of the scoring call for special mention. First, a player must count his hand aloud, and if he overlooks any score, either in play or otherwise, his opponent may call 'Muggins', point out the omission, and peg the score for himself. Secondly, if a player reaches the game hole before his opponent has gone halfway round the board a lurch is scored, that is to say the winner scores two games instead of only one.

Points are scored during the play by a player adding the value of the card played by the opponent to a card played from his own hand. Thus if a 10 or court card is led, and a player plays a 5, he scores 15 and pegs two holes (*fifteen-two* as it is called for short). If a 6 is led, and he plays another 6, he scores for a pair and pegs two. Again, a 4 is led, he plays a 6, and the opponent plays a 5: he pegs three for a sequence and two for 15. And so on.

The general principles may be illustrated in an elementary deal.

West   East

East is the dealer.

West holds a sequence of four. As a result the ♣K will go to the crib, and for his other card he must choose between the ♣6 and the ♡9. There is not much in it, but as the ♣6 is of the same suit as the King, there is a slight advantage in discarding the ♡9, because the ♣6 (along with the King) might help to give East a flush in his crib.

East has an easy choice of discards. Indeed, it is obvious that he will discard the ♣A and ♢3.

West cuts the cards, and East turns up the ♠K.

The position is now as in the illustration below.

Start

Crib

West

East

West leads the ◊ 7 and says 'Seven'. It is his best lead because if East plays an 8 and pegs two for 15, West can play the ♣ 6 and peg three for sequence. He will not, of course, play the ♠ 8, because if East holds another 8 he will play it and not only peg for a pair-royal but for 31 as well.

In the event, East cannot play an 8 and score for 15. His best play, therefore, is the ♣ 10, announcing 'Seventeen'. This makes it impossible for a 15 to be scored against him.

West has no better play than the ♠ 8, announcing 'Twenty-five', because the closer the total to 31 the better the chance that East will be unable to play.

East plays the ♠ 5, announcing 'Thirty'.

West says 'Go' and as East has not got an Ace he pegs One for Last.

The hands are now counted.

West is not helped by the start. All he can score is two for 15 and three for sequence. This with his Three for Last (as non-dealer) gives him eight.

East pegs six for 15 (two 10s and the ♠ K in the start, each combined with the ♠ 5) and two for the pair of 10s. In the crib he finds an Ace, a King, a 9 and a 3. With the start this gives him two for the pair of Kings. He therefore pegs 10 holes, making 11 in all as he has already pegged One for Last.

SIX- AND SEVEN-CARD CRIBBAGE

The six- and seven-card variations of cribbage differ very little from the five-card game. There is, in fact, no difference in the play nor in the crib, and very little in the mechanics of the game. The only differences of importance, apart from the number of cards, are that the non-dealer does not receive Three for Last, that the cards are played out to the end (the player failing to score for go leading again, thus giving his opponent the chance of making a pair or 15) and that in the six-card variation the play is twice round the board (121 holes) and in the seven-card three times round (181 holes).

The general principles explained for the parent game hold good at the six-card variation. It is to be noted, however, that in the six-card variation the number of cards in hand and in the crib are the same, from which it follows that it is not so important for the non-dealer to make an effort of trying to baulk the crib by his discard. The two objectives — preserving any values in hand and baulking the opponent's crib — are in this case on the same level, and either objective may be preferred, as the nature of the hand dictates.

THREE-HANDED CRIBBAGE

With three players, five cards are dealt to each player, and an extra one to the crib, to which each player contributes one card only. There is no Three for Last. The start is cut for in the usual way. The player on the left of the dealer plays first, and has first Show. He deals the succeeding hand. The score may be pegged on a triangular board open in the centre, or on the standard board with a pivoted arm that permits a third player to peg. The game is once round the board.

FOUR-HANDED CRIBBAGE

With four players, two play as partners against the other two, the partners sitting facing each other. Each player is dealt five cards and discards one to the crib, which is the property of the dealer. The player on the left of the dealer plays first. The others follow in clockwise rotation. Consultation between partners is not allowed, nor may they prompt each other, but a player may help his partner in the count of the hand or crib. The cards are played out to the end, as in the six and seven-card variations. Game is usually twice round the board (121 holes).

ECARTÉ

*E*CARTÉ *is a gambling game, once one of the most popular in France. It requires a knowledge of probabilities 'only', and to a player with a complete knowledge of these it is a mechanical game.*

NUMBER OF PLAYERS

Ecarté is suitable for two players only.

CARDS

Ecarté is played with a 32-card pack; that is to say with a pack from which the 2s, 3s, 4s, 5s and 6s have been removed. The cards rank in the order: King (high), Queen, Jack, Ace, 10, 9, 8, 7 (low).

The two players are dealt five cards each, either in sets of three and two, or two and three, and the rest of the pack is placed face downwards on the table, between them. To determine the trump suit the top card of the pack is turned face upwards.

THE PLAY

After looking at his cards, the non-dealer either plays or proposes. If he proposes, the dealer has the choice of either accepting or playing, and if he accepts both players may exchange any or all their cards for others from the pack. By agreement the exchange of cards may continue until the pack is exhausted.

The non-dealer has first lead. The

object of the game is to win three tricks, called the Trick. The winner scores one point for this, and if he wins all five tricks (the Vole) he scores two points. The game is won by the player who first wins five points, and it is customary to count a treble if a play wins the game and his opponent has failed to score; a double if his opponent has scored only one or two points, and a single if his opponent has scored three or four points.

So far, then, *Ecarté* appears to be childishly simple. The game, however, lends itself to a number of refinements that raise it to the level of an adult game. If the non-dealer does not propose, but plays, and fails to make the trick, the dealer scores two points instead of only one. In the same way, if the dealer refuses a proposal, and plays, and fails to make the trick, the non-dealer scores two points. The value of the vole (two points) is not affected by playing without proposing.

Another important feature of the game is that if the dealer turns up a King as trumps, or if a player is dealt the King of the trump suit, he scores one point. The point can be scored by the non-dealer only if he declares the

King before he makes the opening lead, and by the dealer only if he declares it before he plays to the first trick. A player is under no compulsion to declare the King, and, indeed, sometimes it is better to sacrifice the point than to disclose to the opponent that this important card is held against him.

With the score West three points, East four points, West deals and the ♠8 is turned up. The hands are as below.

East decides to play and must win the game if he handles his cards correctly. In the event he loses the game by incautious play. He leads ♣K on which West plays ♣7. West does not declare the ♠K because East has played without proposing and, therefore, will lose two points if he fails to win the Trick. On the other hand, if he wins the Trick, declaring the King will be of no help to West.

East is lulled into a false sense of security, and unaware that the ♠K is against him he assumes that it is safe to lead ♠Q. West wins with ♠K, leads ◇Q to force East to win with ♠J, and comes to the last two tricks, and wins the game, with ♠A and ♡A.

There are a number of stock hands,

West   East

holding which a player should play and not propose, and equally refuse the opponent's proposal. The more important of them are set out below. In all cases spades are trumps:

Any three trumps supported by two inferior cards in outside suits — ♠ J, 10, 7; ♡ 8; ◇ 10.

Any two trumps supported by three cards in one outside suit — ♠ 10, 8; ♡ J, 8, 7.

Any two trumps supported by the King and a low card in an outside suit, and one indifferent card in another suit — ♠ A, 8; ♡ K, 7; ◇ 9.

Any one trump supported by four cards headed by the King (or Queen) in an outside suit — ♠ J; ♡ K, 9, 8, 7 (or Q, J, 8, 7).

Any one trump supported by three cards headed by a court card in an outside suit, and any high court card in another suit — ♠ 10; ♡ J, 10, 7; ◇ Q.

Any hand that contains three Queens (or better) and even though it may lack a trump card — ♡ Q, 7; ◇ Q, 7; ♣ K.

Any hand that contains four high cards (King, Queen, Jack) and even though it may lack a trump card — ♡ K ◇ Q J; ♣ Q, 7.

These stock hands are based on the law of probability, supported by the experience of the best players, who set great store on them. So far as the dealer is concerned, they are the minimum types of hands for him to play on. In a number of cases he may do better if he follows his luck, or decides to play on what is called a hunch, but the non-dealer should never propose when holding a hand similar to one of the above types. The reason is that he has the opening lead, and, at *Ecarté*, the opening lead is of vital importance.

East deals and the ♠ 10 is turned up. The hands are shown below.

West plays and if he leads ♡ Q he wins the Trick no matter how East plays.

If, however, West had dealt, East would be on lead and if he led the ◇ K he would win the Trick no matter how West played. In fact, West would be hard put to save the Vole, and, indeed, would do so only if he retained the ♣ J and not the ♡ Q. An experienced player would, of course, retain the ♣ J (although the ♡ Q is a higher card)

West   East

because he holds three hearts and only one club, and since there are only eight cards in a suit it is about seven to five on that East's last card is a club and not a heart.

The deal is of some interest because it illustrates the danger of leading the Queen of trumps, unless the King has been turned up as trumps. It will be seen that if West decides to lead the ♠Q, East wins with the ♠K, runs his diamonds (scoring the Trick) and West will save the Vole only if he retains the ♣J. On the other hand, it is to be noted that the lead of the single-ton King of trumps is nearly always a good lead, and rarely damages the leader's hand.

As a general rule it is best for a player to play when he cannot see his way to discarding more than two cards; but if a player's hand guarantees him the Trick, or virtually so, he should propose or accept, because if the proposal is refused he is on easy street (since the Trick is more or less in his pocket) and if the proposal is accepted he has the opportunity to convert his hand into one on which he may win the Vole.

EIGHTS

*E*IGHTS *is a game of the Stops family, and is regarded as one with better opportunities for skill than other members of the family. It probably originated in the United States where it is also called Swedish Rummy, although there is no connection with games of the Rummy family. The game is also called Switch (usually with Jacks rather than 8s being the most significant cards).*

NUMBER OF PLAYERS

The game is best for two players, although three can play, and four can play in two partnerships, as explained later.

CARDS

The full pack of 52 cards is used.

Each player draws a card, lower deals (Ace high). Thereafter the deal alternates with each hand. The dealer shuffles, the non-dealer cuts, and the dealer gives seven cards, one at a time, to each player. The remainder of the pack is placed face down to form the stock, and the top card then turned face up beside the stock to become the starter.

THE PLAY

The non-dealer plays first. He must begin a talon pile by laying onto the starter a card from his hand of either the same suit or the same rank as the starter. If he is unable to, he must draw cards one at a time from the top of the stock until he can.

When a player has laid a card, his opponent takes his turn and play continues alternately. If the stock becomes exhausted, a player unable to make a turn passes.

The game gets its name from the fact that all 8s are wild. An 8 may be played at any time, whether or not the player holding it could play another card. The player laying an 8 can specify which suit it represents (but not which rank). He can thereby change the suit or stipulate that the previous suit continues.

A player may choose to draw from the stock even if able to play, but he must eventually lay a card if able – he cannot pass while holding a card which can be played.

The winner is the first to get rid of all his cards. If the stock is exhausted and neither player can play, the game ends in a block, but is still valid for scoring.

A player is debited for the cards in his hand when his opponent goes out, on the following scale: an 8 counts 50 points, a King, Queen or Jack counts ten points, and all other cards count their pip value (Ace counts one point). If the game ends in a block, each player is debited for the cards in his hand. When a player's debit score reaches 100, his opponent wins the game, and wins by 100 points plus the difference between the two totals. Settlement is made on the basis of an agreed amount per ten points, the difference being rounded up to the nearest ten.

Good play comes from keeping count of the number of cards played in each suit, in deciding when to change the suit, and in particular in the use of the 8s. It is best to keep an 8 for emergencies, and it might sometimes be worth drawing from stock rather than playing an 8. A player with the last 8 who knows a suit is exhausted might deliberately call for that suit to cause a block, if he is confident that his opponent holds cards counting more than he does himself.

EIGHTS FOR THREE PLAYERS

This version is played cut-throat style, i.e. each player for himself. After deciding dealer, the deal passes to the left. Each player is dealt five cards (not six as with two players) one at a time, and the player to the dealer's left plays first. Play continues in turn to the left. When one player's debit score reaches 100, each player's score is rounded up to the nearest ten, and the players settle with each other according to the difference between them at a rate agreed beforehand. There is no bonus for winning the game.

EIGHTS FOR FOUR PLAYERS

This version is played in partnerships of two, each player sitting opposite his partner. Each is dealt five cards. For a partnership to win a hand, both partners must get rid of their cards. The side which fails to go out is debited with the cards held in the hands of the players on that side (there might be one hand or two to count). When one partnership is debited with 100, the winning partnership score the difference in the two totals (rounded up to the nearest ten) plus 100 for game. Each winning partner collects from his opponent on his right settlement at an agreed rate per ten points based on the winning margin (i.e. if the margin is 130, each loser pays to his right-hand opponent 13 units).

GERMAN WHIST

*G*ERMAN WHIST *was invented for two players who like Whist and cannot find another pair. It is a simple game but to play it well requires a good memory.*

NUMBER OF PLAYERS

German Whist is essentially a game for only two players.

CARDS

The full pack of 52 cards is used. Cards rank from Ace (high) to 2 (low).

Each player is dealt 13 cards. The remaining 26 cards are placed face downwards between the players and the top card is turned face upwards to denote the trump suit.

THE PLAY

The non-dealer leads to the first trick. Thereafter the player who wins a trick leads to the next, and so on. A player must follow suit if he can. If he cannot he may either trump or discard. The winner of a trick takes into his hand the exposed card from the top of the stock; the loser takes the next card from the stock (he does not show it to his opponent) and turns up the next card of the stock.

When the stock is exhausted, the

players play out the remaining 13 cards, and at this stage of the game the player with a good memory will know exactly which cards his opponent holds.

The game is complete in one deal, and the player who wins the majority of tricks receives an agreed number of points per trick for all in excess of those won by his opponent. If both players win 13 tricks, there is, of course, no score.

Although German whist is a simple game it offers good memory training for those who aspire to succeed at more advanced games, and, at the same time, gives exercise in the technique of card play.

If a player holds a strong trump suit he should lead his trumps early in the game so as to command the game in the later stages of the play, and if the exposed card is a trump it is always good play to make an effort to win it.

On the other hand, it is not always good play to win a trick. Much depends on the value of the exposed card. The ◇ 9 is exposed. West leads the ◇ 7 and East holds ◇ Q, 6, 3. East should play ◇ 3, and allow West to win the

Stock   West

trick. It is not worth while wasting the ◇ Q which should be kept in hand for better things later in the game. By contrary, if the ◇ J is the exposed card, East should win the trick with the ◇ Q, because now he is exchanging the ◇ Q for an equivalent card and adding a trick to his total.

It is advisable to hold command of as many suits as possible, because it enables one to take a trick whenever the exposed card is worth winning, without losing control of the suit.

West holds the hand in the illustration. Spades are trumps, and the exposed card is ♣K.

The ♣K is worth winning, but leading the ♣A is not the best play. West will win the trick, but the value of his hand will remain unchanged. West should prefer to lead the ◇ K, because if it wins the trick his hand will be that much better, and if East is able to win the trick with the ◇ A, West's ◇ Q has been promoted to top diamond.

GIN RUMMY

*T*HE invention of Gin Rummy has been credited to E. T. Baker in a New York club in *1909. It is a variant of the parent game Rummy, which is frequently shortened to Rum, and acquired its name Gin by extension of the alcoholic drink theme. It became very popular due to the publicity it received when taken up by film stars in Hollywood in the 1940s.*

NUMBER OF PLAYERS

Gin Rummy is a game for two players only. There are forms of Rummy for more players – see under Rummy on page 184.

CARDS

The full pack of 52 cards is used, cards ranking from King (high) to Ace (low).

Dealer is determined by the players each drawing a card from the pack: higher has choice of dealing first or not. If cards of equal rank are drawn, the suit determines precedence in the order: spades (high), hearts, diamonds, clubs. After the first deal, the winner of each hand deals the next.

The dealer deals ten cards to each player, one at a time, beginning with his opponent. The remainder of the pack is placed face down between the players to form the stock. The top card of the stock is placed face up beside the stock and becomes the upcard, at the same time beginning a discard pile.

THE PLAY

The object of the play is to form the hand into sets of three or more cards. A set may be of two kinds: three or four cards of the same rank, or three or more cards in sequence in the same suit (Ace being in sequence with 2, 3, not King, Queen).

The non-dealer may take the first upcard into his hand or refuse it. If he refuses, the dealer has the option of taking it or refusing it. If the dealer also refuses it, the non-dealer draws the top card from the stock and takes it into his hand, discarding a card (the new upcard) face up on the discard pile. The discarded card may, in fact, be the card picked up, and the player may merely look at it and discard it immediately. Thereafter each player in turn draws a card, either the upcard or the top card of the stock, and discards, so that the number of cards in each player's hand remains at ten.

Cards which are not included in a set are 'unmatched' cards. After drawing (and only then), a player may 'knock', i.e. terminate the hand, whenever the pip value of the unmatched cards in his hand total ten or less. For this purpose, court cards (King, Queen, Jack) count as ten points each, the Ace counts as one, and the other cards as their face value.

Knocking involves laying down the hand, arranged in sets, with the unmatched cards separate, and making the usual discard. The count of the unmatched cards represent points against the player. If all ten cards are in sets, the player is said to 'go gin', and the count against him is nought.

If the player drawing the fiftieth card discards without knocking (i.e. there are only two cards left in the stock) the hand is abandoned and there is no score for that deal.

When a player knocks, there is one further stage before the calculation of the score, and that is the 'laying off', The opponent of the knocker lays down his cards in sets, and, unless the knocker has gone gin, may lay off any of his unmatched cards on the sets of the knocker, thereby reducing the count against him.

The illustration on page 43 shows a completed deal in which the opponent of the knocker can lay two unmatched cards on the knocker's sets.

SCORING

If the knocker has the lower of the two counts in unmatched cards, he scores the difference in the counts (in the illustration the knocker scores eight points). It is possible that the player who did not knock has the lower count. In this case he 'undercuts' the knocker and scores the difference in the count plus a bonus of 20 points. Should the count be equal, the opponent of the knocker still undercuts him, scoring the bonus 20 points, but no-

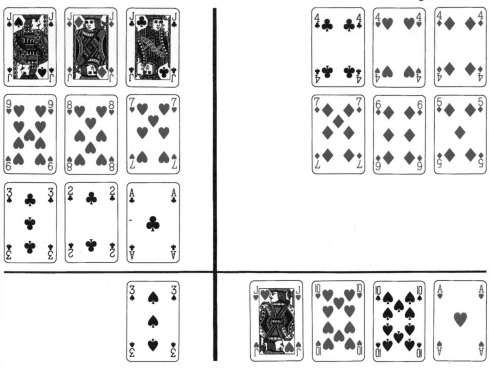

Knocker (left) goes out with a count of three. His opponent lays off with ♡ J, 10, and has a count of 11.

thing for difference in point count. The illustration overleaf shows a completed deal, in which the knocker is undercut.

It must be remembered that cards cannot be laid off on a knocker who goes gin. Going gin therefore guards against being undercut.

A player who goes gin scores a bonus of 25 on top of the point count.

The first player to score 100 points wins the game, but scoring does not end there. The winner of the game adds 100 points bonus to his score. Each player then adds 20 points to his score for each of his 'boxes' – each deal

he won. The winner wins by the difference in the two scores. This difference is doubled if the lower did not score a point. This is called a 'shut-out' or 'schneider'. The score of a completed game is illustrated overleaf.

There is a more complex scoring system, which was used in the days of popularity in Hollywood and which is known as Hollywood scoring.

The scores are recorded on a sheet of ruled paper. The first time a player wins a deal he enters the points in the first column only. The second time he enters the points in the second column

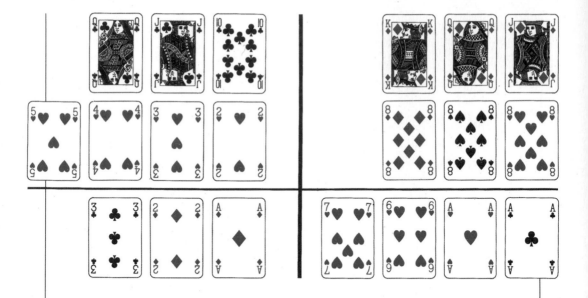

Knocker (left) is undercut when opponent lays off with ♡A, ♡6 and ♡7 on his sequence.

and also adds them to the score in the first column. The third time he enters the points in the third column and adds them to the score in the first two columns. Thereafter points won are added to the scores in all three columns. The illustration below represents a game in progress, showing some scores entered.

When the score of a player in a column reaches 100 or more, the column is closed. The player winning it scores a bonus of 100 points, and each player scores 20 points for each box won, as in the orthodox scoring. The winner wins by the difference in the scores, and if the loser fails to score in a column the difference is doubled. A player who is shut out in the first column must clearly make his first

A completed score card.

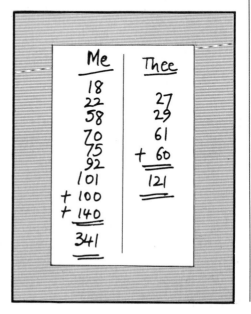

entry in the second column. A game ends when all three columns are won.

STRATEGY

Players must use judgement in deciding how long to hold high cards presenting a good chance of a set. For three or four draws it might pay to hold them, as high cards are likely to be discarded by the opponent. Many gin hands are won after only five or six draws, however, with six or seven cards in sets, and three or four unmatched. At this stage, therefore, a player should consider discarding these high cards in favour of lower ones.

Low cards, if drawn, ought to be retained, as clearly they reduce the loss if your opponent wins, and they enable a player to knock as soon as he holds two or three sets.

A player in a position to knock will have to weigh the chances of being undercut. In the first four turns, a player might feel safe in knocking as

Hollywood scoring, with a game in progress.

	Me	Thee	Me	Thee	Me	Thee
Box 1	25	17	2	3	12	
Box 2	27	20	14		18	
Box 3	39		20			
Box 4	45					
Box 5						
Box 6						
Box 7						

soon as he can. From about the eighth turn, however, he might decide to knock only with a count of, say, five or lower. In deciding whether to knock he will consider the upcards which both players have taken and try to calculate how many sets his opponent has and what he might be able to lay off.

With an opportunity to knock with a low count it is usually a mistake to wait for gin. If your opponent goes gin first it is a costly error.

HONEYMOON BRIDGE

*H*ONEYMOON BRIDGE *is a game invented for Bridge fanatics who find themselves as a pair rather than a foursome.*

NUMBER OF PLAYERS

As with all honeymoons, two is the only suitable number.

CARDS

The full pack of 52 cards is used, cards ranking from Ace (high) to 2 (low).

Thirteen cards are dealt to each player and the remaining 26 cards are placed face downwards between them, to form the stock.

THE PLAY

The non-dealer leads to the first trick. Thereafter the player who wins a trick leads to the next. A player must follow suit if he can. The winner of a trick takes the top card of the stock, the loser takes the next card. The first 13 tricks are played without a trump suit, and do not count in the final score.

When the stock is exhausted, the two players bid as in Bridge (see page 103) the dealer first; bidding continues until one player passes a bid, double or redouble. The player who does not make the final bid leads to the first trick, and the play continues as in the parent game. The players score as in Bridge.

If a player revokes during the play of the first 13 tricks, or if he draws a card out of turn, or sees more than one card when drawing from the stock, his opponent, when it is his turn to draw from the stock, may look at the two top cards and take either. Other irregularities are governed by the laws of Bridge.

HONEYMOON BRIDGE WITH A WIDOW

In this version of the game, the players sit in adjacent seats and the cards are dealt into four hands (as in the standard game) of 12 cards each. The remaining four cards (the widow) are placed face downwards in the centre of the table.

The players bid as in the standard game (the dealer bids first) and when a bid has been passed, doubled or redoubled, the player who has won the declaration takes up the widow hand and, without showing it to his opponent, takes one card into his own hand, one into his dummy, and gives the other two cards to his opponent to take one into his hand and the other into his dummy.

The player who has won the declaration may demand the opening lead to be made either by his opponent or by his opponent's dummy.

SEMI-EXPOSED HONEYMOON BRIDGE

The players in this version sit in adjacent seats and the cards are dealt as in the standard game, except that the first six cards to the dummies are dealt face downwards in a row, the remaining cards, six face upwards on top of them and one face upwards by itself.

The dealer bids first, and the bidding ends when a bid has been passed, doubled or redoubled. The hand on the left of the player who has won the declaration leads to the first trick. The play and scoring are as in the parent game, except that a player may play from his dummy only a face-upwards card. When a face-upwards card has been played, the card under it is turned face upwards, and is available for play.

47

JO-JOTTE

*A*LTHOUGH *Jo-jotte was invented by Ely Culbertson in 1937, it is not altogether a modern game, but a variation of the old French game of Belotte, in itself very similar to Klaberjass (see page 51) and its several variations.*

NUMBER OF PLAYERS

Jo-jotte is a game for two players.

CARDS

Jo-jotte is played with the short pack, namely a pack from which all cards below the rank of 7 have been removed.

The rank of the cards varies. If there is a trump suit, the cards of the suit rank in the order: Jack, 9, Ace, 10, King, Queen, 8, 7. In plain suits, or if the hand is played in no-trumps, the order is: Ace, 10, King, Queen, Jack, 9, 8, 7.

Each player is dealt six cards (either singly, or in twos or threes) and the 13th card of the pack is placed face upwards on the table. This is known as the turned card.

BIDDING

There are two rounds of bidding. The non-dealer bids first. He may either accept the suit of the turned card as trumps, or pass. If he passes, the dealer has the same option. If both players pass, the non-dealer may name any suit, other than that of the turned card, as trumps, or he may declare no-trumps or he may pass. If he passes for the second time, the dealer has the same option. If both players pass twice the hand is abandoned and the deal passes, but if either player names a suit as trumps, his opponent may overbid it by declaring no-trumps, but not by naming another suit as trumps. Either player may double his opponent's declaration, and any double may be redoubled.

THE PLAY

When the declaration has been determined (doubled, redoubled or passed) the dealer deals three more cards to his opponent and to himself, and he places the bottom card of the pack face upwards on top of the undealt cards of the pack. It has no significance in play but is solely informatory and, therefore, is known as the information card.

The player who has made the final declaration is known as the declarer: his opponent as the defender.

At this stage of the game the defender may announce that instead of defending against the declarer's contract he will himself become declarer at a nullo contract; a contract, that is, to lose every trick. The declarer may now declare a slam, a contract to win every trick either in the suit originally named by him (he cannot change the suit) or in no-trumps.

The defender then announces his melds, if he holds any. A meld is four of a kind (except 9s, 8s and 7s at no-trumps, and 8s and 7s in a suit declaration). A meld carries a score of 100 points and is scored (as at Bridge, see page 103) above the line. Only the player with the highest-ranking meld may score for it, and he may score for a second meld if he holds one.

Next, beginning with the defender, the players score for sequences, and for this purpose the cards take their normal rank of Ace (high), King, Queen, Jack, 10, 9, 8, 7. For a sequence of five cards the holder scores 50 points above the line, for a sequence of four 40 points, and for a sequence of three 20 points. If two sequences are of equal length, that headed by the highest card takes precedence. If both sequences are equal, a sequence in the trump suit wins over one in a plain suit; if both sequences are in plain suits neither is scored for. Only the player with the higher-ranking sequence may score for it, and he may score for any other sequences that he may hold.

In the top illustration below, clubs are trumps. Defender scores 200 points above the line for his melds of 10s and Queens, and the declarer cannot score for his meld of Kings because in the trump suit the 10 is higher than the King.

Defender   Declarer

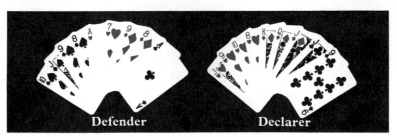

Defender   Declarer

In the lower illustration on page 49, hearts are trumps. Neither player has a meld. Defender declares his four-card sequence in spades but he cannot score for it because the declarer has an equal sequence in the trump suit (hearts). The declarer, therefore, scores 40 points above the line for his four-card sequence in hearts and a further 20 points for his three-card sequence in diamonds.

Finally, it is to be noted that if the declarer elects to play the hand in the same suit as the turned card, either player if he holds the 7 of the suit may exchange it for the turned card.

The player who leads to a trick may lead any card that he chooses. The second player is limited in his play; for he must obey the three rules that follow:

He must follow suit if he can.

If a trump has been led he must not only follow suit if he can, but win the trick by playing a higher trump if he holds one.

If a plain suit has been led and he is unable to follow suit, he must win the trick by trumping if he can.

Second player may discard a worthless card only when he is unable to obey one or other of these three rules.

Winning a trick has no value in itself. What counts is winning tricks with certain cards in them; these are scored as follows:

Jack of trumps	20
9 of trumps	15
Any Ace or 10	10
Any King or Queen	5
Last trick (except at nullo)	10

The example that follows is a simple one to illustrate the mechanics of the game (see hands illustrated below).

Hearts are trumps. The turned card is ♠ K: the information card ♢ Q.

Defender leads ♣ A, and the play is:

Defender	Declarer
♣ A	♣ Q
♣ 10	♡ 10
♢ 8	♢ A
♢ J	♢ 7
♣ 8	♡ 8
♡ 9	♢ 9
♠ 10	♠ 9
♠ Q	♡ A
♡ 7	♡ J

Declarer scores for taking:

Jack of trumps (♡)	20
♡ A	10
♢ A	10
♡ 10	10
♣ 10	10
♠ Q	5
Last trick	10
	75 points

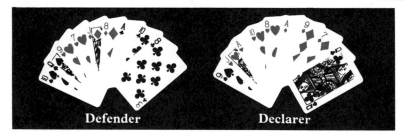

Defender   Declarer

Defender scores for taking:

19 of trumps (♡)	15
♣A	10
♠10	10
♣Q	5
	40

In addition to the above, if a player holds the King and Queen of the trump suit (if there is one) he may score 20 points provided he announces 'Jo' when he plays the King and later 'Jotte' when he plays the Queen. He cannot score for the combination if he plays the Queen before the King.

Game is won by the player who first scores 80 points below the line, which may be made in one hand or in a series of part-scores, and the player who wins the rubber (best out of three games) scores a bonus of 300 points.

The declarer of a nullo contract scores a bonus of 200 points if he loses every trick; if he takes a trick, however, his opponent scores 200 points for the first and 100 for every subsequent trick.

The declarer of a slam scores a bonus of 500 points if he wins every trick; and if a player wins every trick but has not bid slam he scores a bonus of 100 points.

Scoring below the line, towards game, is calculated as follows:

1. If the declarer's total score, including melds, sequences, trick scores and bonuses (if any) is greater than the defender's total score, he scores his trick score below the line, and the defender scores his trick score above the line.

2. If the defender's total score is greater than the declarer's, the two trick scores are added together and scored by the defender below the line.

3. If the contract is doubled or redoubled, the player with the higher total scores both his and his opponent's trick score, doubled or quadrupled, below the line.

4. If there is a tie in total points, the trick scores of both players are put in prison and awarded to the player who obtains the higher total in the following deal.

KLABERJASS

KLABERJASS *is probably better known in America than in Britain, because under the names of Clabber, Clobber, Clubby, Klab and Klob, it occurs in Damon Runyon's amusing stories, and in 1937 a variation of the game, under the name of Jo-jotte (see page 48) was publicized by Ely Culbertson. Despite the similarity of names it is not identical with the*

Hungarian game of Kalabriás, which is a game for three or four players. There may have been a common ancestor, or possibly the game was taken to the New World by Central European immigrants and there adapted as a two-handed game with Klaberjass as a bowdlerized version of Kalabriás.

NUMBER OF PLAYERS

Klaberjass is primarily a game for two players, but can be played by four, in two partnerships, as described later.

CARDS

The game is played with a pack from which the 6s, 5s, 4s, 3s and 2s have been removed. In the trump suit the cards rank in the order Jack, 9, Ace, 10, King, Queen, 8, 7; and in the other three suits Ace, 10, King, Queen, Jack, 9, 8, 7.

Six cards are dealt to both players, in two lots of three cards each. The next card of the pack is turned face upwards on the table (it is known as the turn-up card) and the rest of the pack is placed face downwards so as partly to cover it.

BIDDING

The non-dealer bids first. He may take-it (i.e. accept the turn-up card as the trump suit); pass (i.e. refuse to accept the turn-up card as the trump suit); or schmeiss (i.e. offer to play with the turn-up card as the trump suit or throw in the hand, as his opponent prefers). If the opponent says 'Yes' to a schmeiss there is a fresh deal; if he says 'No' the hand is played with the turn-up card as the trump suit.

If the non-dealer has passed, the dealer may either take-it, pass or schmeiss.

If both players pass there is a second round of bidding. Now the non-dealer may name any one of the other three suits as trumps, or he may schmeiss (i.e. offer to name one of the other three suits as trumps or throw in the hand, as his opponent prefers), or he may pass. If he passes, the dealer may name one of the other three suits as trumps, or throw in the hand.

When a player accepts or names a trump suit, the bidding ends, and the player who has accepted or named a suit as trumps is called the maker.

There is never more than two rounds of bidding, and when the trump suit has been settled, the dealer deals three more cards, one at a time, to the two players. He then turns up the bottom card of the pack and places it on top of the pack. It takes no part in the play, and is put where it is only to be seen.

If either player has been dealt the 7 of the trump suit, he may exchange it for the turn-up card.

THE PLAY

Only sequences are melded, and for melding the cards rank in the order from Ace (high) to 7 (low). A three-card sequence counts 20 points, a four-card or longer one 50 points.

The non-dealer begins by announcing the value of his best sequence. If his best sequence is of three cards he says 'Twenty'; if of four or more cards he says 'Fifty'. If the dealer has a better sequence he says 'No good'; if he lacks a better sequence he says 'Good'; if he has an equal sequence he asks 'How high?' The non-dealer then announces the top card of his sequence. The dealer then says whether it is good, no good, or if he has a sequence headed by an equal card. In this last event neither player scores unless one of the sequences is in the trump suit, which wins over a sequence in a plain suit.

The non-dealer leads to the first trick; thereafter the winner of a trick leads to the next. A player must follow suit if he can, and if he cannot he must play a trump if he holds one. If a trump is led, the second player must win the trick if he can.

After the first trick has been played, the player with the highest meld shows it and scores for all sequences in his hand. His opponent cannot score for any sequences that he may hold.

A player who holds the King and Queen of the trump suit may score 20 points so long as he announces 'Bella' immediately after he has played the second of them to a trick. If a player holds the Jack of the trump suit, as well as the King and Queen, he may score for the sequence as well as for bella.

When all the cards have been played, each player examines his tricks and scores points for winning in his tricks:

Jasz (Jack of trumps)	20
Menel (9 of trumps)	14
Any Ace	11
Any 10	10
Any King	4
Any Queen	3
Any Jack (except Jasz)	2
Last trick	10

If the maker's total, including melds and cards won, is higher than the opponent's, each scores all the points he has won. If the totals of the two players are equal, the opponent scores the points he has won, the maker nothing. If the opponent's total is higher than the maker's, the two totals are added together and the opponent scores them.

The player who first reaches 500 points wins the game.

KLABERJASS FOR FOUR PLAYERS

This game is played in partnership, two playing against two. Eight cards are dealt to each player, and the dealer turns up his last card for trumps.

Each player in turn, beginning with the player on the left of the dealer, may either take-it or pass. There is no schmeiss. If all four players pass, there is a second round of bidding during which each player in turn has a right to name the trump suit. If all four players pass the second round of bidding there is a fresh deal.

The player who names the trump suit becomes the maker, and his side must score more than the opposing side.

The player on the left of the dealer leads to the first trick.

LE TRUC

LE TRUC is an old French gambling game which is very simple to play. Since bluff plays a considerable part it is best when played for stakes (a bluff is easier to attempt if financial penalties would not accompany its failure), but some play the game happily for points.

NUMBER OF PLAYERS

The basic game is for two players, but four may play in partnerships of two, as described later.

CARDS

A short pack of 32 cards is used. Removed from the standard pack are the 8s, 5s, 4s, 3s and 2s. The cards rank in the order 7, 6, Ace, King, Queen, Jack, 10, 9. The suits are immaterial.

Players cut for deal, and lower deals (cards ranking for this purpose normally, i.e. Ace high and 6 low). The deal thereafter alternates with each hand.

The dealer shuffles and non-dealer cuts, and dealer deals three cards to each player, one at a time.

THE PLAY

The non-dealer looks at his hand and may say 'I play', in which case play begins, or he may ask for a new deal. If the latter, dealer has two options. He may accept, in which case both hands are laid aside unexposed, and the dealer deals two fresh hands, or he may refuse, in which case both players play with the cards they have. The non-dealer may ask for new cards once only.

The object in each deal is to win two of the three tricks. There are no trumps and no obligation to follow suit, suits being immaterial. Each player can play whichever card he likes on each trick. The non-dealer leads to the first trick, thereafter the winner of a trick leads to the next. A trick is won by the higher card in it irrespective of suit. Should both players play a card of equal rank, the trick is spoiled and is claimed by the first player to win a trick. Thus if the first trick is spoiled it is claimed by the player to win the second (if that is spoiled too, both are claimed by the player to win the third). If the second trick is spoiled, it is claimed by the player who won the first trick. It is possible that all three tricks are spoiled, in which case that deal is declared a draw and the deal passes to the next player. If a trick is spoiled, the leader to it leads to the next.

Each deal is worth one point, should neither player double, and a game consists of 12 points.

However, it is the doubling which gives the game its appeal, and introduces the opportunity to bluff. At any time a player about to play his card (whether it is first, second or third and whether he is leading or following) may offer to double the value of the hand. If his opponent accepts, the play continues at double value. But a player offered a double may decline it, in which case he concedes the hand at its current value. A hand may be doubled to be worth two points, then four, then eight, but no more. The reason is that a player cannot double the value of the hand beyond a point where, if he won, the value would take his score past the game-winning 12 points. In this case, he can, however, increase the stake to however many points he needs to win the game by saying: 'My remainder'. For example, if his score is seven, and the value of the game is four, he cannot double the stake again because this

would take him past 12, but he can win the necessary five points for game by saying: 'My remainder'. However, this call carries a risk, because if the 'remainder' call is accepted, the points at stake become the opponent's remainder as well, irrespective of how many points he had before the hand was dealt, so the winner of the hand automatically wins the game.

The normal way for a player to double is to state the new value of the game, thus: 'Two if I play?' and 'Four if I play?' and so on. His opponent either says 'Yes' or throws in his cards to concede at the former value.

Each game is a separate entity and is settled as such.

Good play arises first of all for the non-dealer in whether or not to call for new cards. While he might invariably do so with poor cards, he might occasionally do so with good cards, to lure the dealer into a trap. Good play for the dealer begins with making the best decisions on accepting or refusing such calls.

The remaining skill comes in the order of playing the cards in the hand and in the doubling.

Imagine two hands are dealt as in the illustration. The non-dealer

Non-dealer

Dealer

decides to play. If he leads his ♣7, the dealer might spoil the first trick, and when the non-dealer follows with ♡6 he might spoil the second, too, but the non-dealer will win the hand with his ♡A.

On the other hand, when the non-dealer leads his ♣7, the dealer's best play is to play ♡J, deliberately losing. He will now win the hand because, whichever of his two cards the non-dealer plays next, the dealer will beat it and win the last trick.

The non-dealer, despite having the better hand, is similarly doomed if he leads ♡A first. The dealer will win it with ◇6 and then double because he cannot lose. He plays his ◇7 next, and if the second trick is spoiled, which is the worst that can happen, the dealer will take the trick on the strength of having won the first, and thus will win the hand. Would the non-dealer have accepted the double? Well, he could lose only if the dealer held a 7 as well as the 6 already played … or an improbable three 6s.

Although the dealer, by best play, will win the hand if the non-dealer leads ♣7 or ♡A, the non-dealer can be sure of winning by leading ♡6. If the dealer this time throws away ♡J, the non-dealer is certain to win with his ♣7 on the second trick. If the dealer spoils the first trick, he can do no better than spoil the second when the non-dealer leads ♣7, so the non-dealer wins on the third trick. The dealer's best hope is to win the first trick with his ◇7, but whatever he leads to the second trick the non-dealer will beat

and still win the last trick.

While it is generally regarded as vital to win the first trick, in order to guard against spoiled tricks, this example hand shows that this is not always so, and that there is plenty of scope for skill. And as well as the playing of the cards, both sides in this hand could have had decisions to make on whether to double or to accept a double on every card played.

LE TRUC FOR FOUR PLAYERS

This version is played in partnerships of two, each player sitting opposite his partner. Cards are cut to determine partners, the two highest playing against the two lowest, the lowest dealing. The deal passes to the left, as does the turn to play to a trick. One player from each side, the dealer and the player to his left (eldest) are the captains for the hand. Only eldest may call for a new deal, and only the dealer may refuse or accept. Neither may be helped by their partners to reach these decisions. If the dealer accepts a new deal, only he and eldest are dealt new hands – the other players keep theirs. Eldest leads to the first trick.

A spoiled trick is one in which equally high cards are played by both partnerships. If the high cards come from the same partnership the trick is not spoiled but won by that partnership. If three cards of equal rank are highest, the trick remains spoiled, i.e. it is not won by the side which contributed two of the cards.

As before, a spoiled trick is won by the side which first wins a trick, a player winning a trick leads to the next, and a leader to a spoiled trick leads to the next. Where one side contributes equal cards to win a trick, the player who played the first of the two cards leads to the next.

Only the captain of a side may double or remainder, and he must do so before his side plays its first card to a trick. Only the captain of the opposing side may accept the double or concede the hand.

When playing for stakes, it is best if partners are scrupulous about not passing information to each other in any way, but for light-hearted friendly games some schools allow the captain to ask his partner to lead high or low and in very light-hearted games the partner can give his captain information about his holding by various gestures (e.g. a wink for holding a 7, etc).

PINOCLE

*P*INOCLE *is frequently spelt Pinochle, but the Oxford English Dictionary does not sanction the 'h'. It was derived from the old French game of Bezique, and was popular in Europe as a two-handed game. It has become extremely popular in the United States, where it is played by three or more players. The original form is described here and the version for more players is to be found in the later section of this book where card games for four are described.*

NUMBER OF PLAYERS

Pinocle is for two players (but see above).

CARDS

Pinocle is played with a pack of 48 cards, consisting of two Aces, 10s, Kings, Jacks, 9s (in this order) from each of the four suits.

Twelve cards are dealt to each player, either three or four cards at a time, and the next card is turned face upwards to indicate the trump suit. The rest of the pack is placed face downwards on the table to half cover the exposed card.

THE PLAY

The object of the game is to win tricks that include those cards which carry a scoring value when won in a trick, and to meld certain combinations of cards that carry a scoring value.

When taken in a trick each Ace scores 11 points, each 10 scores ten points, each King four points, each Queen three points, and each Jack two points. The player who wins the last trick scores 10 points.

The values of the melds are:

Class A

A, 10, K, Q, J of trumpst	150
K, Q of trumps (royal marriage)	40
K, Q of a plain suit (common marriage)	20

Class B

Pinocle (♠ Q and ♢ J)	40
Dis (9 of the trump suit)	10

Class C

1 Ace of each suit	100
1 King of each suit	80
1 Queen of each suit	60
1 Jack of each suit	40

The non-dealer leads to the first trick. Thereafter the winner of a trick leads to the next. It is not necessary for a player to follow suit to a led card. The winner of a trick replenishes his hand by taking the top card of the stock; the loser of the trick takes the next.

After a player has won a trick and before drawing from the stock, he may meld any of the above combinations. To meld he places the cards face upwards on the table in front of him, where they remain until he decides to play them to a trick, or until the stock is exhausted. Melding is subject to the three rules that follow:

1. Only one meld may be made at a turn.

2. For each meld, at least one card must be taken from the hand and placed on the table.

3. A card already melded may be melded again so long as it is in a different class, or in a higher-scoring meld of the same class. That is to say, if hearts are trumps a player may meld ♡K, Q and score for the royal marriage, and later he may add ♡A, 10, J and score for the sequence. He cannot first declare ♡A, 10, K, Q, J and score for sequence and later declare the royal marriage.

If the dealer turns up a dis as the trump card he scores 10 points. Thereafter a player holding a dis may count it merely by showing it when winning a trick. He may count the dis and make another meld at the same time. After winning a trick, the holder of a dis may exchange it for the trump card.

The player who wins the twelfth trick may meld if he is able to. He then draws the last face-downwards card of the stock and must show it to his opponent. The loser of the trick takes the card exposed on the table.

The last 12 tricks are now played off. During this period of play a player must follow suit if he can to the card led; if he cannot he must trump the trick if he holds a trump. If a trump is led the second player must win the trick if he can.

Melds are scored when they are

declared. The score for cards won in tricks are added after the hand has been played out; a total of seven, eight, or nine points is counted as ten.

Every deal may constitute a game, or the players may prefer that the winner will be he who first reaches an agreed figure.

At pinocle skill and experience count for much. An ability to remember which cards have been played contributes much towards success.

When it comes to playing off the last 12 cards, the experienced player will never be in any doubt about which cards his opponent holds. Thus, when playing to the last trick before the stock is exhausted, a player should be able to weigh up the merits of winning the trick and melding, preventing his opponent from melding, or losing the trick and so obtaining the exposed trump card to add to his trump length in the final play off.

PIQUET

*P*IQUET *is probably the best known of all card games for two players; there is no doubt that it is more skilful and interesting than any other.*

NUMBER OF PLAYERS

Although Piquet has been adapted for three or four players, these variations are not described, as it is essentially a game for two.

CARDS

Piquet is played with the 32-card pack, i.e. the standard pack from which the 6s, 5s, 4s, 3s and 2s are removed. Cards rank from Ace (high) to 7 (low).

Players cut for deal, and the higher has the right of first deal; he would be advised to take it because there is some advantage to be gained from it.

Twelve cards are dealt to each player in either twos or threes, and the remaining eight cards (talon) are placed face downwards on the table between the players. The non-dealer may now exchange any five of his cards with the five top cards of the talon. He need not exchange as many as five cards, but he must exchange at least one, and, if he has not exchanged five cards, he may look at those that he was entitled to draw. The dealer may exchange cards up to the number that remain in the talon. He, too, must exchange at least one card. If he does

59

not exchange all the cards, he may look at those that he was entitled to, but he must show them to his opponent if he does. The players place their discards face downwards on the table in front of them. The discards of the players should not be mixed together as, during the play of the hand, the players are entitled to look at their own discards, but not their opponent's.

The score is made up in three ways: the count of the hand; the count during the play of the cards; the extraordinary scores.

The hand is counted in the following way:

The point, which is the number of cards held in the longest suit. The player who holds the longest suit wins the point, and scores one point for each card that he holds in it. If the number of cards in the suits held by the players is the same, the player with the highest count (Aces 11, Kings, Queens and Jacks 10 each, and other cards at their pip values) wins the point. If the count is equal neither player scores.

Sequences, which must not be of less than three cards of the same suit, are won by the player who holds the most cards in one sequence. As between sequences of equal length, the highest wins. For a sequence of three (tierce) three points are scored; for a sequence of four (quart) four points are scored. For a sequence of five (quint) 15 points are scored; for a sequence of six (sixième) 16 points; for a sequence of seven (septième) and for a sequence of eight (huitième) 18 points.

Quatorzes and trios are any four or three cards of the same rank higher than the 9. The player who holds the superior quatorze or trio wins. Thus, a player who holds a trio of Aces will win even though his opponent may hold trios of Kings *and* Queens. In the same way, a player who holds trios of Aces, Kings, Queens and Jacks will score nothing if his opponent holds a quatorze of 10s. Quatorzes are scored at 14 points each; trios at three points each.

The count of the hand must be declared in the order: point, sequence, quatorze and trio, and, on demand, a player must show any combinations of cards for which he has scored. In practice, however, this is rarely necessary, because the opponent is usually able to infer from his own cards what cards are held against him by his opponent.

When counting the hand a player is not compelled to declare all that he holds. It is in order, and sometimes the very best play, to mislead one's opponent by declaring less than one holds in order to conceal one's strength. The practice is known as sinking. The player who holds a quatorze of Aces may declare only a trio. The opponent may inquire which Ace is not being reckoned, and the player may name any Ace he chooses, because the explicit reply: 'I do not count the Ace of Clubs' is not a guarantee that the player does not hold this card.

THE PLAY

After the non-dealer has counted his hand he leads a card. The dealer then counts his hand and plays a card to the non-dealer's lead. Two cards constitute a trick, and it is compulsory for the second player to follow suit to the led card if he can do so. If not he may play any card he chooses, because there is no trump suit. The player who leads to a trick scores one point, and if his opponent wins it he scores one point for doing so (except in the case of the last trick, when he scores two points) and leads to the next trick, scoring one point for the lead. After all 12 tricks have been played, the player who has won most tricks scores 10 points for having done so (Ten for the Cards, as it is called). There is no score to either player if they win six tricks each.

There are four extraordinary scores: Carte blanche. If a player is dealt a hand that contains no court card he may claim carte blanche and score 10 points. It takes precedence over any other scoring combination, but the player must announce his carte blanche as soon as he picks up the cards dealt to him, and he must show his hand, though he need not do so until after his opponent has discarded.

Pique. If a player scores in hand and plays 30 points, before his opponent scores anything, he wins a pique and scores 30 points for it. Only the non-dealer can win a pique, because he scores one point for the first lead before the dealer counts his hand;

this, of course, automatically rules out the dealer from scoring for a pique.

Repique. If a player scores in hand alone a total of 30 points, before his opponent scores anything, he wins a repique and scores 60 points for it. Either player may score for a repique, because points in hand are counted in priority to those won in play.

Capot. If a player wins all 12 tricks he wins a capot and scores 40 points, not 10, for the cards. The capot, however, is not counted towards a pique because the points are not scored until the hand has been played.

The players deal alternately, and a *partie* (game) consists of six deals (three deals each). At the end of the *partie* the player with the higher score deducts from his score that of his opponent, and adds 100 points to the result. If, however, one player fails to score 100 points, he is rubiconed, and the player with the higher score adds the two scores together, and a further 100 points. If the score after six deals is equal, each player has one more deal, and if the score still remains equal the *partie* is a draw.

Most card games are played in silence. Piquet is a continuous dialogue. When a player counts his hand he declares his point, sequences, quatorzes and trios, and his opponent confirms whether they are 'Good', 'Not good' or 'Equal', and, if equal, the player announces the pip total which his opponent declares 'Good', 'Not

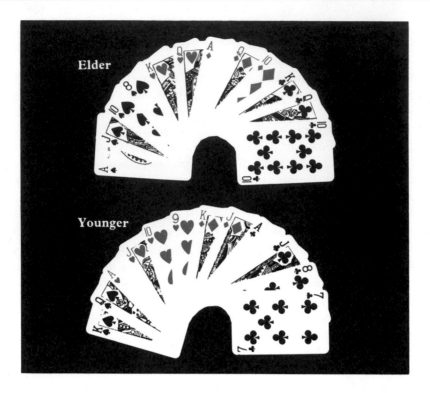

good' or 'Equal'. Then, during the play of the hand, the two players announce their scores as each trick is played.

At piquet it is customary to call the non-dealer the elder (hand) and the dealer the younger (hand). The deal above (after both players have discarded) illustrates the method of scoring and is not to be accepted as an example of good play.

Elder: 'Point of four'.
Younger: 'Making?'
Elder: 'Thirty-nine'.
Younger: 'Not good'.
Elder: 'Queens and Tens – six'. (He counts his score for his trios without waiting for younger to confirm that the

count is good. He knows that his trio of Queens is good because, from his own cards, he can see that younger cannot hold a quatorze or a better trio than one of Jacks. His announcement 'Queens and Tens' means that he holds three Queens and three 10s. If he held four Queens and three 10s he would announce 'Fourteen Queens and three Tens'.)

Elder, who has no more to count, leads the ♠A: 'Seven'.

Younger now counts his hand.

Younger: 'Point of four – forty', (Elder has a right to ask in which suit the point is. In this case, however, he has no need because he knows from his own cards that it can only be in hearts) 'and tierce to the Jack – seven'. (Here, again, elder has no need to ask because, from his own cards, he knows that the tierce must be in hearts.)

Younger plays the ♠Q on elder's ♠A, and repeats his score – 'Seven'.

The rest of the play is:

Elder		Younger	
♠J	'Eight'	♠K	'Eight'
♡Q	'Eight'	♡A	'Nine'
♡K	'Nine'	♡J	'Ten'
♠10	'Ten'	♣7	'Ten'
♠8	'Eleven'	♣8	'Ten'
♣K	'Twelve'	♣A	'Eleven'
◇10	'Twelve'	♡10	'Twelve'
◇Q	'Twelve'	♡9	'Thirteen'
♣Q	'Thirteen'	♣J	'Fourteen'
◇A	'Fourteen'	◇J	'Fourteen'
♣10	'Fifteen'	◇K	'Fourteen'

Elder, winning the trick: 'Sixteen, and the cards twenty-six'. This ends the deal with the score at elder 26, younger 14.

A player's first consideration must be the point. The importance of scoring for the point cannot be overestimated, because not only does it add to a player's score, but it protects him against a pique or repique, and, of course, scoring for point diminishes the opponent's score to the same ex-

tent. Normally, therefore, a player should retain his longest suit intact and discard from shorter suits. This, however, does not always hold good, particularly if the longest suit consists mainly of low cards, and the shorter suits of high ones. The inexperienced player who is dealt the hand below will be tempted to retain the spades, and discard from the other suits, with a view to scoring for point and sequence. The experienced player will know that the better course is to discard all five spades, because the ♠J is the only card that will raise the suit from a quart to a sixième, and the odds are about three to one against drawing it. It is likely that retaining the spades will win the point, but almost certainly it will result in the loss of the cards. This will make a big difference to the score, and the cards must always be considered together with the point. If the non-dealer holds a long suit headed by top cards, usually it guarantees the point and the cards. The suit, therefore, must be preserved at all costs, but this is of much less importance for the dealer because he may never obtain the lead.

A good general rule emerges. The discards of the non-dealer should be made towards obtaining an attacking

hand; that of the dealer towards obtaining a defensive hand; that is to say a hand in which there is some strength in as many suits as possible.

Subject to these considerations, it is best to discard from as few suits as possible, and, once a player has made up his mind to discard from a suit, he should discard the whole of it, unless it is necessary to retain the suit guarded. Sequence cards should be retained in preference to non-sequence cards, and, of course, cards that help to make up trios and quatorzes should never be discarded if it is to be avoided.

Playing to the score is very important, particularly in the last deal of a *partie*. As an example: if a player is well ahead, and sees the opportunity to gain a rubicon, he should discard cautiously and play so as to prevent his opponent from saving the rubicon by scoring 100 points. On the other hand, if a player is in danger of being rubiconed, he should be prepared to take some risks, since only a big score will save him. It must be remembered, however, that if a player is rubiconed his score is added to that of his opponent, so if there is no chance of saving the rubicon he should play to keep his score down. To this end he should declare only equities or those scores that will save pique and repique, and he should aim to divide the cards.

AUCTION PIQUET

This version originated in Oxford, and was developed by some British prisoners of war during the First World War.

The bidding takes place before the discard. It is opened by the non-dealer. He may pass, and if he does and the dealer does also, there is a redeal by the same player. The lowest bid that may be made is one of seven. It is an undertaking to win, or lose, seven of the 12 possible tricks. There is no penalty for a bid out of turn or for an underbid, because these irregularities merely give information to the opponent.

The most interesting feature of the game is the minus bid. It is an undertaking to lose the stated number of tricks. It ranks neither above nor below a normal (plus) bid. In a minus deal the player scores everything good in his opponent's hand. A player may double a bid made by his opponent, and the player who has been doubled may redouble or shift to a higher bid.

After bidding, the players discard. The routine is the same as in the parent game except that there is no compulsion for the players to discard at least one card.

The declarations follow, and the players may declare the point, sequences, trios and quatorzes in any order they choose. Sinking is allowed in plus deals but not in minus ones.

The scoring is as follows:

The value of point, sequences, trios, quatorzes, cards and capot, are the same as in the parent game.

In plus deals pique (30 points) is obtained on the score of 29 and repique (60 points) on the score of 30. In minus deals both pique and repique are obtained on the score of 21.

The *partie* (six deals) is worth 150 points, and rubicon is under 150 points. In the event of a tie a seventh deal is played and the *partie* ends if it is tied.

A player scores 10 points for every trick won in a plus deal (or lost in a minus deal) above (or below) the declared contract.

If a player fails to make his contract the opponent scores 10 points for every trick by which he is short.

Overtricks and undertricks are effected by doubling and redoubling, but scores in hand and play are not.

Although a player scores one point for winning a trick he does not score for leading a losing card, nor an additional one point for winning the last trick.

RUSSIAN BANK

*R*USSIAN BANK *is similar to some patience games, in that cards are built on foundations, but it is a competitive game. It is also called Crapette and Stop!*

NUMBER OF PLAYERS

Russian Bank is for two players.

CARDS

Two full packs of 52 cards with different backs (for ease of sorting into two packs afterwards) are used. The cards rank from King (high) to Ace (low).

Each player draws a card from one of the packs. The player with the lower card plays first. Each player has one complete pack, and each player shuffles his opponent's pack and places it face down before his opponent. Players sit opposite each other.

The first player deals 11 cards face down to a pile to his right, turning the 12th card face up and placing it on top of the pile. This is his depot. He deals the next four cards face up in a column to his left so that the column runs from his left hand to his opponent's right hand. This is his file. He places the rest of his cards face down to his left. This is his stock.

THE PLAY

The object is to pack onto the cards in the files in descending sequences of alternate colours. Cards should be packed outwards from the centre. Any Aces are played to a foundation column to the right of the file. The Aces in the foundation column are built up to King, as cards become available, in suit sequence. The cards

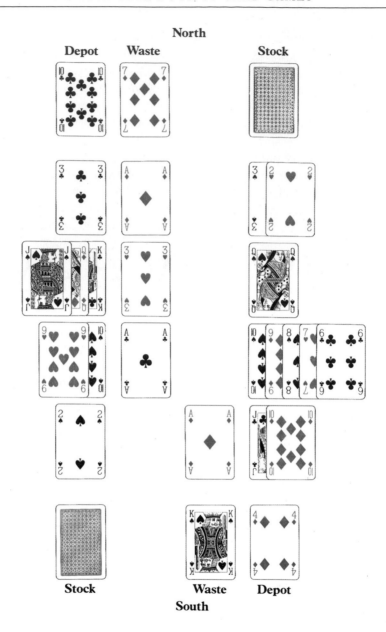

Russian Bank – a game in progress.

initially available are the cards in the file and the card face up on the depot. One card in the file can be packed on another, and when a card in the file is packed upon, it is still available, and can be packed onto another card in the file provided all the cards packed on it are transferred with it. Players of the patience game Demon (or Canfield) will recognize the principles.

When the first player has completed his layout as described, he first moves any Ace from the file to its foundation space. The space created in the file is filled by the top card of the depot, and the next card in the depot is turned face up. He then makes any further plays available, filling spaces created from the depot each time, until no further plays are possible. He then turns over the first card of his stock. If he can build it onto a foundation or pack it onto a file he does so and turns the next card and so on. When he finally turns a card which cannot be played to a foundation or file, he plays it to a waste heap to his right, next to his depot. He then turns the next card from the stock face up to the waste heap ready for play on his next turn, and his current turn ends.

The second player then deals a depot, a file and a stock in the same way, so that his cards interlock with the first to form a complete tableau (the illustration shows a game in progress). The second player makes his moves as the first, but he has the advantage of also being able to build to his opponent's foundations, and pack onto his opponent's files. He can also play from his own depot and file onto his opponent's waste heap in either ascending or descending sequence, irrespective of suit or colour. However, he cannot pack onto his opponent's waste heap from his own

waste heap or stock. Each player from now on has these options on his turn. Cards available for play are those exposed at the top of a file, depot or waste heap. A turn ends when a player cannot play a card from stock except onto his waste heap.

When a player's stock is exhausted, he turns over his waste heap (without shuffling) to form a new stock. When his depot is exhausted, he fills spaces in his file from his stock.

Plays must be made in the following order:

A space in a file must be filled before any other play is made.

A player must play from his depot before he plays from his file or waste heap.

When a card is played from the depot, the next card must be turned face up before the next play is made.

A player must play to a foundation if possible, before playing to a file.

A player must play to a file if possible, before playing to a waste heap.

A player who sees his opponent violate any of these rules or make any other mistake may cry 'Stop!' before his opponent has made a further play, and thus bring his turn to an end. He then points out the mistake, retracts the wrong play and makes the play his opponent failed to. He then takes over the turn himself.

The winner is the first player to get rid of all the cards in his stock and waste heap.

TABLANETTE

*T*ABLANETTE *is a game that is easy to learn and worth learning because it is remarkably fascinating to play.*

NUMBER OF PLAYERS

Tablanette is for two players but can be played by three, as described later.

CARDS

The full pack of 52 cards is used. Cards have their pip values, except that Ace can count as 11 or 1 at the discretion of the holder. King counts as 14 and Queen as 13. The Jack has no value, but plays a special part in the game, as will be seen.

Six cards are dealt face downwards to the two players, and four cards face upwards to the table between them. The rest of the pack is temporarily set aside. If any Jacks are dealt to the table they are removed, placed at the bottom of the pack, and the spaces filled with cards from the top of the pack.

THE PLAY

The non-dealer plays first. If he plays a card of the same rank as any of the four cards on the table, he takes the card; or, if there are any two or three cards on the table whose values if added together equal that of the card played, he takes these cards.

If the cards on the table and the player's hand are as illustrated on page 68 he will play the ♡K and take the ♠K from the table. If he holds the cards in the upper of the two illustrations below he will play the ♡A and take the ♡2 and ♣9 from the table, because together they total 11, the value of an Ace.

The cards played and those taken from the table are kept in a pile, face downwards, on the table by the player who took them.

If at any time a player is able to take all the cards on the table (there may be only one, or there may be more than four) he announces 'Tablanette' and scores the total value of all the cards taken plus the value of the card he has played. If, for example, the cards on the table are as illustrated below,

and a player holds any of the other three Kings, he will be able to announce 'Tablanette', because his King will take the ♠K and the other three cards whose values total 14. The score for this will be 42 points (i.e. 14 × 3).

The special function of the Jack is that playing it allows the player to take all the cards on the table, but it does not allow him to score for a tablanette. Obviously, therefore, a Jack is an excellent card to hold, because playing it compels the opponent to play a lone card to the table and when there is only one card on the table the player whose turn it is to play is in a good position to score a tablanette.

The players play in rotation until they have exhausted their six cards. The dealer then deals another six cards to each, and so on until the pack is exhausted.

When the last batch of six cards has been played, any cards left on the table are taken by the player who last took a card from the table.

The players examine the cards they have taken, and score one point for the ♣2 and for every Ace, King, Queen, Jack and 10 (except the ◇10 which scores two points). Finally, if a player has taken 27 or more cards he scores three points.

The deal passes in rotation, and the game is won by the player who first scores a total of 251 points.

There is more skill in the game than may be apparent at first sight. If, for example, there is only an 8 on the table and the player holds the cards shown at the top of the page, his best play is the

♡4, because no one card has a value of 12 and the opponent, therefore, cannot score a tablanette.

As at all card games it is very important to keep in mind the cards that have been played. The opponent has scored a tablanette and the player holds:

He has to play a card to the table, and the natural tendency is to play the ♡3, because this will give the opponent a minimum score if he can again announce 'Tablanette'. But if no 3s have been played, but a 10 has, then it is better to play one of the 10s, because the chances are against the opponent holding the remaining 10, and there is a possibility that he holds one of the remaining three 3s.

TABLANETTE FOR THREE PLAYERS

Should three wish to play, the game is played in the same way as the parent game, except that the players are dealt four cards (instead of six) at a time.

GAMES FOR THREE PLAYERS

BLACK MARIA

*B*LACK MARIA, *sometimes known as Black Lady and sometimes as Slippery Anne, is very similar to Hearts and its several variations (see page 139).*

NUMBER OF PLAYERS

Black Maria is best played by three players, but can be played by four or five as described later.

CARDS

The full pack is used minus the ♣2, making a pack of 51 cards. Cards rank from Ace (high) to 2 (low).

Seventeen cards are dealt to each player. The deal passes in rotation clockwise. After a player has looked at his cards, he passes three of them to his right-hand opponent and receives three from his left-hand opponent, which he must not look at before he has passed his three on.

THE PLAY

When the exchanges of cards have been made, the player on the left of the dealer leads to the first trick. Thereafter, the player who wins a trick leads to the next. A player must follow suit to the led card provided he can do so. Otherwise he may discard any card he chooses. There is no trump suit.

The object of the game is to avoid winning a trick which contains a penalty card. These cards, and the penalties that go with them, are:

All hearts	1
♠A	7
♠K	10
♠Q (Black Maria)	13

The game introduces two features: the discard and the play of the cards.

The inexperienced player, if he is dealt a high spade, will assume that he cannot do better than pass it on to his right-hand opponent. It is, however, not always the best play. Provided a number of low spades are held in

support of the high ones, it is very often better to retain the high cards with a view to controlling the suit during the play of the hand. Indeed, a player who has been dealt any spades or hearts lower than the Queen would be well advised to keep them in order to protect himself against any top cards in the suits that may be passed on to him. The main principle of discarding should be to try and set up either a void suit – in order to get rid of penalty cards by discarding them during the play – or at obtaining long suits, provided low cards in them are held. A player who has been dealt the hand illustrated above cannot do better than pass on the three diamonds. The

spades must be kept to protect against receiving a high card in the suit, the hearts are adequately protected, and there is nothing to fear in clubs.

An ability to count the cards is the first essential to success. Towards the end of a deal an experienced player will know pretty well which cards are still left to be played, and he will be able to make a shrewd guess who holds them. It is in the end-play, therefore, that opportunity comes for skilful play.

A three-card ending is illustrated at the bottom of page 72. After 14 tricks the players should know who holds the remaining cards.

West is on lead and leads the ♠6, North plays the ♠2 and East, perforce, wins with the ♠K. Now, if East returns the ◇5, West must win with the ◇7 and North saddles him with the ♠Q (Black Maria). If, however, East returns the ♣3, North will have to win with the ♣6 on which West will have played the ♠A.

East's play will be directed by the score, and whether it is more advan-

tageous to him to saddle West or North with all 20 points. The strategy is quite ethical so long as East puts his own interest first and is not moved by malice aforethought.

FOUR-HANDED BLACK MARIA

With four players the game is played in the same way as the parent game, except that no card is removed from the pack, and every player, therefore, receives 13 cards. The players may play all against all, or two in partnership against the other two.

FIVE-HANDED BLACK MARIA

Five players can play in the same way as in the parent game, but the ◇2 as well as the ♣2 is removed from the pack. Each player, therefore, is dealt ten cards.

CALABRASELLA

CALABRASELLA is played with what is now usually called the Spanish pack of 40 cards, but which was also the Italian pack, and the game might have come originally from the province of Calabria, in the extreme south of Italy. It is a game usually played for stakes.

NUMBER OF PLAYERS

Calabrasella is for three players, although four often play in rotation, the dealer giving no cards to himself, and sitting out the hand.

CARDS

The Spanish pack of 40 cards is used, made from the standard pack by discarding the 10s, 9s and 8s. The remaining cards rank in the order 3, 2, Ace, King, Queen, Jack, 7, 6, 5, 4. In the game the Ace is worth three points, the 3, 2, King, Queen, Jack one point each.

Players draw for deal, the lowest dealing first. The deal thereafter passes in rotation to the left. Dealer deals 12 cards to each hand in twos. The four cards remaining are set aside face down to form a widow.

THE PLAY

The object is to make tricks containing cards of a counting value (see above). Players study their hands, and the player to the left of the dealer announces either 'I play' or 'I pass'. Should he pass, the next player has the same option, and if he passes, the dealer. Should all pass, the hand is abandoned, but if any player announces 'I play', the play begins.

The player electing to play is called the Player. He first specifies by suit any 3 not held in his hand. If either of the other players hold that 3 he must pass it

to the Player, who may exchange for it any card he wishes from his own hand, not showing it to the third player. If the Player holds all four 3s, he may specify any 2, and so on. If the card he specifies is in the widow, no exchange takes place.

The Player next discards face down any number of cards from his hand from one to four (he must discard at least one). The widow is then exposed, and the Player selects from it sufficient cards to restore his hand to 12 cards. The remainder, plus the Player's discards, are set aside, and are later claimed by the winner of the last trick.

The game now becomes a trick-taking game, with the other two combining in a temporary partnership against the Player. He to the left of the Player makes the opening lead, and may lead any card he likes. The others follow in a clockwise direction, and are obliged to follow suit to the card led if able; if unable to they may discard. There are no trumps. The winner of a trick leads to the next.

The winner of the last trick takes the four cards not used in the trick-taking phase, and is also awarded a bonus of three points. As there are eight points in each suit, the total points available in each deal is 35.

The side which wins the majority of the points (18 or more) collects from the other side the difference in the two totals. If the Player scores 20 points and his opponents 15, the Player receives five units from *both* opponents. If the opponents had scored the 20 points, each would receive five units from the Player. The amount to be paid per point must obviously be agreed beforehand. The game can be played for recreation only by keeping a running profit and loss score with pencil and paper.

Calabrasella offers opportunities for skill. Much depends on the decision whether or not to play. Of prime importance are stoppers in all suits. Should one of the opponents be able to run off a long suit, the other will be able to discard high-scoring cards (Aces) on it. Should the Player win all the cards in one suit, he might score only eight points from the tricks,

whereas an opponent with the same cards will get scoring discards from his partner. The Player can gain the advantage of calling in a 3, but should not rely on much from the widow. In order to keep guards in each suit, he might not be able to discard more than two cards. It is important for him to remember which cards he discards, since only the Player knows which cards are not in play, and thus which suits are short. The disadvantage of playing against two players is a big one, and the commonest mistake is to play with too weak a hand.

CUT-THROAT BRIDGE

*M*ANY *suggestions have been made to make Bridge (see page 103) suitable for three players. The most satisfactory is Towie (see page 99) but what has become known as Cut-throat Bridge is the original and the simplest of the three-handed variations.*

NUMBER OF PLAYERS

This game is specifically designed for three players unable to find a fourth for Bridge.

CARDS

The full pack of 52 cards is used.

The players take seats at random and after drawing for deal, shuffling and cutting in the usual way, the dealer deals 13 cards each to the three players and to a fourth hand that is temporarily set aside.

THE PLAY

The auction, beginning with the dealer, is conducted as in the parent game, and when a player's bid, double or redouble has been passed by the other two players, the player on his left leads to the first trick. The player who has obtained the final contract then sorts the fourth hand, spreads it in front of him on the table, and plays it as his dummy, against the other two players in partnership with each other.

The play and scoring are the same as in the parent game, except that if a player loses his contract both his opponents score the penalty points. The winner of a rubber receives a bonus of 700 points if neither opponent has won a game, but 500 points if either has.

Very clearly the game is a gamble, because the players must bid in the hope of finding the cards they need in the dummy hand.

A variation designed to make the game less speculative is for every player to be dealt 17 cards and the 52nd card face downwards to the dummy. After looking at their cards, and before bidding them, every player contributes four of them, face downwards, to the dummy. This way every player knows four out of the 13 cards that he is bidding for.

In another variation, instead of bidding for the dummy, an agreed number of deals (that must be divisible by three) is played, and, in turn, every player plays the dummy against the other two playing in partnership.

In this variation rubbers are not played, but the player who bids and makes game scores a bonus of 300 points. There is no vulnerability.

FIVE HUNDRED

FIVE HUNDRED is a trick-taking game invented early this century which was very popular for a long time in the United States.

NUMBER OF PLAYERS

The game is designed for three players, but may be played by two to five, as described later.

CARDS

The usual short pack of 32 is required, plus the Joker, making a pack of 33. From a standard pack the 6s, 5s, 4s, 3s and 2s are removed.

The game is played with a trump suit, and the cards in the trump suit rank as follows: Joker, Jack (called right bower), Jack of the same colour as the trump suit (called left bower), Ace, King, Queen, 10, 9, 8, 7.

The cards in the plain suits rank normally: Ace, King, Queen, Jack, 10, 9, 8, 7, except that the suit of the same colour as the trump suit will not contain a Jack. Therefore the suits have an unequal number of cards: the trump suit has ten cards, the suit of the same colour has seven cards and the other two suits have eight cards.

In addition, the suits are ranked, as follows: hearts (high) diamonds, clubs, spades.

Players draw for deal, the lowest dealing. For this purpose the cards rank in their usual order, but Ace counts low, and Joker lowest of all. The dealer shuffles, the player on his right cuts, and the dealer deals three cards to each hand, beginning on his left, then three to the centre to form a widow, then four to each hand, then three to each hand. Each player therefore has ten cards, with the extra three being in a widow.

THE PLAY

The players examine their cards and a round of bidding begins. A bid is an offer by a player to make a stated number of tricks with a specified trump suit or without a trump suit (a bid in 'no-trumps'). Each bid must be higher than the previous bid. The values of the bids are as follows:

	Six	Seven	Eight	Nine	Ten
Spades	40	140	240	340	440
Clubs	60	160	260	360	460
Diamonds	80	180	280	380	480
Hearts	100	200	300	400	500
No-trumps	120	220	320	420	520

Eldest begins and may bid or pass, and bidding continues until two players in succession pass, whereupon the last bid made constitutes the contract. (In some schools the bidding is not continuous, and each player is allowed one bid only, while in other schools the bidding is progressive but a player who passes cannot re-enter the bidding.)

Should none of the players bid, the deal is abandoned, and passes to the next player.

Once a player has won the contract, he picks up the widow, and discards three cards face down to keep his hand to ten cards.

The ten tricks are now played out, with the player with the contract leading to the first trick. The winner of a trick leads to the next. The normal rules of trick-taking apply: each player must follow suit to the lead, and if unable to he may trump or discard. A trick is won by the highest trump played, or if there is none by the highest card in the suit led.

In a no-trump contract, the Joker remains a trump – the only one. It can be played only if its holder cannot follow suit. If the Joker is led in a no-trump contract, its player specifies the suit it represents, and the other players must play cards of that suit if able to. The Joker always wins the trick.

The object, so far as the declarer is concerned, is to make at least as many tricks as he contracted to do. His opponents score individually for the tricks they make, so are playing for themselves, but they should also play in partnership, because defeating the contract will cost the declarer more than the points they can make individually for themselves.

If the declarer makes his contract, he scores its value as set out in the table above. There is no bonus for overtricks, with one possible exception, which is that a player who takes all ten tricks scores a minimum of 250 points. So if a player's contract is worth less than 250 (i.e. eight spades or less), he will earn a bonus by taking all ten tricks.

If the declarer fails to make his contract, he loses the value of his bid. A player can thus have a minus score, which is recorded with a circle round it, and the player is said to be 'in the hole'.

Each of the two players opposing the declarer scores separately for the tricks they make – ten points per trick, and there is no bonus for defeating the declarer. Game is to 500 points (hence the name). It is rare for a player to win without making at least one contract, so, as stated earlier, the ten points per trick are of less significance than the making or defeating of contracts.

Should the declarer and an opponent pass 500 on the same deal, the declarer is the winner. Should the two opponents pass 500, the one who took the trick to take his score to 500 first is the winner.

It is customary to set a limit to the 'hole', say 500. Should a player reach 500 in the hole, the opponent who is leading at the end of the deal is the winner. This is to prevent a player in the hole bidding recklessly and pre-

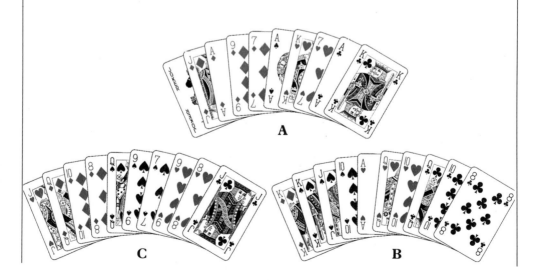

A

C

B

venting his opponents from making a contract, and in effect spoiling the game.

To outline the mechanics of the game, suppose hands are held as in the illustration. Player A has bid seven diamonds, and has been lucky enough to find ♣A in the widow. He decides to lead trumps immediately, hoping to lose one only, to ♡J (left bower), which will ensure his contract. Play proceeds as follows:

	Player A	*Player B*	*Player C*
1	Joker	◇K	◇8
2	◇J	♣8	◇10
3	♣A	♣10	♣J
4	♣K	♣Q	◇Q
5	♡K	♡A	♡8
6	♡7	♡Q	♡9
7	◇7	♡10	♣7
8	◇A	♣10	♡J
9	♣A	♣J	♣9
10	◇9	♣K	♣Q

From trick 2, when ◇J (right bower) failed to drop ♡J, Player A knew that his best chances were that Player C held the ♡A, which would give him a chance of making ♡K, or that Player C could be forced to lead his remaining trumps (in which case Player A would lose only one trump) or that the defenders would make a mistake with their discards. As it happened, the defenders played well, and Player A was forced to lose both hearts and two trumps.

Player A therefore failed to make his contract of seven diamonds, and scored 180 points in the hole. Players B and C each made two tricks, so each scored 20 points.

Strategy in playing the cards is similar to most trick-taking games. The main skill in Five Hundred lies in the bidding. As the trump suit consists of ten cards, one player must hold at least four, so four trumps is the minimum requirement for a bid, and even then they must be good ones and supported by side Aces. Unless six or more trumps are held in the deal, the chances are slightly in favour of at least one more being in the widow, but this should not be relied upon. As a rough guide, a player might count any of the top four trumps (Joker, right and left bower, Ace) as one point each, all trumps held in excess of three as one point each, all master cards in side suits as one point each, and a guarded King in a side suit as half a point, and bid accordingly. In the example above, Player A held three points in top trumps, two more with the ◇9, 7, one more with ♣A, and two half-points with guarded Kings, the ♡K and ♣K (he found ♣A in the widow). He therefore had seven points and bid seven diamonds. The ♣A would usually have made his contract a good one, but as it happened the outstanding trumps were badly split for him, and the ♡A was badly placed.

A variation often played is to allow an extra bid, called nullo. This is a contract to win no tricks at all. There are no trumps. The value of the bid is 250, placing it between eight spades and eight clubs. A player holding the Joker can play it only when void of the suit led. If the Joker is led, its player specifies the suit it represents. The Joker always wins the trick in which it is played. When the declarer makes nullo, he scores 250 and his opponents score nothing. When he fails he is debited 250, and his opponents score ten points each for each trick he makes.

Five Hundred for Two Players

The cards are dealt as for the three-handed game described, the third hand being put to one side and taking no part. With ten cards being dead, the game is much more one of chance than the three-handed version.

Five Hundred for Four Players

With four players the pack must be enlarged to allow each player to have ten cards. The 6s, 5s, and two red 4s are added to the 33-card pack. Play is in partnerships, partners sitting opposite each other. Bidding proceeds as before, and the player making the highest bid leads to the first trick. Each side keeps its tricks separately, and scoring is as before.

Five Hundred for Five Players

The full pack is used, plus the Joker, so that each player receives ten cards and there are three in the widow as before. Each player plays for himself, but the player who wins the contract calls upon one of the others to be his temporary partner, and the two play that hand against the other three. In some schools the declarer names the player he wants as his partner, who will possibly be a player who has bid, and who therefore is known to have a good hand. More usually, the declarer calls upon the holder of a specific card to be his partner. This will usually be the highest missing trump, but it might be an Ace in a side suit. The holder of the card does not announce it, so until he plays the card only he knows that he is partnering the declarer. With neither method does the partner of the declarer change his seat.

Each partner trying to make a contract scores the relevant points if successful and is debited with them if unsuccessful. The opponents each score ten points for each trick taken.

500 RUM

THE game of 500 Rum is much more closely allied to the Rummy family than to Five Hundred.

NUMBER OF PLAYERS

The game is best for three, which is the version described here, but it can be played by any number from two to eight, as described later.

CARDS

The full standard pack of 52 cards is used (with five or more players two packs are used). Cards rank in the order: King, Queen, Jack, 10, 9, 8, 7, 6, 5, 4, 3, 2, Ace. Cards also have values for scoring points as follows: King, Queen, Jack are each worth ten points, Aces are worth 15 points each if melded as Aces, but one point if used in a sequence of Ace, 2, 3. All other cards score according to their pip value.

Each player draws a card to decide dealer; lowest deals. The dealer shuffles the pack, which is cut by the player to his right, and deals seven cards, one at a time, to each player, beginning with eldest. The remaining cards are placed face down to form the stock, and the top card is turned face up and placed beside the stock to begin the discard pile.

THE PLAY

The object of the game is to form sets of three or four cards of the same rank, or sequences of three or more cards of the same suit. Sequences stop at Ace at one end and King at the other: Ace, King, Queen is not a sequence.

Beginning with eldest, each player may take either a card or cards from the discard pile, or the top card of the stock. After drawing, the player may meld as many cards as he likes by placing sets and/or sequences on the table in front of him, and he then discards one card to the discard pile and the turn passes. Should a player draw from the discard pile, he *must* meld, and he must use the card taken from the discard pile in his meld. In other words a card cannot be taken from the discard pile unless it is used immediately in a meld.

This game differs from most other variations of Rummy in that *all* the cards in the discard pile are available, therefore the discard pile is not strictly a pile but a collection of cards spread out so that all their indices can be seen

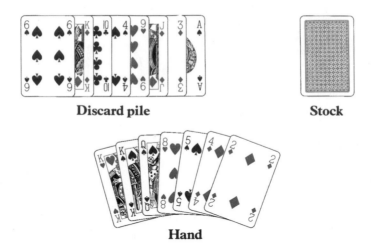

Discard pile   **Stock**

Hand

The player holding this hand will be advised to pick up ◇ 3. He can immediately meld ◇ 2, 3, 4; ♠ 4, 5, 6; ◇ K, ◇ ♡, K ♠. He must leave ◇ J, ♡ 9 and ♣ 10 on the table before him for one round, and should discard ♠ Q.

(see illustration). When a player takes a card from the discard pile, he must also take all the cards above it. After melding with the card taken, he leaves on the table for one round any other cards taken from the discard pile which he has not melded, so that all other players may memorize them. On his next turn he takes them into his hand.

A player may on his turn add cards to any meld on the table, whether it is his meld or an opponent's. These cards are not actually attached to the melds, if they be opponents' melds, but kept on the table before the player, who will score for them later. It may happen that a card thus placed on the table would fit onto two existing melds, in which case the player must state which meld he is fitting his card or cards to. This is important because other players may subsequently add to the melds further.

Play continues until one player gets rid of all the cards in his hand or until the stock is exhausted. When the last card is drawn from stock, and the drawer has discarded, play may continue if the next player can draw from the discard pile and meld, and again if the next player can, and so on until one player passes.

At the end of the game, each player adds up the values of all the cards he has melded, and from the total he deducts the values of all the cards left in his hand, if any (an Ace in hand counts 15). Once a player has gone out, no further melds can be made by other players, and any sets or sequences held, or cards which might be added to melds, are debited. A player may thus end with a minus score on the hand.

A running total is kept of each player's score, and the first to reach 500 is the winner.

500 RUM FOR TWO PLAYERS

When played by two players, each receives 13 cards. Otherwise the game is played as above.

500 RUM FOR FOUR PLAYERS

The game may be played by four players as cut-throat, each playing against each, or it may be played in two partnerships, partners sitting opposite each other. The play is as above, but partners try to co-operate with each other. Scores are kept for each side.

500 RUM FOR FIVE TO EIGHT PLAYERS

Two packs shuffled together must be used. Otherwise the game is played as above, each player playing for himself.

KNAVES

KNAVES is so called because the four Knaves (or Jacks) are penalty cards and the object of the players is to avoid winning tricks that contain them.

NUMBER OF PLAYERS

Knaves is for three players.

CARDS

The full pack of 52 cards is used, cards ranking from Ace (high) to 2 (low).

Seventeen cards are dealt to each player and the last card is turned face upwards on the table to denote the trump suit. It takes no other part in the game.

THE PLAY

The player on the left of the dealer leads to the first trick; thereafter the player who wins a trick leads to the next. A player must follow suit, if he can, to the card led. If he cannot he may either trump or discard a card of a plain suit.

The player who wins a trick scores one point for it, but four points are deducted from a player's score if he wins the Knave of hearts, three points if he wins the Knave of diamonds, two points if he wins the Knave of clubs, and one point if he wins the Knave of spades. The aggregate score for each deal, therefore, is seven points (i.e. 17 points for tricks minus 10 points for Knaves) unless one of the Knaves is the card turned up to denote the trump suit. Game is won by the first player to score 20 points.

The players play all against all, but skilful play introduces temporary partnerships that add much to the interest of the game. If, for example, one player is in the lead and the other two are trailing behind, they will combine with the aim of preventing the leading player from winning still more, even if they cannot reduce his score by forcing him to win tricks that contain Knaves. In the same way, if two players have an advanced score, and the third is down the course, the two who are ahead will so play that such points as they cannot themselves win will go to the player with the low score rather than to the one with the high score.

The game, therefore, gives ample scope for clever play. Until the last Knave has been played, a player has to strike a balance between the incentive to take a trick, and so score a point, and the fear of being saddled with a Knave, resulting in a loss.

There is much more in the game than appears on the surface. Consider the hands in the illustration.

No score to anyone.

East deals and the ♣7 is turned up.

With his preponderance of trumps North appears to be in a position to score well. In reality his hand is far from being a good one, because, though the trumps give him the advantage of winning tricks, this advantage is more than offset by the fact that he is in the dangerous position of being forced to take Knaves. Indeed, North

is very likely to come out with a poor score; against good play by West he will be hard put to avoid taking the Knaves of hearts and diamonds – for a loss of seven points – and, in any case, he can hardly avoid taking one of them.

OKLAHOMA

O KLAHOMA is a game of the Rummy family, not unlike Canasta. It is less complex than Canasta but satisfying to those who like to make lots of melds and hold plenty of cards in their hands.

NUMBER OF PLAYERS

Oklahoma is best for three players, as described here, but can be played by two, four or five players without any alteration to the rules.

CARDS

Two standard packs are joined together and a Joker added, making a pack of 105 cards in all. The cards rank from Ace (high) to 2 (low), but all eight 2s and the Joker are wild cards, representing any cards that the player holding them wishes. Ace in a sequence can be either high (as in Ace, King, Queen) or low (Ace, 2, 3) but cannot be used 'round the corner' (King, Ace, 2). The cards have special values in scoring, as detailed later.

Players draw to decide dealer, the lowest card drawn denoting the dealer (the Joker counts low). Thereafter the winner of a hand deals the next.

The dealer deals 13 cards to each player one at a time. The remaining cards are placed face down in the centre to form the stock. The top card is turned over and placed face up beside the stock to begin a discard pile.

THE PLAY

The object is to form sequences or sets as described.

The player to the dealer's left may take the upcard into his hand or refuse it. If he refuses it the second player has the option and if he refuses it the dealer has the option. The card can be taken only by a player who can meld with it immediately, i.e. he can use it to complete a set of three or more cards of the same rank, or a sequence of three or more cards of the same suit, which he lays down on the table in front of him. A player who takes the card and melds completes his turn by discarding another card face up in its place, the turn passing to the next player clockwise. Play then proceeds normally as described below.

Should the turn pass round the table and back to eldest hand again, eldest takes the top card from stock into his hand. He may now meld or not, but completes his turn by discarding a card onto the discard pile. From now on play proceeds with each player having

85

the option of taking the top card of the discard pile into his hand, or the top card of the stock.

There are two obligations for a player taking the top card of the discard pile. He must immediately meld with it, either by using it to form a new meld or by adding it to a meld he already has on the table. Players may at any time on their turn add cards to their own melds (but not to their opponents'). Having melded with the top card, the player is obliged to take the rest of the discard pile into his hand. He may then make as many melds with these cards as he pleases. His turn does not end until he discards, which he does by beginning a fresh discard pile.

A melded sequence can be as long as 14 cards (a complete suit with an Ace at each end), but a set of cards of the same rank cannot be of more than four cards, whether or not it includes wild cards.

When a wild card is used in a sequence, its user must announce the card that it represents, and it cannot be changed. Thus a player using a 2 to form a meld of, say, ♡9, ♡8, ♧2, specifying the ♧2 as being the ♡7, cannot later add the ♡7 to the meld and use the ♧2 as the ♡6 or ♡10. However, the Joker has a special property. If a player uses a Joker in a meld, and later acquires the card that the Joker represents, he can, on his turn, replace the Joker with the card and take the Joker into his hand for use a second time. A player can take the discard pile if it is headed by the card his Joker represents, by taking the card to re-

place his Joker.

When discarding, a player is not allowed to discard the ♧Q, unless it is the only card left in his hand.

The deal ends either when one player goes out (i.e. melds all his cards and discards) or when the stock is exhausted. A player taking the last card of the stock is allowed to meld, if able, and discard, whereupon the deal ends, and no further melds are allowed.

A player cannot go out without discarding. It follows that a player with two cards only in his hand cannot go out by drawing a card from stock to form a set or sequence with them, because this would leave him with no card to discard, so his only chance is to acquire cards to add to his existing melds. When a player goes out, his opponents cannot add cards from their hands to their melds.

At the end of the deal, each player scores for the cards in his melds, with the cards still held in his hand debited against him. Cards have values as follows:

Joker: melded 100; in hand −200.

♧Q: melded 50; in hand −100.

Ace; melded 20; in hand −20.

K, Q, J, 10, 9, 8 (excluding ♧Q): melded 10; in hand −20.

7, 6, 5, 4, 3: melded 5; in hand −5.

2: melded, the value of the card it represents (except if it represents ♧Q, when it is worth 10); unmelded −20.

A player who goes out is given a bonus of 100, but not if he goes out on his first turn. A player who goes out (except on his first turn) who has not previously melded is said to go out 'concealed', and gets an additional bonus of 250, which, however, does not count towards his game score. The game score is 1,000 points, the game ending with the deal on which a player passes that score. If two or three pass 1,000 on the same deal, the highest score wins the game. The winner receives a bonus of 200 for game (if two or three are equal the bonus is shared).

OMBRE

*O*MBRE *is a Spanish game of considerable antiquity. It was introduced into England by Katherine of Braganza, who married Charles II in 1662, and it immediately became very popular. Nowadays it is rarely played in Great Britain, but it is popular in Denmark (which saw the publication of a book about it in 1965) and it is played in Spain under the name of Tresillo and in Latin America as Rocamber. It deserves to be more popular.*

NUMBER OF PLAYERS

Ombre is a game only for three players.

CARDS

The game is played with a pack of 40 cards, i.e. the standard pack from which the 10s, 9s and 8s have been removed. It is not a difficult game to play, but it is first necessary to master the rather involved and unusual order of the cards.

In plain suits the cards in the red suits rank in the order: King, Queen, Jack, Ace, 2, 3, 4, 5, 6, 7; those in the black suits rank in the normal order: Ace, King, Queen, Jack, 7, 6, 5, 4, 3, 2.

In trump suits if a red suit is trumps the order of the cards is: ♠A (Spadille), 7 (Manille), ♣A (Basto), A (Punto), K, Q, J, 2, 3, 4 5, 6; if a black suit is trumps the order of the cards is: ♠A (Spadille), 2 (Manille), ♣A (Basto), K, Q, J, 7, 6, 5, 4, 3.

The three top trumps, Spadille, Manille and Basto, are collectively known as Matadores. The holder of one need not follow suit with it to a trump lead, but he must play one if a higher Matador is led and his hand contains no other trump card.

To determine the dealer, a card is dealt face upwards to each player in turn, and he who is first to receive a black Ace is dealer. It is here to be noted that, as in all games of Spanish origin, in dealing and play the game progresses anti-clockwise.

Nine cards are dealt to each player in threes. The remaining 13 cards are placed face downwards in the centre of the table.

THE PLAY

Each deal is complete in itself. One player (ombre) plays against the other two playing in partnership. The player on the right of the dealer has first option of being ombre. It carries two privileges: he names the trump suit, he may discard from his hand as many cards as he chooses and draw fresh cards from the stock. If the player on the right of the dealer wishes to become ombre he says 'I play'. His right-hand neighbour may then announce that he wishes to become ombre, and, by so doing, he tacitly agrees that he will play without exchanging any of his cards. The first player may then reconsider the position, and is entitled to remain ombre if he is willing to play without exchanging any of his cards. If the second player passes, the third player (the dealer) may announce that he wishes to play without discarding. Again, the first player has a right to reconsider and may remain ombre without discarding.

If all three players pass, that is to say if none wishes to play ombre, the deal is abandoned.

If the first player is allowed to play

ombre unopposed, he discards as many cards as he chooses from his hand, and draws cards from the stock to replace them. The second player does the same, and then the dealer. If any cards are left in the stock after the three players have made their exchanges, the dealer is entitled to look at them. If he does he must show them to the other two players: if he does not, the other two may not.

Ombre now names the trump suit and leads a card. The game proceeds, anti-clockwise, every player following suit, if he can, to the led card, or trumping or discarding if he cannot. The winner of a trick leads to the next, until all nine tricks have been played.

At the beginning of a deal each player puts an agreed sum in a pool. Now:

Sacardo. If ombre wins more tricks than either of his opponents individually, he takes all that is in the pool.

Codille. If one of the opponents wins more tricks than ombre, ombre pays him a sum equal to the amount in the pool, and the amount in the pool is carried forward to the next deal.

Puesta. If ombre and one, or both, of his opponents win the same number of tricks, ombre doubles the amount in the pool and it is carried forward to the next deal.

After every deal the dealer for the next is determined by dealing the cards, face upwards, until one player receives a black Ace.

The deal that follows is a simple one to illustrate the mechanics of the game:

West	North	East
♡ K,7	♡ none	♡ 4,5,6
◇ 6	◇ 7	◇ 2,3,4,5
♤ 7,5	♤ J,6,4,3,2	♤ Q
♧ Ma,Ba,	♧ Q,J,6	♧ 7
K,5		

North deals.

West says: 'I play'. East and North pass.

West discards ♡ 7, ◇ 6, ♤ 7, ♤ 5. He draws ♡ 3, ◇ Q, ◇ A, ♧ 4.

East discards ♡ 4, ♡ 5, ♡ 6. His hand is of no value and he hopes to end with a void suit. He draws ♡ Q, ♡ A, Spa.

North discards ◇ 7, ♤ J, ♤ 6, ♤ 4, ♤ 3, ♤ 2. He draws ♡ J, ♡ 2, ◇ K, ◇ J, ♤ K, ♧ 3.

The hands are now:

West	North	East
♡ K,3	♡ J,2	♡ Q,A
◇ Q,A	◇ K,J	◇ 2,3,4,5
♤ none	♤ K	♤ Q
♧ Ma,Ba,	♧ Q,J,6,3	♧ Spa,7
K,5,4		

West names clubs as the trump suit.

His hand is none too good, but the lead of a trump is called for. He, therefore, leads ♤ K, and East wins with Spadille, because West would hardly have led the King of trumps if he did not hold Manille, and probably Basto as well. East has no better return than ♧ 7, on which North plays ♧ J. West allows it to win, by playing ♧ 4, because he is aware that North holds the more dangerous hand, and that sooner or later a trick in trumps must be lost to him. North must keep his top diamonds and ♤ K, and he cannot safely lead a heart. He, therefore, leads a club. West wins with Basto, draws North's last trump with Manille, and continues with ♧ 5. It puts North on the spot. If he discards ◇ J, West will lead the suit and later win ♡ K and a diamond; if North discards ♡ 2 or ♤ K, West will win ♡ K, and continue with ♡ 3, so that he will either win ◇ Q, or North and East will divide their tricks three-two. Either way it is sacardo, and West scoops the pool.

SCHAFKOPF

*S*CHAFKOPF *is an old game which lent some of its principles to the highly organized game of Skat. Schafkopf is less complex and is enjoyed widely without having had codified rules.*

NUMBER OF PLAYERS

Schafkopf is for three players.

CARDS

A short pack of 32 is used, i.e. a standard pack from which are removed the 6s, 5s, 4s, 3s and 2s.

There is a trump suit which consists of all the Queens, all the Jacks and all the diamonds. The trump suit, consisting of 14 cards, ranks as follows: ♣Q, ♠Q, ♡Q, ◇Q, ♣J, ♠J, ♡J, ◇J, ◇A, ◇10, ◇K, ◇9, ◇8, ◇7.

In the plain suits the cards rank as follows: Ace, 10, King, 9, 8, 7.

The high cards have point values as follows:

Ace	11
10	10
King	4
Queen	3
Jack	2

One player shuffles the pack and deals the cards face up to each player clockwise, and the first to receive a Jack is the first dealer. The deal subsequently rotates to the left.

The dealer shuffles, the player to his right cuts, and the dealer deals first three cards to each player clockwise, then two to the centre to form a skat or widow, then the remainder to the players in lots of four and three.

THE PLAY

The player to dealer's left is called Forehand, and the player to dealer's right is called Middlehand. The object is to win in tricks cards of scoring values as detailed above.

The player who picks up the skat becomes the Player, and plays the hand in opposition to the other two players.

Forehand has the first option, and may pick up the skat or pass. If he passes, Middlehand has the next option, and if he passes the dealer has the option. If all three pass the hand is played as Least, to be described later.

When a player picks up the skat, he discards two cards face down, and a trick-taking phase begins. Forehand leads to the first trick, thereafter the winner of a trick leads to the next. Players are required to follow suit to the card led, and if unable to can trump or discard. The trick is won by the highest trump it contains, or if it contains none, by the highest card in the suit led. The Player adds any points among his discards to his own total.

The Player scores points as follows: if his tricks plus his discards contain cards worth 61 to 90 points, two game points; 91 or more, four game points (known as Schneider). If he wins all the tricks, he scores six game points (known as Schwartz).

For failing to score 61 points, the Player is debited as follows: if his tricks and discards contain 31 to 60 points, he is debited two game points; 30 or fewer, he is debited four game points. If he loses all the tricks, he is debited six game points.

Game is to ten points.

When all three players pass, Least is played. The uninspected skat is set aside, the cards it contains to be added later to those of the player who takes the last trick. Forehand makes the opening lead as usual, but this time the object is to win as few as possible cards of point value. Each player plays for himself, there being no Player.

If one player takes no tricks, he scores four game points. If one player takes all the tricks, he is debited four game points. If each player takes a trick, then the player with the fewest points among his cards scores two game points. If two tie for fewest, the one who collected his last trick earliest wins the two game points. If all three tie with 40 points each among their cards, the dealer wins the two game points.

It should be remembered that of the 30 cards in play, 14, or nearly half, are trumps, so the requirement to pick up the skat is something like seven trumps, including four Queens and Jacks. Remember the odds are very much against a plain suit going round twice, as there are only six cards in each plain suit, and it is actually slight odds against all six being in play. So Ace, 10 in a side suit is likely to make two tricks only if all trumps are drawn first. The Player should consider that high-scoring cards like 10s and Aces might be best left in the skat, where the Player will score for them without risking having them taken in play by the opponents.

SKAT

*O*RIGINATING *in the south of what is now East Germany in the early part of the 19th century, Skat has become a popular pub game over most of German-speaking central Europe. Played at the highest level Skat is one of the most skilful of all card games, and it is particularly recommended for people who play Hearts (Black Maria, Chase the Lady, etc.) but find that game too straightforward.*

NUMBER OF PLAYERS

Skat is a game for three players.

CARDS

The pack is of 32 cards (as used for Piquet, Euchre, etc.), and consists of four suits: clubs, spades, hearts and diamonds, each suit containing Ace, King, Queen, Jack, 10, 9, 8, 7.

The four Jacks are always part of the trump suit in Skat, and they always rank in the order: clubs, spades, hearts, diamonds (clubs are high). The 10 ranks between Ace and King.

The order of the trump suit is:
♣J; ♠J; ♡J; ◇J, A, 10, K, Q, 9, 8, 7 (11 cards).

And the order of the other three suits is:

Ace, 10, King, Queen, 9, 8, 7 (seven cards)

There is also a contract, called 'Grand', in which there are, effectively, five suits: the four Jacks, which are trumps, form a small suit by themselves, and the other four suits have seven cards each.

(Note that in all contracts the Jacks are treated exactly as ordinary members of the trump suit for the purposes of play, so that, for example, if hearts are trumps and the ◇ J is led, the other players are forced to follow with hearts [or Jacks] if they have any.)

The cards have widely differing values as follows:

Ace	11
10	10
King	4
Queen	3
Jack	2
9, 8, 7	0

This makes a total of 120 points in the pack. The object of the game is to capture half these 'card points' in tricks (Declarer needs 61 points to win, the defenders need 60 to beat him).

The skat counts as part of the declarer's tricks, so that if he discards two 10s for example, he already has 20 points — almost a third of his target.

Note that the Jacks, which are the most powerful cards for winning tricks, are not in themselves worth many points — this special feature of Skat is responsible for much of the strategic richness of the game.

To determine the dealer for the first hand, cards are dealt out one at a time by whoever happens to hold them, face up, one to each player. The first person to get a Jack is dealer. The dealer shuffles, then someone else cuts, then the dealer deals, clockwise starting with the player on his left, three cards to each player, then two to the skat, then four cards each, then another three each (the peculiar English habit of dealing cards one at a time is rare in central Europe). The deal moves round to the left on subsequent hands. The player on Dealer's left is called 'Forehand', the other player is called 'Middlehand'.

BIDDING

The bidding consists of an auction between the three players. The bids are numbers, and represent the number of points the player contracts to score if he becomes the declarer. If someone else eventually becomes the declarer then there is no obligation on the bidder. If the declarer makes a higher score than he bid then that is fine — he scores the higher number. Note that these bids are scores, not numbers of card points — the contract is always to make 61 card points (unless Schneider is announced).

The process of bidding is for one player to call numbers in ascending order while a second player says 'Yes' after each bid. Eventually one of them drops out of the auction by saying 'Pass'. The auction begins with

Middlehand bidding and Forehand saying 'Yes' (or 'Pass'), then when one of these two has passed, the dealer starts bidding and the other says 'Yes' (or passes).

One may only bid numbers which it is possible to score. The full bidding sequence starts with:

diamonds with, or without, one Jack	18
hearts with one	20
spades with one	22
null	23
clubs with one	24
diamonds with two	27
hearts with two	30
spades with two	33
null hand	35
clubs with two or diamonds with three	36
hearts with three or grand with one	40
spades with three	44
diamonds with four	45
null open	46
clubs with three	48
hearts with four	50
diamonds with five	54
spades with four	55
null hand open	59
clubs with four, hearts with five or grand with two	60

and so on up to

grand hand with four with Schwartz announced	200

and theoretically

club hand with Schwartz announced	204

In practice the auction never gets past 60 among skilful players.

A typical auction might go:

(M Middlehand, F Forehand, D Dealer).

M: 18	F: Yes
M: 20	F: Yes
M: 22	F: Yes
M: 23	F: Yes
M: 24	F: Pass
D: 27	M: Yes
D: Pass	

The result of this auction is that Middlehand has contracted to make at least 27 points.

If all three players pass, the hand is thrown in and the deal passes on.

If the declarer overbids, either by accident or because he was hoping to play without several Jacks and finds one in the skat, then it is possible that he has absolutely no way to make his contract, even by making Schwartz. In this case he loses the next higher multiple of his base value above his bid. Suppose, for example, that a player holding:

♡ 10, K, Q, 9, 8, 7

♧ A, 10

♤ A, K

plays hearts in hand, after bidding up to 59 points. He makes 82 card points, but the ♤ J proves to be in the skat. Far from being 'without five' as he had hoped, he is only 'without one' and so scores only 30 (without one, game two, hand three). He loses 60 points for this, since that is the next multiple of 10 above his bid. It is always a bit dangerous trying to go without the Jacks because of the risk of finding one in the skat.

THE PLAY

Skat is a trick-taking game, like Bridge, Solo Whist and Hearts. Play proceeds in a series of tricks, in each of which one player leads a card, and the other two, in turn clockwise round the table, follow with one card. The player leading can choose any card he likes, but the others are forced to play cards of the suit led, unless they have no such card when they are free to choose any card. The trick is won by the highest card of the suit led, except that one suit (called the trump suit) always beats the other suits and a trick to which trumps are played is won by the highest trump irrespective of the suit led.

The winner of each trick keeps the three cards it contains face down in front of him, and leads to the next trick. The player on the dealer's left ('Forehand') leads to the first trick.

SCORING

Adding up the value of the cards captured and seeing whether the declarer has achieved 61 card points determines whether he has won or not. The amount of money he gets for doing so (or the score he gets if you are not playing for money) is determined in an unlikely sounding manner which takes a little getting used to. It is the product of two numbers which we shall call the 'base value' and the 'multiplier'.

The base value depends only on the trump suit:

Diamonds	9
Hearts	10
Spades	11
Clubs	12
Grand	20

The multiplier depends mostly on the number of top trumps the declarer holds, but various bonuses may be added:

If declarer holds the ♣J (the top trump), the multiplier is the number of trumps he holds in sequence from the ♣J down.

If declarer does not hold the ♣J, the multiplier is the number of trumps he is missing, in sequence from the ♣J down.

If declarer plays 'in hand', i.e. he does not look at the skat, but just puts the two cards in his pile of tricks, he adds one to the multiplier. If declarer makes 'schneider', i.e. he takes 90 or more card points in his tricks, he adds one to the multiplier. If declarer announces that he is going to make schneider at the beginning of the hand, then he adds another one to the multiplier in addition to the one for making schneider. It is illegal to announce schneider except when playing in hand. If declarer announces schneider and takes fewer than 90 card points, then the multipliers for schneider and schneider announced still apply, but he lose. If declarer makes 'schwartz' (German for black – he takes all the tricks), then he gets another one added to the multiplier in addition to the one for schneider.

If declarer announces schwartz then he gets yet another one added, but, as for schneider, he may only announce Schwartz when playing in hand.

One is always added to the multiplier 'for the Game'.

If declarer fails to make his contract he loses double the score he would have won, except when playing in hand.

Let us consider some examples:

The declarer plays in hearts, holding ♣J, ♠J, ◇J, and he takes 76 card points. He is 'with two' Jacks (the ♡J is missing) and claims:

'With two, game three, times 10, makes 30.'

The declarer plays a Grand holding ♡J, ◇J, and he makes 59 card points (not enough) and announces:

'Without two, game three, off six, times 20, loses 120.'

The declarer plays in spades, in hand, holding ♣J, ♠J, ♡J; and he announces Schneider. He makes 87 card points (not enough), therefore loses:

'With three, game four, hand five, schneider six, announced seven, times 11, loses 77.'

The declarer plays in clubs, in hand, holding ♣J, ♡J, ◇J, and the Ace of clubs. He makes 96 card points, and the ♠J proves to have been in the skat (lucky). He claims:

'With five, game six, hand seven, schneider eight, times 12, makes 96.'

In addition to the normal trump contracts, there is a contract called null, which is a contract to take no tricks at all. Card points do not count, and the hand stops immediately if the declarer takes a trick (he has lost).

The order of the cards is different in null. There are no trumps, and the four suits each have eight cards: Ace, King, Queen, Jack, 10, 9, 8, 7 in that order (the 10s and Jacks are back where you would expect them to be).

In null it is possible to play 'open': the declarer exposes all his cards, and plays with them face up on the table. There are four contracts, depending on whether declarer looks at the skat:

Null	23
Null Hand	35
Null Open	46
Null Hand Open	59

As with ordinary contracts, the declarer loses double the number of points if he has looked at the skat, but just loses what he would have won if he plays in hand.

Skat scoring is designed for players who use piles of money on the table in front of them, and settle up after each hand – the rule is that the declarer is paid by (or pays if he has lost) each of the other players.

If you intend to play for honour (or if you, or the publican, do not like having money on the table) then the score can be kept on a piece of paper. After each hand add the score for that hand to the total under the declarer's initial. At the end each player pays each other the difference between their scores. (If you are not playing for money it's just the player with the biggest score who wins, which is simpler).

Requirements to bid a suit contract. The important cards are Jacks and Aces, and the average hand has $1\frac{1}{3}$ of each of them. The advantages of getting the skat, discarding, and choosing trumps almost outweigh the disadvantage of being one player against two, and most hands with three cards which are Jacks or Aces can reasonably be bid up to the value of their lowest ranking long suit.

To bid grand. Here Jacks and Aces are especially important. Normally you need five of them (or perhaps four if you are Forehand, and have the lead). Tens to support your Aces are much better than 10s by themselves.

To bid null. You need 7s. Competent defenders will nearly always force you to take a trick if you have a three-card suit containing the Ace or King, or a four-card suit missing the 7, or a single card of a suit which is not 7, 8 or 9.

Going in hand. If you have a rock-crushing collection of Aces and Jacks you might as well go in hand to score for the extra multiplier, but there are two common reasons for not doing so:

(a) a holding which is almost sure to make game in hand can be converted, using the skat, to one which is absolutely sure to make game and almost sure to make schneider – the extra multiplier for schneider is just as good as the one for hand, and you are insured against dangers like a 5–0 trump split.

(b) many holdings which would make game in hand in a suit could be converted into a grand given one more Ace or Jack from the skat. Since grand is so much more valuable than the suit contracts it is often worth forgoing the multiplier for hand in the hope of something bigger. If there are four particular cards any one of which would let you make grand, the chance of finding one of them in the skat is about one in three.

Discarding the skat. The declarer should try to create void suits where he holds one or two cards without the Ace. One odd low card can cost 21 card points. It is much better to have two low cards in one suit than one in each of two suits. Never discard an Ace.

Counting. Counting is quite important in Skat. If you can only remember one number, then count trumps. If you can manage two, then count trumps and the number of card points the defenders have collected.

Choosing trumps. If you have two suits of equal length, then choose the weaker one as trumps, which avoids devaluing your Aces.

The following example hand (see illustration) covers a number of other aspects of skilful play – you may find it easier to follow by laying the cards out on a table.

First, let's consider what the players should be prepared to bid:

Forehand: He has no chance in anything except null. His clubs and hearts are safe, but he might be forced to take a trick either in spades or diamonds (the diamonds are about as worrying as the spades – any long suit missing the 7 is a liability in null). He has a reasonable chance of improving one or both these suits if he looks at the skat, so he can bid up to 23.

An example deal in Skat.

Middlehand: He has a reasonable hand for playing in clubs (he can even consider playing in hand) but he would feel much happier if he could see the skat, and find another club, or a Jack, or an Ace. He can bid up to 24 (clubs without one).

Dealer: He has quite a good hand. He, can consider playing hearts in hand, but the ♠ 10 is a severe embarrassment – it is almost sure to be caught by the Ace. Ideally the dealer would like to look at the skat. If he finds an Ace, or possibly a Jack, he will be strong enough to play grand, and if he can discard the embarrassing ♠ 10 into his trick pile, then hearts are almost cast-iron. In a hand like this, with few losers, it is worth doing a calculation to see how many points the defenders can collect. In this case we would suppose that the defenders catch the ♠ 10 with the Ace and King, for 25 points, that they catch the ◇ Q with the Ace and 10, for a further 24 points making 49, and then we are left with the question of whether they can collect 11 points in trumps (assuming hearts are trumps, of course). There are four trumps outside the dealer's hand, and he should be prepared for them to divide three—one between the opponents. In this case the defenders can arrange for at least one trick to happen when one of them is winning a trump, while the other is out of trumps and can throw on some valuable card like the ♣10. This will make up the required 11 points and the dealer will lose. Of course, in practice, the defenders will rarely manage to put the maximum possible number of points on his losing cards, but the calculation shows that the dealer is not quite safe playing hearts in hand.

The bidding goes as follows:

Middlehand: 18	Forehand: Yes
M: 20	F: Yes
M: 22	F: Yes
M: 23	F: Yes
M: 24	F: Pass
Dealer: Pass	

The dealer decides to pass since his hearts hand contract is not quite safe and he has very good chances of defeating any contract Middlehand might try. This is rather cowardly – most players would bid up to 30 with the dealer's cards.

Middlehand looks at the skat, fails to find any of the key cards he was hoping for, and discards ♡K and ♠Q, getting 7 points home and creating a void in hearts.

Middlehand then announces his contract: 'clubs are trumps'.

The play proceeds as follows (F = Forehand, M = Middlehand, the Declarer, D = Dealer):

Trick 1: F leads the ♠A. Normal practice is for the player in front of the declarer to play long suits, while the other defender plays short suits – the reason soon becomes apparent. M fol-

lows the ♠9 and D plays the ♠10.
Score: M 7 points, Defenders 21.

Trick 2: F leads the ♠K. This is the position the defenders have been trying to create, with D, void of the suit led, playing after the declarer. This means that if M trumps the card led, D can overtrump, while if M throws away some odd card, D can put something valuable on (in this case, the ♡A). M decides to trump with the ♣Q, and D overtrumps with the ♣A.
Score: M 7 points, Defenders 39.

Trick 3: D leads the ♡A. He expects M to trump this card, but it is far better to force M to trump than to allow him an opportunity to get rid of an odd card. F plays the 7, and M trumps with the ♣10.
Score: M 28 points, Defenders 39.

Trick 4: M leads the ♢J. It is almost always best for the declarer to get rid of trumps as soon as possible. D wins with the ♡J, and F plays the ♣7.
Score: M 28 points, Defenders 43.

Trick 5: D leads the ♡Q. He is saving the ♡10 for later, in case F is taking a diamond trick which he (D) will want to put a valuable card on. F plays the ♣9. He is not expecting to win this trick, since M will probably want to trump anyway, but the ♣9 is worse than useless – if his partner wins another trump trick then F wants to be free to put the ♢10 on, and not to be forced to follow suit with the ♣9 which is worth no points. M wins with the ♣K.
Score: M 35 points, Defenders 43.

Trick 6: M leads the ♣8 – he makes sure that D's trump goes on a nice cheap card, and hopes that it is D, not F, who has the outstanding trump so that D will be embarrassed by having to lead diamonds. D wins with the ♣J, and F decides to play the ♣7, since he has been counting the points carefully. If he played the ◇10 the defenders would get to 55 points but would not have much chance of getting any more – he is hoping the ◇10 will take a trick.

Score: M 35 points, Defenders 45.

Trick 7: D leads the ◇Q. This brilliant play depends on his having worked out that F and M both have three diamonds (do you see how?). F plays the 9, and M, who rather enjoys having D on lead, plays the 7.

Score: M 35 points, Defenders 48.

Trick 8: If D now plays a small heart then M will throw away his ◇K, and win the rest of the tricks. D therefore plays his ♡10, to force M to trump. F plays the ♣8, and M trumps with the ♣J.

Score: M 47 points, Defenders 48.

Trick 9: M plays the ◇A, hoping that he has miscounted the points. D plays the ♡8, and F follows with the ◇8.

Score: Declarer 58 points, Defenders 48.

Trick 10: M plays his last card, the ◇K. D plays his heart, and F wins with the ◇10.

Final score: M 58 points, Defenders 62.

So Forehand and Dealer win 'without one, game two, off four, times 12, loses 48'.

VARIATIONS IN THE RULES

The rules of Skat described above are among those most commonly used across central Europe, but Skat is the type of pub game in which local variations are common, such as the base value for grand is often taken as 24, not 20.

TOWIE

*T*OWIE was originated by J. Leonard Replogle as a variation of Bridge (see page 103).

NUMBER OF PLAYERS

The game is played by three active players, and so is most suitable for that number, but can be played by more, as described later.

CARDS

The full pack of 52 cards is used.

Four hands of 13 cards each are dealt in the usual way; the one to the quarter opposite the dealer is the dummy hand to be bid for. After dealing, the dealer chooses (without looking at them) six cards from the dummy hand, and turns them up.

THE PLAY

The players, beginning with the dealer, bid as in the parent game, but part scores are not reckoned and if the bidding ends without a game or higher contract being reached, there is a goulash deal, with further goulashes if necessary.*

When the bidding ends the player on the left of the declarer makes the opening lead. The dummy hand becomes the property of the declarer who sorts it, exposes it on the table, and plays it against the other two players in partnership, as in the parent game.

The scoring is the same as in Bridge with the following differences:

1. In no-trump contracts the trick score is 35 points a trick.
2. For winning a first game the declarer scores a bonus of 500 points and becomes vulnerable. For winning a second game – and with it the rubber – a player scores 1,000 points.
3. The declarer who makes a doubled or redoubled contract scores a bonus of 50 points if not vulnerable, and 100 points if vulnerable.

---

*For a goulash deal the players sort their cards into suits (the dealer sorts the dummy hand) and the hands are placed face downwards in a pile, one on top of the other, in front of the dealer. The cards are cut without being shuffled, and the same dealer deals the cards.

4. For undoubled overtricks the declarer scores 50 points each. If doubled or redoubed he scores for them as in the parent game.
5. The penalties for undertricks are:

Not vulnerable

Undoubled: 50 points per trick
Doubled: 100 points for the first and second tricks
           200 points for the third and fourth tricks
           400 points for the fifth and subsequent tricks

Vulnerable

Undoubled: 100 points for the first trick
           200 points for the second and subsequent tricks
Doubled: 200 points for the first trick
           400 points for the second and subsequent tricks

If the contract is redoubled the scores for doubled contracts are multiplied by two.

Large penalties are not uncommon in Towie because a player has no partner during the auction period and cannot do more than bid on the strength of his own hand, the six cards that he sees in dummy, and the seven cards that he expects to find there. Over-bidding is frequent, but risks must be taken, and the game is not for the chicken-hearted or cautious bidder. The play of the defence offers scope for

The dummy hand after the face-down cards have been exposed.

skill, but, on the whole, the main object of a player must be to play the dummy, particularly when five are in the game (see overleaf).

Consider the hands and dummy as dealt in the illustration below.

South and East were vulnerable, and South dealt. He bid a cautious One Spade, and, after a pass by West, East bid Three No-Trumps. South lacked the courage to bid Four Spades, and East, with dummy's cards opposite him, had an easy ride for his contract.

Dummy

West

South

East

TOWIE FOR FOUR OR MORE

If there are more than three players participating in the game the inactive players are opponents of the declarer. They take no part in the bidding or play, but participate in the scoring, losing when the declarer makes his contract, and scoring the undertrick penalties when the declarer's contract is defeated.

At the end of a deal the declarer, whether he has won or lost his contract, retires from the table and his place is taken by one of the waiting players. The inactive players come into the game in turn, replacing the declarer of the previous deal. No vulnerable player, however, may re-enter the game if a non-vulnerable player is waiting to play.

The game ends when one player has won two deals.

GAMES FOR FOUR PLAYERS

AUCTION PITCH

*A*UCTION PITCH, *commonly known as Pitch and sometimes as Set Back, is a variation of* All Fours *(see page 9)*.

Each player is dealt six cards in two lots of three each. No card, however, is turned up to determine the trump suit.

NUMBER OF PLAYERS

Auction Pitch is at its best and most popular when played by four players, each playing for himself. It can, however, be played by any number from two to seven.

CARDS

The full pack of 52 is used and cards rank from Ace (high) to 2 (low).

THE PLAY

The player on the left of the dealer bids first, and each player, in his turn, may either make a bid or pass. A bid must be for at least two points, and for more than the preceding bid, except for the dealer, who is entitled to buy the hand for the same number of points as the preceding bid. The maximum number of points in a deal is four, and a player who expects to win them bids smudge. The dealer cannot take the declaration from him.

The successful bidder is known as the maker, and he pitches (leads) to the first trick. The card that he leads determines the trump suit.

At each trick a player must follow suit to the card led, if he can, otherwise he may discard or trump. The winner of a trick leads to the next.

As in the parent game, points are scored as follows:

High. The player who holds the highest trump scores one point.

Low. The player who holds the lowest trump scores one point.

Jack. The player who wins the trick that contains the Jack of the trump suit (if it is in play) scores one point.

Game. Counting the Ace as four, the King as three, the Queen as two, the Jack as one and the 10 as ten, the player with the highest total in the tricks he has won scores one point. If there is a tie no-one scores the point.

Every player records what he scores, and if the maker fails to reach his bid he is set back by the full amount of it. He records the score and if it reduces him to a minus score he encircles it and is said to be in the hole.

The game is won by the player who first reaches seven points, and if the maker and one or more of the other players reach seven points in the same deal, the maker wins. As between the other three players, the points are counted in the order High, Low, Jack, Game.

A player who smudges and wins all four points automatically wins the game regardless of his score, unless he was in the hole when he smudged. In this event he scores only four points.

BRIDGE

MODERN BRIDGE, more precisely Contract Bridge, but the 'Contract' has for long been dropped, was developed out of Auction Bridge and introduced to card players in the early 1920s. It took firm root quickly, and made rapid progress, to become the most popular game in the history of card-playing. To-day, half a century after its début, it is played by millions, rich and poor, from peers to peasants, and it has attracted to itself a vast literature in most European languages.

NUMBER OF PLAYERS

Bridge is a game for four players, two playing in partnership against the other two, players sitting opposite each other.

CARDS

The full pack of 52 cards is used. Although only one pack of cards is necessary, it is customary to use two, of different design or colour, and while one is being dealt the other is shuffled by the partner of the dealer, in readiness for the next dealer.

The cards rank in the order Ace (high) to 2 (low), and the Ace, King, Queen, Jack and 10 of a suit are known as the honour cards. The suits rank in the order spades, hearts, diamonds, clubs; the spade and heart suits are known as the major suits: the diamond and club suits as the minor suits.

To determine partners, a pack is spread on the table. The four players draw cards from it, and the two who draw the two highest cards play in partnership against the other two. If two players draw cards of equal rank, precedence is determined by the rank of the suits. The player who draws the highest card has choice of seats and cards, and deals first. Thereafter the deal passes round the table clockwise. His partner sits opposite to him; the other two partners sit one on each side of him. It is usual to denote the four players by the cardinal points of the compass.

BIDDING

During the bidding, which the two partnerships compete against each other to establish which suit shall be made trumps or whether the hand shall be played without a trump suit.

The dealer bids first, and the bidding continues round the table clockwise. When a player bids he states the number of tricks in excess of six that he undertakes to win, and in the denomination that he undertakes to play. The lowest bid, therefore, is a bid of One (a contract to win seven tricks) and the highest is a bid of Seven (a contract to win all 13 tricks). As no-trumps takes precedence over the suits, the lowest possible bid is One Club, and the ascending scale is: One Club, One Diamond, One Heart, One Spade, One No-Trump, Two Clubs, Two Diamonds ... Seven Hearts, Seven Spades, Seven No-Trumps. A contract of Six (to win 12 tricks) is called a small slam; a contract of Seven (to win all 13 tricks) is called a grand slam.

In turn each bid must name either a greater number of tricks than the previous one, or an equal number of tricks in a higher denomination. If a player has no wish to contract to win tricks he says 'No Bid', and if all four players do so, the hand is thrown in and the deal passes.

In his turn any player may double a bid made by an opponent. The effect of a double is to increase the score whether the contract succeeds or fails: and the partnership whose contract has been doubled may redouble thereby increasing the score, win or lose, still further. Doubling and redoubling, however, do not increase the size of a contract: e.g. a bid of Four Clubs is inferior to a bid of Four Diamonds and remains inferior to it even though it may have been doubled and redoubled.

The bidding period continues until the last and highest bid has been followed by three passes. The player who first mentioned the denomination in the final contract then becomes the declarer.

Bridge is not a difficult game unless a player makes it so by ill-advised bidding. Its most important feature is that a player scores towards game only for the tricks that he has contracted to win, and, by a logical extension, he scores the big bonuses for slams only if the necessary amount of tricks has been contracted for. It follows that it is of paramount importance for the partners to estimate the trick-taking power of their combined hands, and not only must a player estimate as accurately as possible the position of the adverse high cards and distribution (as revealed by the bids of the other players) but convey by his bidding as much information as possible to his partner. In short, bidding may be defined as a conversation between the partners, and both must speak the same language.

OPENING BIDS

Most modern players value their hands by means of the well-known Milton Work count of 4 for an Ace, 3 for a King, 2 for a Queen, and 1 for a Jack. *Suits*
The player who opens the bidding with a bid of One of a suit promises to make a further bid if his partner responds with One in a higher-ranking suit, or Two in a lower-ranking suit.

For this reason a player should not open unless he can see a sound rebid in his hand over his partner's most likely response.

The strength to justify an opening bid varies, but in general it may be said that a hand totalling at least 13 points should be opened. It is clear, however, that the more points a player holds the less length does he need in the trump suit, and the fewer points in the hand the greater must be the length in the trump suit. With less than 13 points in the hand the practice is to open an 11- or 12-point hand with a reasonable five-card suit, and with only 10 points in the hand, sometimes less, a player needs a reasonable six-card suit, or two five-card suits.

Open One Heart. The hand totals only 11 points, but the heart suit is worth showing and if it is not shown at once it may be too late.

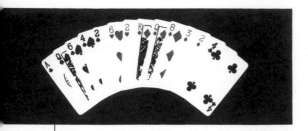

Open One Spade. The hand totals only 11 points, but is strong by reason of its distribution. With two suits of equal length it is proper to bid the higher-ranking before the lower-ranking one.

Trumps over Three Spades, Hearts or Diamonds. Either bid invites partner to bid his best suit.

When an opponent has bid a suit at the level of One, a player should enter the auction only if he can be reasonably sure that his bid, if passed out, will not be defeated by more than two tricks if vulnerable and three if not vulnerable. This general rule, however, must be accepted with some reservation. It would, for example, not be wrong for a player who holds

Open One Spade. The hand totals a mere 10 points, but the six-card spade suit is too good to be held back.

A pre-emptive bid is defined as an opening bid at the level of Three or higher. It is a bid of great value because either it prevents the opponents from entering the auction or compels one of them to bid at a level that is dangerously high when he has no notion of what cards his partner may be holding. Postulating that the bid of Three is weak and that an opponent holds strength in the other three suits, the most practical way of countering the pre-empt is to bid Three Diamonds over Three Clubs and Three No-

to bid One Heart over an opponent's One Diamond. The bid might prove costly, but not very often, and it is cowardly not to contest the part-score for fear of the worst happening. A player has a right to assume that even if his partner has a blank hand and only two or three low hearts, the hand will win three tricks in hearts and one in each of the black suits.

No-trumps

A bid of One No-Trump is advised with a total of 16 to 18 points. The bid should never step outside the stipulated range, because your partner needs to rely on it for his response. With nine points he will jump to Three No-

Trumps; with seven or eight he will bid Two No-Trumps and leave it to the opener to pass with a minimum, but bid Three with a maximum. A no-trump range of 16 to 18 points is known as a strong no-trump. Some experienced players favour, particularly when not vulnerable, a range of 12 to 14 points. It is known as a weak no-trump. Whether a strong or a weak no-trump is played is a matter of personal choice, but it must be agreed between the partners before play begins, because if a weak no-trump is played partner must increase his responses by four points.

In the same way, an opening bid of Two No-Trumps is advised on 20 to 22 points, leaving it to partner to raise to Three if he holds five points, and to pass with less.

Opening bids of One No-Trump and Two No-Trumps postulate a balanced distribution of 4–3–3–3 or 4–4–3–2. A bid of Three No-Trumps is tactical. It shows a hand containing a solid minor suit, and altogether a hand that has a reasonable prospect of winning nine tricks if partner has one or two top cards in the right places.

The hand qualifies for an opening bid of Three No-Trumps. There is every

prospect of making the contract; if not it will not cost a lot and there is the consolation that it has probably stopped the opponents from bidding a game that would have been a greater loss.

Weak and strong bids

An opening bid of Three of a suit is a weakness bid. It is made with a hand that has little, if any, defensive strength, offers small chance of success of game, and with one long suit that, if trumps, is unlikely to be defeated by more than two tricks if vulnerable and three if not vulnerable.

This type of hand qualifies for an opening bid of Three Spades if only because, even if doubled and partner has no support, it cannot cost more than 500 points (two down). It is a reasonable loss if the opponents have a game in one of the other suits.

There is also a range of strong bids. The strongest of all is an opening bid of Two Clubs. It is strictly conventional and may be made even if the player is void in the suit. The bid guarantees either five or more high cards and distributional strength, or 23 or more points and a balanced distribution. With one exception the bid is forcing to game. Partner must respond no matter how weak his hand is, and with a weak hand he bids Two Diamonds. Any other response by him shows an Ace and a King or two King-Queen combinations or the equivalent in high cards. The exception to the bid not being forcing to game occurs when the opener has bid Two Clubs with a balanced hand and, after the negative response of Two Diamonds, has rebid Two No-Trumps.

West	East
♠ K, J, 3	♠ Q, 6, 2
♡ A, Q, 6	♡ 9, 7, 4
♢ A, K, 4	♢ 8, 5, 3, 2
♣ A, Q, J, 2	♣ 7, 4, 3
Bidding	Bidding
2 ♣	2 ♢
2 No-Trumps	No Bid

West, with 24 points, is too strong to open with any other bid than Two Clubs, and over East's negative response he cannot do better than rebid Two No-Trumps. East with only two points in his hand does well to pass, but another point in his hand would make a big difference and with three points or more he would bid Three No-Trumps.

The opening bid of Two in any other suit is forcing for one round, and

shows a hand containing not fewer than eight playing tricks and at least one powerful suit.

The hand at the foot of the page is best opened with Two Spades. If it is opened with One Spade there is no satisfactory way of coping with a response of Two Hearts.

A strong two-suited hand also qualifies for an opening bid of Two. The higher-ranking suit is bid first.

A one-suited hand may also be opened with a Two bid. This hand should be opened with a bid of Two Spades, and Three Spades should be bid over any response made by partner.

As well as an opening bid of Two Clubs there are several other bids that are forcing to game. The most frequent is a jump bid in a new suit.

West	East
♠ Q, 8, 4	♠ A, K, 6
♡ 9, 2	♡ A, Q, J, 10, 6, 4
◇ A, J, 3	◇ 8, 2
♣ A, K, 9, 3, 2	♣ J, 4

Bidding	Bidding
1 ♣	2 ♡

The situation is typical. East's bid of Two Hearts sets up a forcing situation. It is true that a bid of One Heart by East cannot be passed by West, but it is better for East to get the hand off his chest, and by bidding Two Hearts he makes certain that the bidding will not be dropped until a game level is reached.

It is much the same if the opener makes a jump in a new suit over his partner's response:

West	East
♠ K, J, 6	♠ A, Q, 9, 2
♡ A, K, J, 7, 4	♡ 10, 8, 3
◇ 6	◇ K, Q, 9
♣ K, Q, J, 7	♣ 10, 6, 3

Bidding	Bidding
1 ♡	1 ♠
3 ♣	

In this situation (or a similar one) West's bid of Three Clubs is a game force and East cannot pass it.

In many cases a forcing situation is set up by reason of the logic behind the bidding.

West	East
♠ A, K, 9, 6, 3	♠ Q, 7, 4, 2
♡ K, J, 9, 2	♡ Q, 10, 8, 3
◇ A, 8, 4	◇ K, 6, 2
♣ 9	♣ 5, 4

Bidding	Bidding
1 ♠	2 ♠
3 ♡	?

As West rebid at the level of Three, over East's weak response of Two Spades, and when there was no need for him to rebid, he must have a very strong hand, and East must make a further bid. He bids Four Hearts and West passes.

An inferential force is even more pronounced in a sequence such as:

West	East
1 ♡	1 ♠
2 No-Trumps	3 ♡
?	

West must not pass because East is very clearly inviting him to choose between playing the hand in Three No-Trumps or Four Hearts, whichever contract best suits him.

Bidding slams

There are 40 points in the pack and experience has taught that if the combined hands have a total of 25 points game will be made, if 33 the small slam, and if 37 the grand slam. There are, of course, exceptions, but in the long run the rule is to be relied on.

When the bidding of the partners shows that they hold between them the balance of strength, they should consider bidding a slam. As a guide it may be said that prospects of a slam are good when a player holds enough to make a positive response to a forcing bid; or when the point count of the combined hands totals at least 33; or when a player has enough for an opening bid opposite a partner who has opened with a bid of Two, or who has opened the bidding and made a jump rebid.

Before a slam can be bid with a measure of safety, it is essential for the partners to find out if they hold between them control of the vital suits. The Blackwood convention has been designed to enable the partners to learn how many Aces and Kings are held by the partnership.

When the trump suit has been agreed either directly by support or by implication, or if a forcing situation has been set up, a bid of Four No-Trumps by either partner asks the other to bid Five Clubs if he lacks an Ace or holds all four, Five Diamonds if he holds one Ace, Five Hearts if he holds two and Five Spades if he holds three. If the player who has bid Four No-Trumps, after his partner's response continues with a bid of Five No-Trumps, he is showing that he holds all four Aces and is asking his

partner to bid Six Clubs if he lacks a King, Six Diamonds if he holds one King, Six Hearts if he holds two, Six Spades if he holds three and Six No-Trumps if he holds all four. Look at the hands at the foot of the page. Bidding:

West	East
1 ♠	2 ♡
3 No-Trumps	4 ♠
4 No-Trumps	5 ♡
6 ♠	No Bid

Once East has shown that he has support for spades, West, with support for hearts, visualizes a slam. His bid of Four No-Trumps asks East how many Aces he holds, and East's response of Five Hearts tells West that he holds two. It is important for West to bid the slam in spades, because if East plays in hearts and his two Aces are in hearts and clubs (as they are) the opening lead of a diamond from South may break Six Hearts out of hand. When West plays in Six Spades, the ◇ K is protected against the opening lead and 12 tricks are assured.

As West knows that there is an Ace against the hand the grand slam is out of the question and West, therefore, has no need to bid Five No-Trumps to ask East how many Kings he holds.

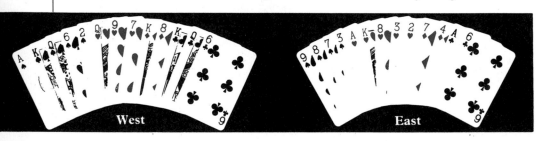

West   East

The convention is a very useful one, but it must be used with discretion, because if partner lacks the necessary Aces the partnership may find itself carried out of its depth. As a rule, it may be said that if the final contract is to be in clubs the bid of Four No-Trumps should not be made unless the bidder holds at least two Aces, and if the contract is to be in diamonds he should hold at least one Ace.

A limit bid is a bid that informs partner of the precise strength of the hand, and so permits him to estimate the combined strength of the partnership, and drop the bidding if he can see no future for it.

No-trump bids are limit bids because they are made on an agreed number of points in the hand. A single raise of partner's suit is a limit bid that shows moderate strength and support for the suit; a double raise of partner's suit shows that the hand is too good for a mere simple raise and invites him to bid game if his hand is above average; a triple raise is distributional, it promises good support for the suit and a few scattered points, but no more because with good support for the suit coupled with high-card strength it would be more in order to make a gradual advance to a possible slam.

RESPONDING BIDS
Suits

A jump overcall shows strength, and, though it is not forcing, partner is expected to take action if he holds the values that would justify a response to a bid of One.

An overcall should be based on a five-card or longer suit, though it is reasonable to overcall with A, K, Q, x or K, Q, J, x at the level of One. It is nearly always very unwise to overcall with a broken suit.

In general, when an opponent has opened the bidding with a bid of One of a suit, it is better to counter it with a take-out double than with a weak overcall. A double in this situation shows weakness in the suit doubled and a total of about 13 or 14 points with a balanced hand and 11 or 12 with an unbalanced one. If the doubler's partner has not bid (if he has the double is for a penalty) the doubler invites partner to bid his best suit.

West	*East*
♠ K, J, 9, 6, 2	♠ 5, 3
♡ K, J, 9, 2	♡ A, Q, 8, 3
♢ 6	♢ K, 7, 2
♣ A, Q, 7	♣ 10, 8, 6, 2

If South has bid One Diamond, West should double. East bids hearts and the good fit has been found. If West bids One Spade over South's One Diamond the heart fit will never be found and a good result will be exchanged for a bad one.

If partner's best suit is the one that has been doubled, either he bids no-trumps or passes for a penalty if he holds length in the suit.

A double of One No-Trump is made with a balanced hand and a count of about two points more than the no-trump bidder's average. With a weak hand partner will take out into his best suit, but if the combined count totals 23 or more he will pass for a penalty.

The responses to opening Two bids (of suits other than clubs) are not so well-defined and clear-cut as the responses to an opening bid of Two Clubs. In general, if partner holds a biddable suit he should bid it at the lowest level. If he lacks a biddable suit, but has a total of from 10 to 12 points, he should bid Three No-Trumps. If he lacks a biddable suit and insufficient points to bid Three No-Trumps, but has adequate support (i.e. x, x, x or Q, x) for partner's suit and a count of five, he should give a simple raise in partner's suit. If he lacks a biddable suit, insufficient points for Three No-Trumps, and insufficient support for partner's suit, he should make the negative response of Two No-Trumps.

No-trumps

The partner of the player who opens the bidding with No-Trumps raises on a very precise number of points. The number of points, however, may be reduced slightly if the responder holds a five-card suit. Over a bid of One No-Trump, partner holds:

The hand totals eight points and nine points are normally necessary to jump to Three No-Trumps. Here, however,

the jump to Three No-Trumps is justified on the length of the spade suit, and the good intermediate cards. It is unwise to bid spades because if it is assumed that partner holds a balanced 16-point hand he is just as likely to win nine tricks in No-Trumps as the responder is to win ten in spades. If Three No-Trumps cannot be made there is no reason to suppose that Four Spades can.

A jump take out into a suit is a game force. It does not, however, promise a very strong hand: rather it means that the responder, who knows the precise strength of his partner's bid, can foresee game for the partnership but cannot tell whether the combined hands will play better in No-Trumps or in a suit.

West	*East*
♠Q, J, 4, 3	♠K, 10, 9, 7, 2
♡A, Q, 2	♡J, 6, 4
◇K, 9, 3	◇A, J, 8, 2
♣A, 7, 6	♣8

Bidding	Bidding
1 No-Trump	3 ♠
4 ♠	No Bid

Over West's opening bid of One No-Trump (16 to 18 points) East who has 9 points has enough to jump to Three No-Trumps. He prefers Three Spades, however, which West raises to game, because game in spades can hardly fail, but in No-Trumps will be defeated if a club is led.

Another important feature of responding to a No-Trump bid is the

Stayman convention. It is a bid of Two Clubs over partner's One No-Trump, or Three Clubs over his Two No-Trumps, made, irrespective of the holding in the suit, to ask partner to bid his better four-card major suit, or, if he lacks one, to bid diamonds.

West	East
♠ K, Q, 2	♠ A, J, 4, 3
♡ A, J, 6, 2	♡ K, Q, 8, 4
◇ Q, 6, 4	◇ 3, 2
♧ A, Q, 4	♧ J, 8, 5

Bidding	Bidding
1 No-Trump	2 ♧
2 ♡	4 ♡
No Bid	

Without the convention East, with 11 points, would have no alternative except to jump his partner's opening bid of One No-Trump (16 to 18 points) to Three. The combined total of 29 points is more than adequate for the bid, but Three No-Trumps may be defeated if a diamond is led and Four Hearts can hardly fail.

There is a large range of bids which show weakness and that may be recognized as such by the logic of the situation.

West	East
1 ♠	2 No-Trumps
3 ♠	?

East's bid of Two No-Trumps shows a count of from 11 to 13 points, and over it West cannot do more than repeat his suit. His hand, therefore,

cannot be strong, and his bid of Three Spades no more than the cheapest way of keeping his promise to rebid, which he made when he opened with One Spade.

In the same way, if the bidding is:

West	East
1 No-Trump	2 ♠
?	

West should pass. East's bid must be showing a weak hand that he considers will play better in a suit than in No-Trumps, otherwise, over an opening bid of One No-Trump, it would be impossible for partner ever to play in Two of a suit.

Or we may consider the following sequences:

West	East	West	East	West	East
1 ♡	2 ♡	1 ♡	2 ♧	1 ♧	1 ♡
3 ♧	3 ♡	2 ♡	3 ◇	1 ♠	2 ♡
		3 ♡		2 ♠	3 ♡

In all these sequences the bid of Three Hearts shows weakness. A player cannot be holding much of a hand when he cannot do better than rebid his suit at the lowest level, and it is particularly pronounced when he rebids it twice.

If we assume that South deals, a sequence of bidding to illustrate some of the points mentioned might be:

South	West	North	East
1 ◇	No Bid	1 ♡	1 ♠
1 No-Trump	2 ♠	3 ◇	No Bid
3 No-Trumps	Double	No Bid	No Bid
4 ◇	No Bid	5 ◇	Double
Redouble	No Bid	No Bid	No Bid

The final contract, therefore, is Five Diamonds, and the hand will be played by South, because he was the first on his side to mention diamonds as the trump suit.

THE PLAY

During the playing, the player who has won the contract strives to make it, playing his own hand and that of his partner exposed on the table, against the 'defenders' striving to prevent him.

The playing period begins by the player on the left of the declarer leading to the first trick. As soon as he has done so, the partner of the declarer places his cards face upwards on the table as dummy. He takes no further part in the play except that he has a right to draw his partner's attention to certain irregularities, such as asking him if he has none of a suit when he fails to follow suit, and warning him against leading out of the wrong hand. The declarer plays the dummy hand as well as his own.

The play follows the normal routine of trick-taking games: if a player is able to do so he must follow suit to the card led; otherwise he may either discard or trump. The trick is won by the player who plays the highest card of the suit led, or the highest trump. The player who wins a trick leads to the next. If a trick is won in the dummy, the next trick must be led from there.

DECLARER'S PLAY

After the opening lead has been made, and the dummy hand exposed, it is of first importance for the declarer, before he plays a card from dummy, to take stock of the position and decide upon the best way to play the cards.

In the deal below, against West's contract of Three No-Trumps, North leads the ♠Q. At first sight it may seem immaterial whether West wins the trick with the Ace in dummy or with the King in his own hand. In the event, it matters a lot in which hand he wins the trick. If West gives consideration to the position he will appreciate that he must win the first trick with the ♠K in his hand, win the ♣K, Q, J, reach dummy, by leading the ♠4 to the Ace, to win dummy's Ace and ♣7, and finally the two red Aces in his own hand. If West wins the first trick with dummy's ♠A, he will lose the contract

West   East

West   East

if the adverse clubs fail to divide three—two, because he has left himself with no side entry to the clubs.

When the declarer is playing a No-Trump contract, usually his first aim should be to establish his longest suit. In many cases, however, it is better to develop a short and strong suit rather than a long and weak one.

In the deal above, North leads a club against West's contract of Three No-Trumps. Consideration shows that West's best play is to win with the ♣K and play on spades to knock out the Ace. This way, West makes sure of his contract with three tricks in spades, three in hearts, one in diamonds and two in clubs. The diamond suit is longer than the spade suit, but West cannot develop East's diamonds without first losing the lead twice. By then the opponents will have set up the clubs and broken the contract; in any case, only three tricks in diamonds will be developed for eight in all, which is not enough.

In a suit contract, it is usually the right play for the declarer to draw the adverse trumps at the first opportunity. Trumps, however, should not be drawn if there is a better use for them.

In the deal illustrated below, West plays in Four Hearts, and North leads a club. West wins the first trick with the ♣A, and if he draws the trumps at once his contract will depend on the

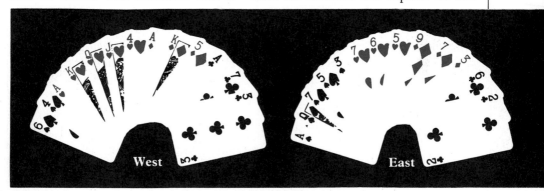

West   East

finesse of the ♠Q being successful. It is no more than an even chance. The contract is a certainty if West, after winning the first trick with the ♣A, leads either the 7 or 3 of the suit. It does not matter whether North or South wins the trick, or what card is returned. Declarer wins the next trick and trumps a club in dummy. Now the adverse trumps may be drawn, and West comes to ten tricks with one spade, five hearts, two diamonds and one club by straight leads, and the ruff (trump) of a club on the table.

A valuable weapon in the armoury of the declarer is the ability to manage a suit to make the most tricks out of it.

West	East
A, 9, 3, 2	K, Q, 10, 5, 4

In this position it is vital to play the King first. Then, if either North or South is void of the suit, there is a marked finessing position over the Jack, and five tricks will be made.

The unthinking player who first plays the Ace, on the assumption that it does not matter which high card he plays first because the outstanding cards will normally divide three–one or two–two, will lose a trick in the suit whenever North is void and South holds J, 8, 7, 6. It will occur about five times in every hundred.

West	East
A, K, 10, 5, 3	9, 7, 6

If West cannot afford to lose more than one trick in the suit, his play is to

win either the Ace or King; if both opponents follow suit, he enters East's hand in a side suit, leads the 7 from the table and if South plays the 8, plays the 10 from his own hand. This protects him against losing two tricks in the suit if South started with Q, J, 8, x.

There is a percentage play or a safety play for almost every combination of a suit, and it may be found by analysing the division of the remaining cards in the suit.

West	East
♠A, K, 4, 2	♠5, 3
♡A, 9, 7	♡10, 6, 2
◇A, 9, 4	◇K, 8, 7
♣K, 7, 6	♣A, 10, 5, 4, 3

Against West's contract of Three No-Trumps, North leads a spade. West can make his contract only if he wins four tricks in clubs. After winning the first trick with the ♠K, the right play is for West to win the ♣K. If North and South both follow suit, West continues with the ♣7 and plays the 4 from the dummy if North plays an honour, but the 10 if North plays a low card. If South follows suit, there is only one more outstanding club and it will fall under East's Ace. If North shows out on the second round of clubs, then South started with Q, J, x, x of the suit and West cannot do anything about it. The directed play, however, guarantees that he will win four tricks in the suit if North originally held Q, J, x, x of the suit.

Most important of all, however, is an ability to count the cards. It is not all that difficult, and, in the main, is largely a matter of drawing deductions from the bidding and previous play of the cards, coupled with training oneself to think along the right lines.

♠ K,8
♡ Q,10,4
◇ 9,6,2
♣ Q,9,6,4,3

♠ Q,J,9   N   ♠ 10,7,5,4,2
♡ K,7   W   E   ♡ 5,3
◇ Q,10,8   ◇ A,K,J,7,4
♣ K,J,10,8,5   S   ♣ 2

♠ A,6,3
♡ A,J,9,8,6,2
◇ 5,3
♣ A,7

West deals at love all, and the auction is:

West	North	East	South
1 ♣	No Bid	1 ◇	1 ♡
2 ◇	2 ♡	2 ♠	4 ♡
No Bid	No Bid	No Bid	

West leads diamonds and East wins the first two tricks with the Ace and King of the suit. A third round of diamonds is ruffed by South with the ♡ 8.

As South has lost two tricks, it would seem that his contract is doomed, because West, by reason of his opening bid and lacking either the Ace or King of diamonds, must surely be holding the Kings of hearts and clubs.

South, however, has a partial count of the hand that will enable him to make his contract if he knows how to take advantage of it. On the assumption that West almost certainly started with three diamonds and probably five clubs, he cannot have more than five cards in spades and hearts. South, therefore, wins the ♡ A (in case the King is singleton) and when the ♡ K does not come down, he leads a spade to dummy's King, a spade from dummy to the Ace in the closed hand, and then trumps his last spade with dummy's ♡ 10. As West played the ♡ 7 under South's Ace and followed to the three rounds of spades, South may reconstruct the position as:

♡ Q
♣ Q,9,6,4,3

♡ K   N   ♠ 10,7
♣ K,?,?,?,?   W   E   ♡ 5
   ◇ J,4
   S   ♣ ?

♡ J,9,6,2
♣ A,7

Now, by leading the ♡ Q from dummy, West is put on lead with the King, and as he must return a club, South wins two tricks in the suit.

DEFENDERS' PLAY

Leading

When the bidding period ends, and the playing period begins, the player on the left of the declarer leads to the first trick. It is only after he has led that the partner of the declarer exposes his hand on the table as dummy. It follows, therefore, that the opening lead has to be made in the dark, since the player can see only his own hand and is left to judge the best lead from it, coupled with the information that he has obtained from the bidding. The opening lead must be chosen with care. It is of great importance, because quite often the choice of a good or bad lead will decide whether or not the declarer's contract will be made.

Against a No-Trump contract, if partner has bid a suit, leading it usually offers the best chance of defeating the contract, unless the player on lead holds only a singleton in the suit or he has a good suit of his own.

With two cards of partner's suit the higher should be led; with three cards the highest should be led, unless the suit is headed by the Ace, King, Queen or Jack, when the lowest should be preferred. With two honours in partner's suit the higher should be led; with a sequence (a combination of three or more cards of adjacent rank) the highest should be led. In all other cases the fourth highest should be led.

When a player leads his own suit, he should lead the fourth highest of his longest suit, unless he holds a sequence (when he should lead the highest), a long suit headed by the Ace and King and an entry in another suit (when he should lead the King), or an intermediate honour sequence, e.g. A, Q, J, x or K, J, 10, x (when the higher of the two touching honours should be led).

The reason for leading the fourth highest card of a suit is that if partner subtracts the number of the card from eleven, the remainder will be the number of higher cards held by the other three players. The Rule of Eleven.

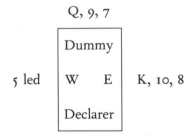

Q, 9, 7

Dummy

5 led — W E — K, 10, 8

Declarer

West leads the 5. As $11 - 5 = 6$, and East can see six cards higher than the 5 in dummy and in his own hand, he will know that the declarer cannot hold a card higher than the 4, so that whichever card is played from dummy he can win the trick with the card just higher.

Against a suit contract it is usually best to lead partner's suit, if he has bid one. If he has not, and the player on lead has to lead from his own suit, he should give preference to leading the top card of an honour sequence. He should avoid leading a card that may cost a trick, e.g. leading the King from K, Q, x, or a card that might enable the declarer to win a trick with a card that might have been captured, e.g. leading the Ace from A, Q, x. The lead of a trump is a good lead if the bidding has suggested that the dummy will be able to trump side suits.

Play

The play of the defenders is more difficult than that of the declarer, because a defender has to combine his hand with that of the unseen one held by his partner. They have the slight advantage of a partnership language that enables them to exchange inform-ation and advice, but, for the most part, success in defence comes mainly from drawing the right deductions from the bidding, and the cards that have been played to previous tricks.

To lead the highest card of a se-quence, to win with the lowest, and to follow suit as the situation dictates, is a general rule that does not need to be enlarged on. Most of the general rules for defence play, however, have been handed down from the days when whist was the fashionable game. At bridge reservations have to be made, because the bidding and the exposed dummy hand allow for modifications.

To return the suit that partner has led is not always the best play. Some-times it is more important to take time by the forelock.

♠ 8, 3
♡ 10, 2
♢ K, Q, J, 6, 3, 2
♣ A, 8, 5

♠ A, 6, 2
♡ K, Q, 9, 3
♢ 10, 9
♣ 6, 4, 3, 2

N
W   E
S

♠ Q, J, 7, 4
♡ A, 5, 4
♢ 8, 7, 4
♣ 10, 9, 7

♠ K, 10, 9, 5
♡ J, 8, 7, 6
♢ A, 5
♣ K, Q, J

South deals and opens the auction with One No-Trump (12 to 14 points)

and North jumps him to Three.

West leads the ♡ 3 and East wins with the Ace. If East returns a heart, South has no difficulty in making nine tricks, because dummy's ♡ 10 protects the Jack in the closed hand and the defenders cannot win more than one trick in spades and three in hearts. With the ♡ 2 on the table, East should appreciate that his partner cannot hold more than four hearts and that they cannot be better than K, Q, 9, 3, because if they were K, Q, J, 3 he would have led the King and not the 3. As once East gives up the lead he can never regain it, he must take advantage of the time factor, the tempo, and lead the ♠ Q. The only chance of defeating the contract is to find West holding the ♠ A, and as South's bid of One No-Trump postulates a maximum of 14 points, East, who holds seven points and can count 10 on the table, can count West with just enough room for the ♠ A as well as for the ♡ K, Q.

To cover an honour with an honour may be good play in many cases, but it is not when the honour has been led from a sequence.

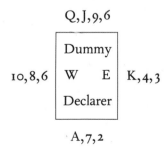

Q, J, 9, 6

10, 8, 6   K, 4, 3

A, 7, 2

The Queen is led from dummy. If East covers with the King, the declarer will win four tricks in the suit by winning with the Ace and returning the suit to finesse against West's 10. East, therefore, should not cover. The Queen will win, but now the defenders will always win a trick in the suit because if the declarer continues with dummy's Jack, the lead is no longer from a sequence and East covers it with the King. With K, x only, East should cover the Queen, otherwise the declarer, after winning dummy's Queen may continue with a low spade (not the Jack) from the table and East's King will be wasted.

Second hand plays low; third hand plays high, is another general rule that has been handed down from the past. It is, perhaps, a rule worth remembering, because exceptions when second hand should play high are few and far between, and when third hand sees only low cards on his right, there are virtually no exceptions to his playing high.

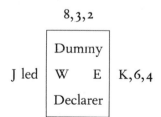

8, 3, 2

	Dummy	
J led	W E	K, 6, 4
	Declarer	

West leads the Jack. East should play the King. He knows that the declarer holds the Queen (otherwise West would have led it in preference to the Jack) and if declarer holds the Ace as well the King is doomed. East, therefore, must play on the chance that West has led from A, J, 10, x and that

declarer holds Q, x, x.

A very important weapon in the armoury of the defenders is the echo or peter, sometimes called the come-on or high-low signal. Reduced to its simplest terms, when a defender plays a higher card followed by a lower one of the same suit, it is a request to partner to play the suit. In many cases a defender can afford to play the suit only once. In such a case to play a 7 or a higher card is an encouragement to partner, and to play a lower card is a discouragement to him. Against a trump contract, the high-low play in a side suit shows that a doubleton is held and that the third round can be trumped. If the play is made in the trump suit itself, it shows that three trumps are held. Against a No-Trump contract, the echo shows length in the suit, usually four cards.

The defenders are frequently compelled to discard, and nearly always discarding presents them with a problem. The general rules to follow are not to retain the same suit as partner; not to discard from a suit in which you have the same length as dummy or suspect the declarer has in his hand; and never to discard so that the declarer is given information.

Counting the cards is, of course, as important to the defenders as it is to the declarer. In some ways, however, the defenders have it a bit easier. If the declarer is in a No-Trump contract he will have limited his hand to an agreed number of points. It follows, therefore, that if the declarer's limit is 16 to 18 points and he has shown up with 15 points, the defenders know that he has left in his hand no more than a King or its equivalent. In much the same way, in a suit contract the declarer and his dummy will rarely hold less than eight trumps between them. It follows, therefore, that if a defender holds three trumps, he knows that his partner is probably holding not more than two.

In conclusion, it may be said that good defence consists in playing those cards that give as much information as possible to partner, and making things as easy as possible for him; by contrary, in playing those cards that give as little information as possible to the declarer and making things as difficult as possible for him. Whenever it is possible to do so, a defender should play the cards that the declarer knows are in his hand, and retain those of which he knows nothing. If all this comes as a counsel of perfection – the best Bridge players are perfectionists.

SCORING

When all 13 tricks have been played, the players record their scores, and those of their opponents, on a marker, or sheet of paper, as illustrated.

The main object is to win a rubber, which is the best out of three games.

When a player makes his contract, the score for tricks won is entered below the horizontal line. All other scores are entered above this line.

A game is won when a partnership scores 100 points below the horizontal line, either in one or more deals.

A partnership that wins a game becomes vulnerable and is subject to higher bonuses if it makes its contract, and increased penalties if it fails. Vulnerability does not affect the points for winning the tricks contracted for.

If a partnership scores less than game in one deal, it is said to have a part-score and if the opponents then score game the part-score cannot be carried forward towards the next game. When a partnership wins a game a line is drawn across the score sheet below it, and both partnerships begin the next game from a love score.

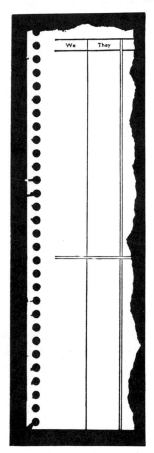

Tricks

If a partnership has bid and made its contract, it scores:

In No-Trumps: 40 points for the first trick and 30 points for each subsequent trick.

In Spades and Hearts: 30 points for each trick.

In Diamonds and Clubs: 20 points for each trick.

The scores for winning tricks are doubled if the contract has been doubled, and quadrupled if the contract has been redoubled.

If a partnership has made tricks in excess of its contract, it scores:

If undoubled: trick value for each trick.

If doubled: 100 points for each trick if not vulnerable. 200 tricks for each trick if vulnerable.

If redoubled: 200 points for each trick if not vulnerable. 400 points for each trick if vulnerable.

If a partnership has failed to make its contract, it loses:

If undoubled: 50 points for each trick if not vulnerable. 100 points for each trick if vulnerable.

If doubled: 100 points for the first trick; 200 points for each subsequent trick if not vulnerable.

200 points for the first trick; 300 points for each subsequent trick if vulnerable.

If redoubled: 200 points for the first trick; 400 points for each subsequent trick if not vulnerable.

400 points for the first trick; 600 points for each subsequent trick if vulnerable.

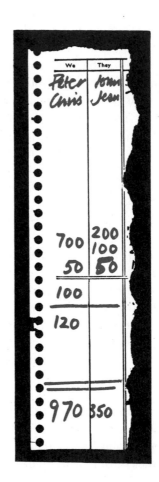

Bonuses

Winning rubber:

    in three games   500

    in two games   700

Grand slam bid and made: vulnerable 1,500; not vulnerable 1,000.

Small slam bid and made: vulnerable 750; not vulnerable 500.

150 points if either partner holds all four Aces in a No-Trump contract, or all five honours in a suit contract.

100 points if either partner holds any four honours in a suit contract.

50 points if a partnership makes a doubled or redoubled contract.

BRINT

*B*RINT was originated by J. B. Chambers in 1929. It is a hybrid of Bridge (see page 123) and Vint, the national card game of Russia.

NUMBER OF PLAYERS

Brint is for four players.

CARDS

The full pack of 52 cards is used.

THE PLAY

Brint is played in the same way as Bridge. It has been described as Bridge with Vint scoring, because the score that counts towards game, and recorded below the line, depends entirely upon the level to which the bidding has been carried. No-trumps and the suits retain their rank, but each trick (over six) at the level of One is worth 10 points, at the level of Two 20 points, and so on up to Seven when each trick is worth 70 points.

The full scoring table is set out at the top of the next page.

The score for tricks made is unaffected by a double, but if a doubled contract is redoubled the trick score, as well as the bonus and penalty for a doubled contract, is doubled. The bonuses and penalties are increased by 100 points each if the player is vulnerable.

A game is won by the pair that first reaches a trick score of 160 points.

The bonuses for bidding and making slams and games, and for holding honours, recorded above the line as at Bridge, are set out at the foot of the next page.

THE SCORING TABLE FOR BRINT

		When the declarer is not vulnerable		
		Undoubled	Doubled	
When the contract is at the level of:	Each odd-trick (whether doubled or not) is worth:	Penalty for each undertrick	Bonus for contract and each overtrick	Penalty for each undertrick
One	10	50	50	100
Two	20	50	50	100
Three	30	50	50	100
Four	40	100	100	200
Five	50	150	150	300
Six	60	200	200	400
Seven	70	250	250	500

THE BONUSES IN BRINT

Successful bid of Seven   1,000
Successful bid of Six   500
Successful bid of Five   250
Successful bid of Four
  vulnerable   500
  not vulnerable   250
4 Aces in one hand in no-trump
  contract   150

5 honours in one hand in suit
  contract   200
4 honours in one hand in a suit
  contract   100
They are unaffected by vulnerability, doubling and redoubling.

CALYPSO

CALYPSO was invented by R. W. Willis of Trinidad: it dates from the mid-1950s, and though designed on entirely new lines, inevitably borrows some of the best features of Bridge (see page 103) and Canasta (see page 127).

NUMBER OF PLAYERS

Calypso is for four players playing in two partnerships, but can be played cut-throat by three, as described later.

CARDS

The game is played with four packs of cards (with identical backs) shuffled together, but the cards are shuffled only at the start of a game, and a player holds only 13 of them at a time.

It is a novel feature of the game that each player has his own trump suit. Spades and hearts play in partnership against diamonds and clubs. The players cut for seats and trump suits. The highest has the choice of both, and his partner takes the corresponding suit and sits facing him. The choice of a trump suit conveys no advantage; it is purely a matter of personal preference.

Thirteen cards are dealt to each player, and the dealer places the rest of the pack to his left, ready for the next dealer after the hand has been played.

THE PLAY

The object of the game is to build calypsoes. A calypso is a complete suit (from Ace to 2) in a player's trump suit.

The player on the left of the dealer leads to the first trick. Thereafter the lead is made by the player who wins a trick. When playing to a trick a player must follow suit if he can; otherwise he may either discard or trump by playing a card of his own trump suit.

A trick is won by he who has played the highest card of the suit led, or by he who has trumped it, or over-trumped it by playing a higher trump of his own trump suit. If two or more players play identical cards, the first played takes priority for the purpose of winning tricks, and perhaps the most important feature of the game is that if a player leads a card of his own trump suit, he wins the trick automatically unless it is trumped by another player or over-trumped by another. To illustrate:

North ♣	East ♠	South ♦	West ♥
♥ 8	♥ J	♥ 10	♥ 3

North has led the ♡8, and East wins the trick because he has played the highest heart.

North ♣	East ♠	South ◇	West ♡
◇4	♠6	◇7	◇3

North has led the ◇4, and East wins the trick because he has trumped. South has merely followed suit to North's lead.

♡3	♠4	◇6	♡J

North has led the ♡3, and South wins the trick, because although East has trumped, he has over-trumped. West has merely followed suit to North's lead.

♣9	♣J	♣6	♣5

North has led the ♣9 and wins the trick because clubs is his own trump suit. That East has played a higher club does not score.

♣6	♠7	◇9	♣5

North has led the ♣6, East has trumped, but South wins the trick because he has over-trumped.

♡6	♡Q	♡Q	♡10

North has led the ♡6, and the trick is won by East as his ♡Q was played before South's.

When a player wins a trick, he leaves exposed on the table, in front of him, any cards that will help him to build a calypso, passes to his partner any cards that will help him to build a calypso, and discards the others, face downwards, on his right.

North (whose trump suit is clubs) leads the ♣4 and wins the trick:

♣4	♣6	♣J	♣6

North places the ♣4, ♣6 and ♣J face upwards on the table in front of him, and discards the second ♣6. He then leads the ♣8 and the trick is:

♣8	♣J	♣7	◇8

Again North wins the trick. He keeps the ♣7 and ♣8 for his calypso, passes the ◇8 to his partner for his calypso, and discards the ♣J because he already has one.

The play continues until all 13 tricks have been played; the next player then deals another hand of 13 cards each.

A player may build only one calypso at a time, but once a calypso has been built the player may begin another. He may use any cards in the trick with which a calypso has been completed, but he cannot use any cards from his discard pile. These cards are dead.

The game ends when each player has dealt once. The score is then made up as follows:

For the first calypso — 500 points.

For the second calypso — 750 points. | When obtained by the individual players.

For any subsequent calypso — 1,000 points. |

For each card in an incomplete calypso — 20 points.
For each card in the discard pile — 10 points.

The two partners add their totals together, and stakes are paid on the difference between the totals of the two sides.

A serious view is taken of revoking. A revoke does not become established until a player of the offending side has played to the next trick, and a revoke made in the 12th never becomes established, but if established a revoke suffers a penalty of 260 points.

SOLO CALYPSO

Solo Calypso is played by four players but each plays for himself. The play is more or less identical with the parent game, the main difference between the two is that, in Solo Calypso, the players draw cards for choice of seats and trump suits; the highest has first choice, the lowest takes what is left.

CALYPSO FOR THREE PLAYERS

This variation is played with three packs of cards and one complete suit (it does not matter which) removed from all three packs. The game consists of three deals. Each player plays for himself.

CANASTA

*C*ANASTA *was invented in South America during the early part of this century, and spread rapidly round the world soon after the Second World War. Recently it has declined somewhat in popularity, but it remains an entertaining game, and is easy to learn.*

NUMBER OF PLAYERS

Canasta is best for four players, but can be played by two or three, though not so satisfactorily.

CARDS

Two standard packs are used, together with four Jokers, making 108 cards in all.

If there are four players, each receives 11 cards. With three players each gets 13 cards, and two players get 15 cards each. Cards are dealt one at a time, clockwise round the table starting on dealer's left. The top card of the remaining pack is then turned over to start the discard pile, and the player on dealer's left plays first. Before that, however, all the players holding red 3s put them down and draw replacement cards. The deal moves round to the left in subsequent hands.

If the card turned over by the dealer is a Joker, a 2 or a red 3, then he turns another card to cover it, and the pack is frozen (so that wild cards and cards on the table may not be used to capture it).

THE PLAY

Canasta is a 'draw and discard' game, like Gin Rummy and Mah Jong — each player in turn draws a new card from the pack, and then discards one card, trying to form his hand into matching sets while doing so. It is sometimes possible, instead of drawing a new card from the pack, to capture the entire discard pile, and much of the skill in the game goes towards manoeuvring so as to be able to do this.

If a player is able to form a legal combination including the top card (that most recently discarded) of the discard pile, then he may do so instead of drawing a new card from the pack, and having done so he takes the remainder of the discard pile into his hand. The combination may involve the last discard, cards in the player's hand and combinations previously played on the table by him, but may not involve any of the previous discards. Having made his capture, and picked up the discard pile, the player may put down any further cards he wishes — these may include some of the cards he just picked up — and then discards to complete his turn. There is

no restriction on discarding captured cards immediately.

It is illegal to make a capture using a wild card unless the player already has a wild card on the table before the start of his turn — otherwise the last discard must be matched with at least two plain cards of the same rank.

If a black 3 is discarded, it is always illegal for the next player to capture the pile — the main function of black 3s in the game is to act as safe discards.

If a wild card is discarded, then the pile is said to be 'frozen'. It is illegal for the next player to capture the pile, as with black 3s, but there are two additional restrictions which continue to apply until the pile is next captured: it becomes illegal to combine the top discard with cards already played on the table — the combination must be with cards from the hand; and it becomes illegal to capture the pile using a wild card, even if a wild card has already been used.

It is normally illegal to put down a set of black 3s, but this may be done by a player on the turn in which he goes out. A set of black 3s may never contain any wild cards.

If the last card in the pack is a red 3, then the player drawing it does not discard on that turn.

Wild cards may be added to completed canastas, provided that they do not break the law that no more than three wild cards should appear in one combination. If wild cards are added to a natural canasta, though, it becomes a mixed canasta and only scores 300 points (it may be necessary to do this in order to go out).

In the early part of the game, the main objective is to be the first to capture the discard pile. Having done this, a player can often continue capturing the pile for the rest of the hand – each time he picks up he recycles the safe discards he has already used.

When a player has succeeded in making the first capture, and has the chance to go out, it is often good not to do so, but to keep going and make a really huge score. If, on the other hand, his opponent has made the first capture, he will often be stuck simply feeding him cards, and it is usually best to try to go out as soon as possible. Going out is a defensive tactic.

Black 3s should not be discarded too early. Capturing a pile of three of four cards is not very devastating, and it is usually better to hang on to black 3s until the pile gets bigger and a safe discard is really needed.

SCORING

The object of the game is to be the first to 5,000 points.

In order to score, a combination of cards must be laid face up on the table. The only combinations allowed are sets of cards of the same rank – there are no sequences in Canasta. A combination must contain at least three cards. Jokers may be used to substitute for 'plain' cards, and 2s may also be used like Jokers in this way. We refer to 2s and Jokers collectively as 'wild cards'. However, a set may never

contain more than three wild cards, and the plain cards must always outnumber the wild cards in one set.

A set of seven or more cards is called a canasta, and scores a large bonus. 'Natural' canastas (containing no wild cards) score more than 'mixed' ones. Examples are illustrated overleaf.

The 3s are covered by special rules. Black 3s may not normally be used for anything constructive – but are nevertheless good cards to hold – they are discussed later. Red 3s are bonus cards – a player holding one should immediately lay it face up in front of him and draw another card to replace it.

The first time a player puts scoring cards on the table, they must add up to at least a minimum value, which depends on how close that player's side is to the target of 5,000 points. This total may be achieved using several combinations, for example a total of 50 can be achieved with a set of three 5s (15) and a set of two Kings with a 2 (40). If (as usually happens) the first scoring cards are played while capturing the discard pile, this total must be achieved using only the last discard and cards in the player's hand.

The requirements depend on the side's score as follows:

Negative score	No restriction
0–1,495	50 points required
1,500–2,995	90
3,000–4,995	120

This requirement is quite independent of any red 3s laid down. Examples of sets giving the points required are shown in the illustration.

When the game ends, each side adds

A natural canasta (this one worth 535 points) and a mixed canasta (worth 430).

up the value of their cards face up on the table, then subtracts the value of any cards remaining in their hand. Scores are as follows:

7, 6, 5, 4 or black 3	5
K, Q, J, 10, 9 or 8	10
Ace	20
2	20

Sets satisfying the requirements of a first combination, worth 50, 90 and 120 points.

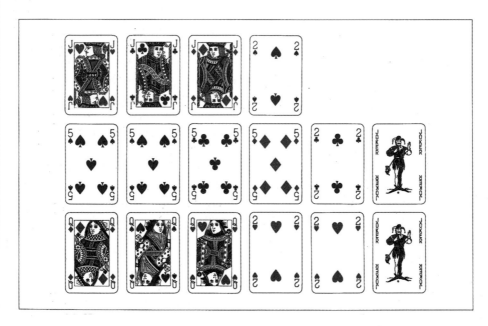

Joker	50
Red 3	100
All four red 3s	800
Mixed canasta	300
Natural canasta	500
Going out	100
Going out 'concealed'	200

FOUR PLAYERS

With two or three players, each plays individually, but four players play as two pairs of partners. Partners sit opposite each other. In this case partners keep their scoring cards separately, and they must meet the requirements to score a certain number of points with their first combinations and to make one canasta before going out separately, but they can add cards to each other's combinations.

The end of the game comes when both partners on one side have gone out (or when the pack runs out). It is normally good play for the two partners to go out in immediate succession, and in order to be able to achieve this it is legal to say 'Shall I go out, partner?' before discarding. If your partner says 'Yes' then you are obliged to go out.

CINCH

CINCH is a game from the All Fours family which was very fashionable in America before Bridge began to oust most other card games of the type. It has some of the attractions of Bridge, like the bidding, without all the conventions, and is a game of skill well worth playing. It is also called Double Pedro and High Five.

NUMBER OF PLAYERS

Cinch is best as a game for four players, as described first, playing in two partnerships, with the partners sitting opposite each other. It can be played by two to six players, and there are variants such as Auction Cinch, described later.

CARDS

The full pack of 52 cards is used. Cards rank from Ace (high) to 2 (low), with the exception of the 5 of the same colour as the trump suit, which is also regarded as a trump and ranks between the 5 and 4. For example, if clubs are trumps, the trump suit ranks as follows:

♣A, K, Q, J, 10, 9, 8, 7, 6, 5; ♠5; ♣4, 3, 2

The 5 of the trump suit is called Right Pedro and the 5 of the same colour is called Left Pedro. Cards in the trump suit have values to players winning them in tricks as follows: Right Pedro five points, Left Pedro five points, Ace (known as 'high') one point, 2 (known as 'low') one point, Jack one point and 10 (known as 'game') one point. On each deal there are thus 14 points at stake.

Players draw cards to determine partners, the two highest playing against the two lowest, the highest being dealer. The dealer shuffles, and the player to his right cuts. The dealer deals nine cards to each player in threes, clockwise from his left. The remaining cards are set aside face down for the moment – they will be used later.

THE PLAY

The object is to take tricks containing the scoring cards, and the trump suit is decided by the side which undertakes to make the most tricks, so the next stage is a round of bidding.

Beginning with eldest hand (to dealer's left), each player in turn makes a bid, or passes. Each player is allowed only one bid. A bid consists of the number of points that the player proposes to make in play, with his partner's help. He can decide which suit is to be trumps, but at the bidding stage he does not announce the suit. The minimum bid is one, and the maximum is 14 (the total points avail-

able). Once a player has bid, any subsequent bid must be for a higher number of points. When the round of bidding has finished, the player who bid the highest names the trump suit (he is not allowed to consult with his partner, and no signals must pass between them). The side bidding highest has now contracted to make the stated number of points with the trump suit as specified.

As with Bridge, expert players have certain systems of bidding, of which the following is an example:

With a Pedro, bid five to show it.

With A, x, x, or A, x, x, x, bid six.
With A, K, bid seven.
With A, K, J, x, x, bid 11.
With A, K, Q, x or better, bid 12.

Should the first three players all pass, the dealer names the trump suit, but he is not obliged to contract to make a certain number of points.

The trick-taking part of the game commences with each player holding six cards, so the next stage is one of discarding, but each player is given the opportunity to improve his hand by drawing new cards from the remaining pack.

Beginning with eldest hand, each player discards as many cards as he wishes, face up, and is given by dealer, face down, enough cards from the top of the pack to bring his hand up to six cards. A player must make at least three discards (if he discards only three, he draws no new cards). No player may discard a trump, unless he is dealt with seven or more, in which case he must discard at least one to bring his hand to six cards.

When it is dealer's turn to discard, he simply 'robs the pack'. He is entitled to look at all the remaining cards and decide which he wishes to take into his hand and to discard accordingly. He announces how many cards he is taking but need not show his discards except that, should there be more than six trumps in his hand and the pack, he must show the other players the trumps that he is forced to discard or not to take into his hand.

In practice, each player will keep all his trumps and usually discard all his non-trumps, because as all the point-scoring cards are trumps, it is impossible to win any points with a plain card.

With all players reduced to six cards, the trick-taking phase begins. The player who named the trump suit is called the maker. The maker leads to the first trick. Subsequently the winner of a trick leads to the next.

When a trump is led, each player must follow suit if able, and must discard if unable. When a plain suit is led, a player able to follow suit may do so *or trump*, but may not discard. A player unable to follow suit may discard or trump.

The object of each side is to take as many tricks containing point-scoring cards as possible, with particular reference to the contract.

When all six tricks have been played, each side counts the number of points won. If the making side has made its contract, i.e. has scored at least the number of points bid by the maker, the side with the higher total of points wins the difference. For example, if the maker bids six and scores nine against the opponents' five, his side scores four points. Notice that even when the maker achieves his contract, it is not necessarily his side which scores. If he bids six and makes six, his opponents having scored eight, his opponents score two points for the difference.

If the making side fails to make its contract, the opponents score the number of points they made, plus the value of the contract. For example, if a side contracts to make ten points, and makes only eight, the opponents score the six points they made plus the ten points of the contract, i.e. 16 points.

When all players have passed, and the dealer names trumps without bidding, the side scoring the more points scores the difference.

Game is to 51 points.

The illustration overleaf shows the nine cards dealt to each hand by the dealer (South).

West bid five (to tell his partner he held a pedro); North, with ♣A, K bid seven; East, with his strong diamonds, bid eight (if his partner's 5 was red, he was certain to make seven, and almost certain to make eight, even without any cards he might draw), while South could only pass.

East announced diamonds as trumps, much to the satisfaction of West, whose ♡5 was now certainly worth five points.

West, North and East each dis-

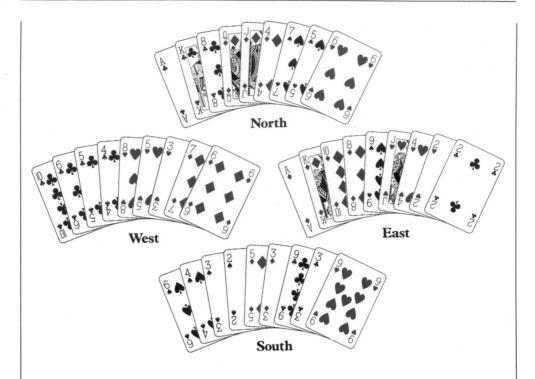

North

West

East

South

carded all their non-trumps, and drew three, three and two cards respectively. South robbed the pack, finding only one trump, the ◇2, and drawing two cards.

The new hands are in the illustration opposite.

Play might proceeds as follows:

East	South	West	North
♠8	♠2	◇6	♠10
◇A	◇3	♡5	◇4
♠A	♡9	◇7	♣Q
◇10	♣3	♠J	◇9
◇K	◇2	♡Q	◇Q
◇8	◇5	♣J	◇J

East led low and his partner West played ◇6 to prevent North winning

the trick and five points should he hold a Right Pedro (West knows he himself has Left Pedro). This play, of third player playing a trump higher than 5 is known as 'cinching the trick'. Knowing that his partner held ◇A, West led Left Pedro for East to take, and West cinched again at trick 3. East played ◇10 at trick 4, because he would not mind losing it to either ◇Q or ◇J in the South hand, as he would be sure then of taking the last two tricks and capturing Right Pedro. It would not have helped North to play ◇Q or ◇J at trick four – East would play low and win the last two tricks, conceding no more than six points. At trick 5 East leads the ◇K knowing he will lose the last trick but that his opponents cannot contribute more than six points to it. East/West thus take eight points, achieve their contract, and score the difference between the two totals, i.e. two points.

It is as well to remember that of the 24 cards in play, 14 will be trumps, and that a player holding four trumps will find at least one other player holding as many. However, it is more important to hold the high trumps than length. A player whose hand consists of six low trumps might not win a point. It is necessary to win at least one Pedro to take the balance of points, and a player can lead a Pedro to a partner holding the master trump, as in the second trick in the example hand on page 134.

It frequently does not pay to draw

trumps, a tactic that is frequently used in other trick-taking games, including Bridge. Had East, with his strong trumps, attempted to do so in the example hand, the play might have proceeded as follows:

East	South	West	North
◇ A	◇ 3	♡ 5	◇ 4
◇ K	◇ 2	◇ 6	◇ 9
♠ 8	♣ 2	◇ 7	♠ 10
◇ 8	♡ 9	♠ J	♣ Q
♠ A	♣ 3	♡ Q	◇ J
◇ 10	◇ 5	♣ J	◇ Q

Each side took seven points, meaning East/West failed to make their contract, and North/South therefore scored their points, seven, plus the

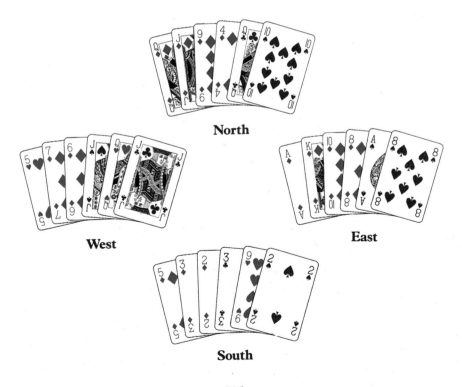

North

West

East

South

value of the contract, eight, making 15.

It is as well to note that a side failing to make a contract must lose at least 15 points, while if it makes the contract it cannot score more than 14. This suggests bids should be made with caution. On the other hand, naming the trump suit is a big advantage.

CINCH WITH A WIDOW

In this variation of the game, after the first three cards to each player, the dealer deals each player a widow of four cards, which remains on the table before them. Players bid as before, whereupon each player picks up his widow. The maker then names the trump suit, and each player discards seven cards to bring his hand to six. Any player who discards a trump or trumps must show them to the other players. Play then proceeds as before.

CUT-THROAT CINCH

Cinch can be played by two, three, five or six players, each playing for himself. With two or three players, the dealer does not rob the pack, but discards and draws like the other players. Obviously not all the trumps will be in play, which makes the bidding and play more of a gamble. With five or six players, each player is dealt six cards only, so draws the same number of cards as he discards.

In Cut-throat Cinch, the maker plays against the other players. With two players, scoring is as in the parent game, which has two sides. With three to six players, if the contract is made, the side with the most tricks (either the maker or the combined opponents) scores the difference between the two totals (each opponent of the maker scores the difference if his side wins). If the contract is not made, each opponent scores the amount of the bid plus the number of points scored by himself personally.

AUCTION CINCH

Auction Cinch, also called Razzle Dazzle, is for five or six players, each playing for himself. Six cards are dealt to each player in bundles of three. Bidding is as in the parent game described, and when the highest bidder has named trumps, each player in turn discards all his non-trumps, and takes cards sufficient to bring his hand back to six cards. The maker then specifies a card not in his hand (usually the highest trump he is missing). The holder of the card acknowledges that he has it, and the two play in opposition against the others. The partner does not change seats, even if sitting next to maker. The scoring of the points in play is as in the parent game. If the maker and his partner make their contract, the side with most points scores the difference between the two totals. Each player on the winning side scores the difference. If the contract fails, each player on the non-contracting side scores the points specified in the contract plus the points he himself took in tricks.

Some schools prefer that the partner of the maker does not acknowledge that he holds the specified card. This brings surprise and uncertainty to the play while detracting from the skill factor.

EUCHRE

*E*UCHRE *is a game always more popular in the New World than in the Old, and made famous by Bret Harte's witty* Plain Language from Truthful James.

NUMBER OF PLAYERS

The standard game is suitable for from two to six players, but is best for four, two playing in partnership against the other two, as described first.

CARDS

The game is played with a 32-card or short pack, that is the standard pack from which the 6s and lower cards have been removed. The cards rank in the order from Ace (high) to 7 (low) with the exception that the Jack of the trump suit (Right Bower) takes precedence over all other trump cards, and the Jack of the suit of the same colour (Left Bower) ranks as the second highest trump.

There is some advantage in dealing. The players, therefore, must draw cards to decide who shall deal. The highest takes first deal, which, thereafter, passes round the table clockwise.

The dealer gives five cards to each player either in bundles of two then three, or three then two. It does not matter which, but he must be consistent throughout the game. The rest of the pack is placed face downwards in the centre of the table, and the top card is turned face upwards.

THE PLAY

The turned up card is the potential trump suit, and, beginning with the player on the left of the dealer, each player in turn has the option of either refusing or accepting it.

To accept it as the trump suit the opponents of the dealer say: 'I order it up'; the dealer's partner says: 'I assist'; and the dealer himself says nothing, but accepts by making his discard. To refuse the card as the trump suit, the opponents and partner of the dealer say: 'I pass'; the dealer signifies refusal by taking the card from the top of the pack and placing it, face upwards, partly underneath the pack.

If all four players pass on the first round, there is a second round. Beginning with the player on the left of the dealer, each player in turn may now either pass, or name any suit he likes (other than that of the turned up card) as trumps. If all four players pass on the second round, the hand is abandoned and the deal passes.

When the trump suit has been settled, the player who has named it (the maker) has the right to go it alone, but he must announce his intention to do so before a card has been led. His partner places his cards face downwards on the table, and takes no active part in the hand. The maker (he is the only one of the four who can go alone) plays his hand against the two opponents in partnership. If he wins the march (all five tricks) he scores four points; if he wins three or four tricks he scores one point; if he is euchred (i.e.

fails to win at least three tricks) the opponents score two points each.

Euchre is a trick-taking game. The player on the left of the dealer (or the player on the left of the maker if he is going it alone) leads to the first trick. Thereafter the player who wins a trick leads to the next. A player must follow suit to the card led if he can, if not he may either discard or trump.

If the partnership that made the trump suit wins the march it scores two points; if it wins three or four tricks it scores one point; if it is euchred the opposing side scores two points. It is customary for each side to keep the score by using a 3 and a 4 (cards not needed in the game) as shown in the illustration. The side that is first to score five points wins.

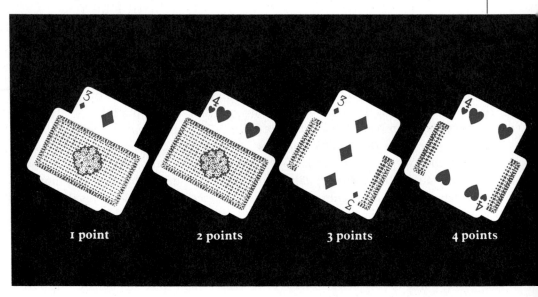

1 point   2 points   3 points   4 points

TWO-HANDED EUCHRE

With two players, the game is played in exactly the same way as the parent game except that the pack is reduced to 24 cards by removing the 8s and all lower cards, and, obviously, there is no declaration of going it alone.

THREE-HANDED EUCHRE

The game for three players is played in the same way as the parent game except that the maker of the trump suit plays against the other two in partnership. If the maker wins the march he scores three points; if he wins three or four tricks he scores one point; and if he is euchred each of his opponents scores two points.

CALL-ACE EUCHRE

This is a variation that may be played by four, five or six players, each playing for himself. It is played in the same way as the parent game with the exception that the maker has the option of either playing for himself or of calling for a partner by saying: 'I call on the Ace of...' and he names a suit. The player who holds the Ace of this suit then plays in partnership with the maker against the other players, but he does not reveal himself. It follows, therefore, that until the Ace is played, and it may not be in the deal, everyone except the holder of the Ace (if it is in play) is left to guess where his interest lies.

The scoring is rather different from that of the other variations as fundamentally the game is all against all. For winning the march a lone player scores one point for every player in the game; in a partnership hand the score is two points each if three or four players are in the game, and three points each if five or six players are in the game. For winning three or four tricks a lone player scores one point; in a partnership hand both players score one point. If a lone player or a partnership is euchred the other players score two points each.

HEARTS

*H*EARTS *and its several variations is very similar in principle to Black Maria (see page 71) because the object of the game is to avoid taking tricks that contain certain specified cards.*

NUMBER OF PLAYERS

The game may be played by any reasonable number of players, but it is at its most interesting and skilful as a game for four, each playing for himself.

CARDS

The full pack of 52 cards is used. However, when the game is played by three players or by more than four, low cards are removed from the pack to reduce it to a number that allows every player to be dealt the same number of cards.

All the cards are dealt out, singly, clockwise.

THE PLAY

The play follows the general principles of trick-taking games: the player on the left of the dealer leads to the first trick, and thereafter the winner of a trick leads to the next; a player must follow suit to the card led if he can, and if he cannot he may discard any card that suits him.

The ♠Q and all cards of the heart suit are penalty cards. Every deal is a separate event, and the usual method of settling is to debit the player who wins the ♠Q 13 points, and those who win hearts one point for each card.

A revoke is heavily penalized. A player may correct a revoke if he does so before a card is led to the next trick; otherwise the revoke is established, the hand is abandoned, and the revoking player is debited all 26 points.

The game is not a difficult one, but it calls for an ability to count the cards,

read the distribution and visualize possibilities. It is instructive to consider the play in the deal illustrated opposite if West has to make the opening lead and assumes that the best lead is the ♡2 because one of the other players will certainly have to win the trick.

Against West's opening lead of the ♡2 the play will be short and sharp, and West will come off worst of all because good play by his opponents will saddle him with the ♠Q.

West	North	East	South
♠2	♡4	♡3	♡8
♡6	♡7	♡10	♡9
♡Q	♡K	♡J	◇A
♡A	♡5	♠Q	◇Q

A more experienced West would have kept off leading a heart. It is probable that his best lead is the singleton diamond, because he has nothing to fear in the spade suit, and, once he has got rid of his diamond, he gives himself the best chance to get rid of the dangerous ♡A and ♡Q.

DOMINO HEARTS

In this version of the game, the players are dealt only six cards each, and the rest of the pack is placed face downwards in the centre of the table. The player on the left of the dealer leads to the first trick, and the game is played in the same way as the parent game except that if a player cannot follow suit to a card that has been led he must draw a

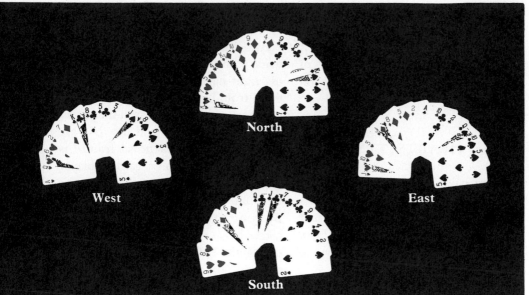

West

North

East

South

card from the stock, and continue to do so until he draws a card of the suit led. Only after the stock has been exhausted may a player discard from his hand if he cannot follow suit to a lead.

Play continues until all the cards have been taken in tricks, each player dropping out as his hand is exhausted. If a player wins a trick with the last card in his hand, the next active player on his left leads to the next trick. The last player to be left in the game retains all the cards left in his hand, and takes into it any cards that may be left in the stock.

The ♠ Q is not a penalty card; only cards of the heart suit are, and one point is lost for each one taken in a trick or left in the hand of the surviving player.

GREEK HEARTS

In this version, as in Black Maria (see page 71) each player, before the opening lead is made, passes three cards to his right-hand opponent and receives three from his left-hand opponent.

As in the parent game the penalty cards are the ♠ Q and all cards of the heart suit, and the penalties for winning them are the same; if, however, a player wins all the hearts and the ♠ Q, instead of losing 26 points, he receives 26 points from each of the other players.

The game calls for some considerable skill, because, before passing on his cards, a player has to decide whether he will take the easy road and play to avoid winning penalty cards, or try for the big prize by winning them all. The decision is never an easy one, because discarding a high heart one may be helping an opponent to a better score, and oneself lose a good score if one receives the ♠Q and a couple of high hearts from one's left-hand opponent.

HEARTSETTE

This variation is played in the same way as the parent game, but with a widow hand. If three or four take part in the game the ♠2 is removed from the pack, and if five or six take part the full pack is used.

When there are three players, each is dealt 16 cards; when four, 12 cards; when five, ten cards and when six, eight cards. The remaining cards are placed face downwards in the centre of the table.

The player on the left of the dealer leads to the first trick and whoever wins it takes the widow and discards from his hand to reduce it to the proper number of cards. No-one else sees the widow nor the cards that have been discarded.

The play continues in the same way as in the parent game with the same penalty cards and penalties for winning them.

OMNIBUS HEARTS

Also called Hit the Moon, this version combines most of the features that have been added to the parent game. Like it, it is at its best when played by four, each playing for himself.

Thirteen cards are dealt to each player, and before the opening lead is made each player passes three cards to his right-hand opponent and receives three from his left-hand opponent.

The play is the same as in the parent game. All the hearts and the ♠Q are penalty cards, but a novel feature is that the ◇10 is a bonus card. A player loses one point for every heart that he wins and 13 points if he wins the ♠Q. By contrary, he wins 10 points if he takes the ◇10, and if he wins all the hearts, the ♠Q and the ◇10 (known as hitting the moon – no longer such a feat as it once was) he wins 26 points instead of losing 16.

The game is won by the player who has the highest plus score, or lowest minus score, when one player reaches a score of − 100.

The game calls for skill both in discarding to the right-hand opponent and in the play. Good discarding is dictated by the fact that only the club suit is neutral and harmless. Every heart is a liability and top spades are dangerous (unless adequately supported by low cards) and though top diamonds are advantageous the low ones may be liabilities.

In play it is necessary to aim at forcing the lead into the hand of the least dangerous opponent. All the time temporary partnerships must be formed. If the score stands at: North − 83, East − 41, South + 32, West + 47, it is obvious that West will be doing his best to win the game by driving North to − 100 as quickly as possible. A skilful South, therefore, will enter into a tacit partnership with North to try and save him by prolonging the game and so give himself more time to pull ahead of West. The strategy is perfectly proper because both players are acting in their own interests.

PIP HEARTS

This version is played in the same way as the parent game, but the ♠ Q is not a penalty card and the penalty for winning a heart is increased to the pip value of the card, the court cards counting Jack 11, Queen 12, King 13 and Ace 14.

PINOCLE

*P*INOCLE *(spelt without the 'h' as explained on page 57) has much in common with Bezique (see page 11) and it originated in Europe. It has, however, long since crossed the Atlantic, and, if we exclude the ubiquitous Bridge (see page 103) it shares with Poker (see page 177) the honour of being the national card game of the U.S.A.*

NUMBER OF PLAYERS

In its original form, Pinocle is a game for two players and is described on page 57. American card-players, however, have developed a number of variations suitable for more than two. The most popular is Auction Pinocle, a rather remarkable game because though fundamentally a game for three it makes a better game when played by four. The four-handed game is de-

scribed first. However, the game can be played by more than four players, and a version is described later.

CARDS

From two packs of 52 cards, the 8s and below are stripped, leaving a pinocle pack of 48 cards. The cards rank Ace, 10, King, Queen, Jack, 9.

The dealer deals 15 cards face downwards to the active players, either in five threes, or in three fours and one three, and after the first round, three cards face downwards to the table as a widow hand.

THE PLAY

In every deal only three players take an active part. If four play (as recommended) the dealer deals no cards to himself; and if five wish to take part the dealer deals no cards to the second player on his left as well as none to himself. The inactive players, as they are called, take no part in the bidding and play, but participate in the settlement.

A bid is a contract to score either by melds, by cards won in tricks, or by both, the number of points named, and the player on the left of the dealer makes the first bid which must be at least 300. After this, each player in turn may either pass or make a higher bid. Bids must be in multiples of ten, and once a player has passed he cannot re-enter the auction. When two players pass a bid the player who made it becomes the bidder, his bid the contract, and the other two players his opponents.

If the opening bid of 300 is passed by the other two players the bidder may concede defeat by throwing in his cards without looking at the widow. He pays three units to the kitty (but nothing to his opponents) and the deal passes to the next player.

If the bid is for more than 300, or if the bidder does not wish to concede defeat, he shows the widow to his opponents and takes the cards into his hand. He then names the trump suit, and places on the table in front of him his melds. They are scored for as follows:

Class A

A, 10, K, Q, J of trumps	150
K, Q of trumps (royal marriage)	40

K, Q of plain suit (common marriage)	20

Class B

Pinocle (♠ Q and ◇ J)	40
Dis (9 of the trump suit)	10

Class C

Ace of each suit	100
King of each suit	80
Queen of each suit	60
Jack of each suit	40

No card may be used twice in melds of the same class, but the same card may be used in two or more melds of different classes. Only the bidder melds. He then discards face down-wards (buries) three cards from his hand in order to reduce it to 15 cards: later the cards that he discards will be counted for him as won in a trick. The discards must be made from the cards in his hand, not from those in his melds, but before he leads to the first trick he may change the cards that he has discarded, change the melds and the trump suit.

When the bidder and his opponents have agreed on the value of the melds and how many more points (if any) he needs to fulfil his contract, the bidder leads to the first trick. If, however, he thinks he will not be able to make his contract he may concede defeat (called *single bete*) and pay to the players, active and inactive, the value of his bid.

When playing to a trick a player must follow suit if he can, and if he cannot he must play to win the trick by trumping or overtrumping it. Only if he has no card of the suit led and no trump card may he discard. If a trump is led, the subsequent players must try to win it. A trick is won by the highest card of the suit led or the highest trump if the led card has been trumped. If two identical cards are played the one first to be played wins the trick, if the trick is to be won by the card.

When all the tricks have been played, the players score for each Ace 11 points, each 10 ten points, each King four points, each Queen three points, each Jack two points, and for winning the last trick ten points. It gives a total of 250 points to be won in tricks.

Every deal is a separate event and settlement is made before the next deal begins. It is usual to reduce the contract to units on which payment is made.

Contract	Unit value	
300–340	3	
350–390	5	If spades
400–440	10	are trumps
450–490	15	the unit
500–540	20	values are
550–590	25	doubled.
600 and more	30	

The bidder pays double (called *double bete*) if his score for melds and cards taken in tricks fails to equal his contract; he receives if his score equals or exceeds his contract, but he does not receive more than the unit value of his contract.

Payment is made to and from all players, active and inactive, and to and from a kitty if the contract is for 350 or more.

The kitty is a separate account and is the common property of the players. They make good any deficiency if it owes, and divide any surplus when the game breaks up.

PARTNERSHIP PINOCLE

This game, as its name implies, is played by four players, two playing in partnership against the other two. The partners face each other.

The 48-card Pinocle pack is used. The dealer gives each player 12 cards in sets of three, and turns up the last card dealt to himself to determine the trump suit. In turn, beginning with the player on the left of the dealer, any player who holds the dis (9 of the trump suit) may exchange it for the turned-up card, and if the dealer turns up the dis as the trump card he scores ten points. Each original holder of a dis, whether or not he exchanges it with the turned-up card, scores ten points for it.

The players expose their melds on the table in front of them, and, in addition to the melds for Auction Pinocle, melds and the scores for them are as follows:

Double trump sequence	
A, 10, K, Q, J	1,500
Double pinocle	300
All eight Aces	1,000
All eight Kings	800

All eight Queens	600
All eight Jacks	400

When the players have shown their melds and scored for them, they return them to their hands. No meld, however, finally counts unless the partnership wins a trick, and when a trick is won both partners score for their melds.

The player on the left of the dealer leads to the first trick, and the play continues as in Auction Pinocle.

When all 12 tricks have been played, the players count ten for every Ace and 10 won, five points for every King and Queen, and ten points for winning the last trick. As in Auction Pinocle the total is 250 points.

The game is won by the partnership that first wins 1,000 points in melds and cards won in tricks, but if both partnerships reach 1,000 or more points in the same deal the game continues to 1,250 points, and, if it happens again, to 1,500 points, and so on.

At any time during the game a player may claim that he has scored 1,000 points or more and won the game. Play is brought to an end and the claim is verified. If the claim is found to be correct his partnership wins the game; if the claim is found to be wrong his partnership loses the game. In either case, what the opposing side has scored makes no difference to the result.

PARTNERSHIP PINOCLE FOR MORE THAN FOUR PLAYERS

This game is played with two 48-card Pinocle packs shuffled together. Six players form two partnerships of three players each sitting alternately at the table: eight players form two partnerships of four players each sitting alternately.

The dealer gives 16 cards to each player in bundles of four each and turns up the last card dealt to himself to denote the trump suit.

The game is played in the same way as Partnership Pinocle, but in addition to the melds above, melds and the scores for them are as follows:

Triple trump sequence	
A, 10, K, Q, J	3,000
Double trump sequence	
A, 10, K, Q, J	1,500
4 Kings and Queens of the same suit	1,200
3 Kings and Queens of the same suit	600
2 Kings and Queens of same suit	300
Quadruple pinocle	1,200
Triple pinocle	600
Double pinocle	300
15 Aces, Kings, Queens and Jacks	3,000
12 Aces	2,000
12 Kings	1,600
12 Queens	1,200
12 Jacks	800
8 Aces	1,000
8 Kings	800

8 Queens	600
8 Jacks	400

FIREHOUSE PINOCLE

This version is played as a partnership game for four, two playing in partnership against the other two. Twelve cards are dealt to each player. As in Auction Pinocle the trump suit is bid for; the player on the left of the dealer bids first; each player has only one bid or pass, and the minimum bid is 200. The bidder makes the trump suit and leads to the first trick. Game is won by the partnership that first reaches 1,000 points. The score of the bidder's side is counted first, and the game is played to the end. A partnership cannot concede defeat.

CHECK PINOCLE

This version was developed some say in Texas, out of Firehouse Pinocle, and is considered one of the best and most skilful of all partnership games, not excluding Bridge.

The game is played by four players, two playing in partnership against the other two, with the regular 48-card Pinocle pack.

Twelve cards are dealt to each player three at a time, and each player in turn, beginning with the player on the left of the dealer, must either bid or pass. The lowest bid is 200, subsequent bids must be made in multiples of ten, and once a player has passed he may

not re-enter the bidding. None of the first three players may make a bid unless he holds a marriage (King and Queen of one suit) but if all three pass the dealer must bid at least 200 and he does not need a marriage to do so; if, however, he wishes to make a higher bid than 200 he must hold one. The bidding ends when a bid has been passed by the three other players, and the bidder then names the trump suit.

The players then expose their melds on the table. The melds and the scores for them are the same as in Auction Pinocle (page 143) and the partners add the values of their melds together and record the total as a single score.

Some melds have what is known as a check (chip) value: a trump sequence (Ace, 10, King, Queen, Jack) and four aces each of a different suit are each worth two checks, four Kings, four Queens, four Jacks each of a different suit, and double pinocle are all worth one check. Check values are paid across the table as the game proceeds.

The players return the melds to their hands, and the play is the same as in Partnership Pinocle. When all 12 tricks have been played a partnership scores 10 points for every Ace and 10 that it has won, 5 points for every King and Queen, and 10 points if it has won the last trick.

The bidding side adds these points to those that it has already scored for its melds, and if the total is at least equal to the bid the contract has been made and the partnership scores for everything that it makes; if its total is less than its bid the amount of its bid is deducted from its score. In all cases the opposing side scores for everything that it makes.

At the end of each deal a partnership is entitled to checks on the following scale:

Contract	If made	
200–240	2 checks	If the contract
250–290	4 checks	is defeated the
300–340	7 checks	bidding
350–390	10 checks	partnership
400–440	13 checks	pays double
and 3 added checks		checks to the
for each series of		opposing
50 points.		partnership.

A partnership that wins all 12 tricks in a deal receives four checks; for winning the game it receives seven checks and one check for each 100 points (or part thereof) by which the score of the winning partnership exceeds that of the losing partnership; and if the losing partnership has a net minus score, the winning partnership receives an additional four checks.

The game is won by the partnership that first scores 1,000 points. The score of the bidding partnership is counted first, and as the game is over when it reaches 1,000 points, the opposing partnership scores nothing in the final deal.

POLIGNAC

POLIGNAC is sometimes called Quatre Valets or Four Jacks.

NUMBER OF PLAYERS

Polignac is for four players.

CARDS

A 32-card pack is used, i.e. a standard pack with the 6s, 5s, 4s, 3s and 2s removed.

Eight cards are dealt face downwards to each player.

THE PLAY

The player on the left of the dealer leads to the first trick. Thereafter the player who wins a trick leads to the next. A player must follow suit to the card led, if he can, otherwise he may discard.

The object of the game is to avoid taking tricks that contain a Jack, and one point is lost for every Jack taken, with the exception of the ♠J (Polignac) which costs the winner two points.

The usual method of scoring is to play a pre-arranged number of deals (that should be a multiple of four) and he who loses the least number of points is the winner.

It is a very simple game, but some skill is called for particularly in choosing the best card to lead after a trick has been won, correct discarding when unable to follow suit, and deciding whether or not to win a trick when the choice is available.

SLOBBERHANNES

If we may judge by its name, Slobberhannes is either of Dutch or German origin. It is a very simple game played in the same way as Polignac. The only difference is that a player loses one point if he wins the first trick, one point if he wins the last, one point if he wins the trick containing the ♣Q, and a further one point (making four points in all) if he wins all three tricks.

QUINTO

*Q*UINTO *is unusual in that three of the suits are trumps. It is a trick-taking game which gives the opportunity for skilful play.*

NUMBER OF PLAYERS

Quinto is for four players, who play in two partnerships, partners sitting opposite each other. It can be adapted for three players, as described later.

CARDS

The standard pack of 52 cards plus the Joker is used. The cards rank from Ace (high) to 2 (low). The Joker has a points value, as will be seen, but does not rank in trick-taking value. The suits also have their rank as follows: hearts (high), diamonds, clubs, spades. Each card in a suit can be used to trump over a card in a lower suit. Thus only spades cannot be used as trumps, spades being the lowest suit. In other words the cards rank from ♡A (high) down to ♣2.

The dealer deals the top five cards to the table in front of him. These are known as the 'cachette'. The remaining 48 cards are dealt clockwise one at a time to the four players, so each has 12 cards.

THE PLAY

Players draw for partners, the two lowest playing against the two highest, the lowest of all being the dealer (cards for this purpose rank as above, so there cannot be any ties). The dealer shuffles and the opponent to his right cuts. After each hand the deal passes to the left.

After examining his hand, each player in turn, beginning with eldest (the player to dealer's left), may double, which doubles the value of all the tricks. When a player has doubled, a succeeding opponent may redouble, which has the effect of quadrupling the value of each trick. A player cannot redouble a double by his partner.

Each trick, if undoubled, is worth five points, if doubled 10, and if redoubled, 20.

Once the value of a trick is decided, eldest leads to the first. Each player in turn must follow suit if possible. If unable to, he may trump with a card of any higher suit or he may discard. It is, of course, impossible to trump a heart, since hearts is the highest ranking suit, or, by the same token, to discard on a spade.

A trick is won by the highest value card it contains. The Joker has no trick-taking value, and can be played by its holder whenever he wishes, irrespective of whether or not he can follow suit. If the Joker is led, succeeding players can play whatever card they wish, the trick, as usual, being won by the highest card played.

As well as points for each trick, there are bonus points for taking tricks containing certain cards. The Joker, known as Quint Royal, is worth 25 points. The 5 of each suit, or any pair of cards totalling five, are Quints (for which purpose Ace counts as one, thus Ace, 4 and 2, 3 are Quints) and winning a Quint in a trick scores points according to the suit. The illustration gives the values of each of the bonuses. To score for the Quints Ace, 4 and 2, 3 the cards must be taken in the same trick.

The winner of a trick leads to the next. The winner of the last trick takes the cachette, which is regarded as an extra trick and scores accordingly, including scoring for any Quints or Quint Royal it might contain.

Two running scores are kept, one for each partnership. All scores for Quint Royal or Quints are entered on the score sheet as they are made, while the scores for tricks are added at the end of each hand. The partnership which scores 250 points first wins the game. It is usual to play a rubber of best of three games. The scores of each game in the rubber (which might be of two or three games) are added together for each partnership and the side which won the rubber adds 100 points. If the game is played for stakes, the losing partnership pays the winning partnership according to the difference between the two totals at an agreed unit per ten points, any odd five points being disregarded.

An example deal is shown in the illustration on page 152. Dealer is South. None of the players has a very

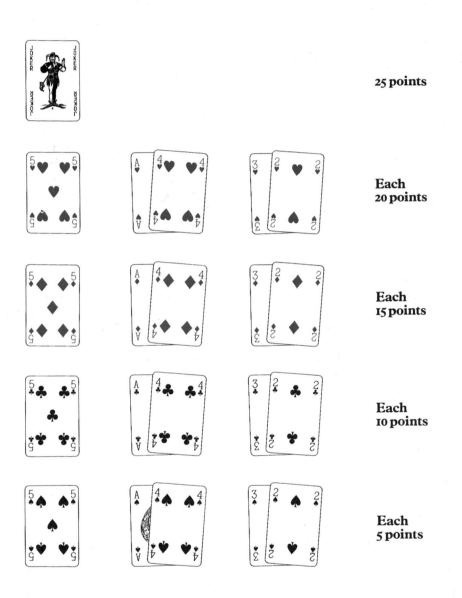

25 points

Each
20 points

Each
15 points

Each
10 points

Each
5 points

strong hand, but East, with prospects of making four tricks himself (with ♡K, Q, J, and ♣A, and a possible small trump on a diamond lead) and also of taking the cachette, decides to take a chance and double. South does not redouble.

West, assuming that his partner holds ♡A, is tempted to lead the Joker immediately and score his side 25 points, but luckily decides it would be more prudent to wait until he knows

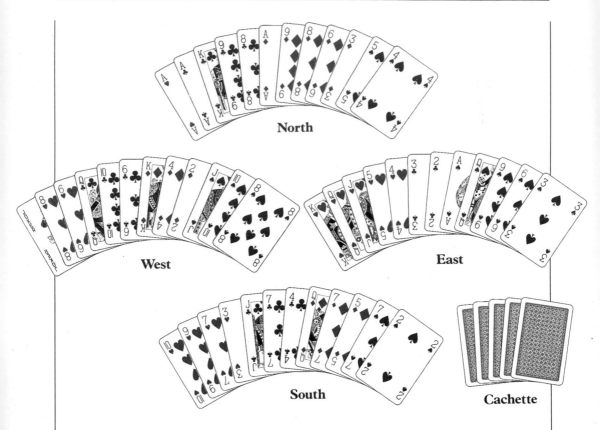

North

West

East

South

Cachette

his partner is certain to win a trick. So he can do no better than lead an unadventurous spade. In view of North's spade holding, this works beautifully for East, who is able to score a Quint on the first lead. Play proceeds as follows:

West	North	East	South
♠8	♠4	♠A	♠7
♣Q	♣K	♣2	♣7
♣6	♣A	♣3	♣4
♣10	♣9	♣3	♣J
♠10	♠5	♠6	♠2
♡6	♡A	♡K	♡3
◇4	◇A	♡5	◇7

♠J	♣8	♠Q	◇5
◇K	◇3	♠9	◇Q
Joker	◇6	♡Q	♡7,
♡8	◇8	♡4	♡10
◇2	◇9	♡J	♡9

East's double was fully justified, as by making sure of the last trick he picked up the cachette, making seven tricks to six in his side's favour. The last trick also contained a Quint, the ♣5.

Eight Quints were scored. To East/West: Joker; ♡5; ♣5; ♠5; ◇A, 4; ♠A, 4; total 80 points. To North/South: ◇5; ♣A, 4; total 25.

So on the first hand, East/West, with tricks worth ten points each, made a total of 150 points to North/South's 85.

QUINTO FOR THREE PLAYERS

Quinto is one four-handed game which can be played very well by three: indeed some people prefer the game with three. Two players play in partnership against a third. Dealer is decided by the method described above, and the first dealer is the player with the dummy, and he remains the player with the dummy for the whole game. The dummy is the hand opposite him, his opponents sitting either side of him and dummy. After the first hand, the deal passes clockwise.

The dealer, on the first hand, must look at his dummy hand first, and can double or redouble either of his opponents on the strength of it. He cannot double or redouble on his own hand, because he will by then have seen both his hands. Similarly, when one of his opponents deals, the player with the dummy must look first at the hand which will lead to the first trick, and can double on it but any doubling or redoubling must be completed before the player with the dummy looks at his second hand.

Before the lead to the first trick, the dummy is displayed on the table, and the player with the dummy operates both his hands.

Because the player with dummy is regarded as having an advantage, his opponents are given a start of 25 points towards game. Each game is regarded as separate (i.e. rubbers are not played) and it is usual to play games in sets of three, so that each player has a turn to have the dummy.

SOLO WHIST

SOLO WHIST, usually just called Solo, is based on the ancient game of Whist (page 158) but it includes a bidding principle and each player plays for himself. It is a betting game.

NUMBER OF PLAYERS

Solo Whist is a game for four players, and cannot satisfactorily be played by any other number.

CARDS

The full pack of 52 cards is used.

Thirteen cards are dealt to each player in three bundles of three cards each, and the last four cards singly. The dealer turns up the last card to indicate the trump suit.

THE PLAY

Each player in turn, beginning with the player on the left of the dealer, must either pass or make a bid. The bids (declarations) are:

Proposal. The player who makes a Proposal asks for a partner with the object of making eight tricks in partnership with him against the other two players. In turn, any other player may Accept, and the two play as partners from the seats in which they are sitting. The declaration of Proposal and Acceptance is usually called Prop and Cop.

Solo is a declaration to win five tricks against the other three players.

Misère is a declaration to lose all 13 tricks. The hand is played without a trump suit.

Abundance is a declaration to win nine tricks against the other three players; the declarer chooses his own trump suit. A player who wishes to play abundance with the turned-up suit as trumps may overcall with Royal Abundance, but the stake value of the bid remains unchanged.

Open misère is a declaration to lose every trick, and after the first trick has been played with his cards exposed on the table in front of him. There is no trump suit.

Declared abundance is a declaration to win all 13 tricks with a trump suit of his own choice.

Every bid must be higher than the previous one, and with the exception of the player on the left of the dealer, who may accept a proposal after passing, no player may re-enter the bidding once he has passed. The bidding ends when a bid has been passed by the other three players.

If the final bid is Declared abundance, the declarer leads to the first trick. Against any other declaration the opening lead is made by the player on the left of the dealer. The play follows the general principles of trick-taking games: a player must follow suit if he is able to, otherwise he may either discard or trump, and the winner of a trick leads to the next.

Stakes are scaled to the value of the bids:

Proposal and Acceptance	2 units*
Solo	2 units
Misère	3 units
Abundance	4 units
Open misère	6 units
Declared abundance	8 units

*Proposal and Acceptance does not carry equivalent stakes to Solo because they are paid by and received from two players, whereas in Solo (and higher declarations) they are paid to and received from three players.

Solo is a combination of whist and nap(oleon). It is a fairly simple game, and by far the simplest of the declarations is Proposal and Acceptance. As no player will propose without some strength in trumps, the partnership hardly ever fails to make eight tricks. It is a notoriously dull contract, therefore, and most modern players reject it.

The declaration of Solo is another that is fairly easy to win, though it must never be forgotten that the player has to compete against three. It is unwise to bid Solo without a good trump suit, and the dealer is in the ideal position to bid it with success because he plays last to the first trick: it gives him the best chance to win it and make an immediate attack on the trump suit.

Misère is not such an easy declaration as it may seem. A five-card suit, unless it contains the 2, is likely to spell defeat. If a player holds 7, 6, 5, 4, 3 of a suit he will usually be defeated if another holds four of the suit including the 2.

Abundance should not be attempted without a very good trump suit, and Declared abundance is best avoided by any except an experienced player.

South deals the cards in the illustration below and turns up the ♠2.

West	North	East	South
Solo	Misère	Abund-ance	Open misère
Pass	Pass	Pass	

West's Solo is the obviously correct bid. He cannot fail to win at least five tricks and it is too much to expect the hearts to develop three tricks to make Abundance a good call.

North's Misère is optimistic. Had he

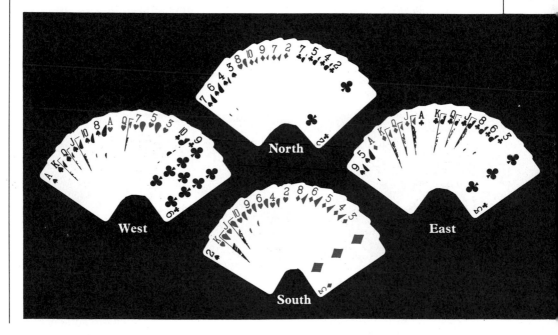

West

North

East

South

been left to play it, the opening lead of a heart would have broken him out of hand.

East's Abundance is a certainty with 11 tricks (and needing only nine) for the taking of them.

South's Open misère is not to be advised. As already pointed out, a five-card suit missing the 2 is a danger spot. As it happens it is the heart suit that proves his downfall.

West leads the ♣10, and the play is:

West	North	East	South
♣10	♣7	♣J	♡K
♣9	♣5	♣A	♡J
♠A	♣4	♣3	♡10
♡A	♡8	◇A	♡6

The position is down to the situation shown in the illustration below.

South is doomed because West wins the ♡7 and ♡5 (on which South plays the ♡4 and ♡2) and continues with the ♡3 which South must win with the ♡9.

AUCTION SOLO

As Solo is limited to a mere handful of declarations, the variation known as Auction Solo is much to be preferred, because it permits of a larger number of declarations and, therefore, makes a more interesting and skilful game. In ascending order the declarations are:

Proposal and Acceptance.
Solo of Five in own suit.
Solo of Five in trump suit.
Solo of Six in own suit.
Solo of Six in trump suit.
Solo of Seven in own suit.
Solo of Seven in trump suit.
Solo of Eight in own suit.
Solo of Eight in trump suit.
Misère.
Abundance of Nine in own suit.
Abundance of Nine in trump suit.
Abundance of Ten in own suit.
Abundance of Ten in trump suit.
Abundance of Eleven in own suit.
Abundance of Eleven in trump suit.

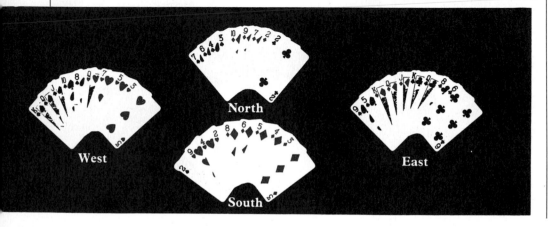

Abundance of Twelve in own suit.
Abundance of Twelve in trump
suit.
Open misère.
Declared abundance with no
trump suit (bidder has the
lead).
Declared abundance in the original
trump suit (bidder does not
have the lead).

Such, at least, are the declarations in
the original version of the game, but
modern players do not recognize all of
them. Proposal and Acceptance are
nearly always omitted, so also are Solo
of Five in own suit, and Declared
abundance in the original trump suit.

Once the players have agreed on
which declarations are admissible and
which not, the game is played in the
same way as the parent game.

Settlement is made in the following
way:

Proposal and Acceptance

For success: receive 6 units each
plus 1 unit for each
overtrick.
For failure: pay 6 units each plus 1
unit for each
undertrick.

Solo

For success: receive 6 units from
each player plus 3
units for each
overtrick.
For failure: pay 6 units to each
player plus 3 units for
each undertrick.

Misère

For success: receive 12 units from
each player.
For failure: pay 12 units to each
player.

Abundance

For success: receive 18 units from
each player plus 3
units for each
overtrick.
For failure: pay 18 units to each
player plus 3 units for
each undertrick.

Open misère

For success: receive 24 units from
each player.
For failure: pay 24 units to each
player.

Declared abundance

For success: receive 36 units from
each player.
For failure: pay 36 units to each
player.

The stake values of Solo and Abundance are unchanged whether the
contract is for five, six, seven or eight,
or nine, ten, eleven or twelve tricks.
Overtricks and undertricks count from
the number of tricks that are contracted for.

The method of scoring appears to
encourage underbidding. In practice,
however, it is not so and as first bidder
a player would be well advised to
declare his full strength at once, especially if his hand is worth no more than
six tricks. With six tricks in a plain suit
a player should bid it at once, no matter
what his position at the table, but if the
tricks are in the original trump suit it is

reasonable to bid only a Solo of Five: he may get away with it, and, if not, a Solo of Six in the trump suit will overcall an opponent's Six in a plain suit. The penultimate player should make it a rule to bid his hand to the limit; if he does not the last player will and then there may be no second chance.

WHIST

WHIST developed out of the 16th century game of Triumph. At first its practice was confined to the lower classes, but in 1718 it was taken up by a party of gentlemen, Lord Folkestone among them, who met at the famous Crown Coffee House, and they, with the help of Edmond Hoyle, introduced the game to fashionable society. At this time the game was known as whisk: soon after it was changed to whist in order to underline the silence in which it was proper to play the game.

During the 18th and 19th centuries it was by far the most popular card game of the English-speaking nations, but at the close of the 19th century it lost much of its popularity due to the introduction of Bridge. It is, however, still extensively played.

NUMBER OF PLAYERS

Whist is played by four players, in two partnerships.

CARDS

The standard pack of 52 cards is used, the cards ranking from Ace (high) to 2 (low).

The partners sit facing each other. The deal passes in clockwise rotation. Thirteen cards are dealt singly to each person, and the dealer exposes the last card to denote the trump suit. He takes it into his hand after he has played to the first trick.

THE PLAY

The player on the left of the dealer leads to the first trick. Thereafter the player who wins a trick leads to the next. A player must follow suit to the card led if he can, if not he may either discard or trump.

The object of the game is to win a rubber (best out of three games), and a game is won when one side has won five points. The first six tricks (the book) do not count for scoring: a side scores one point for each trick that it wins over six. The Ace, King, Queen and Jack of the trump suit are known as honours, and any side that is dealt all four of them scores four points, and any three two points. If, however, at the beginning of a deal a side has a score of four points it cannot score for honours.

Skill at whist is largely a matter of playing in close collaboration with one's partner, and estimating from the cards held and those that have been played, the most likely position of those that remain to be played.

To this end, there are a number of recognized plays which should be departed from only under special circumstances, to be learnt by experience. It is, for example, good tactics for second player to play low and third high; a player should not finesse against his partner; and if an opponent plays an honour it is usually profitable to play a higher honour on it.

A player who holds five or more trumps in his hand should make it a rule to lead one; and if a player fails to lead a trump and wishes his partner to do so, he calls for the lead of one by first playing an unnecessarily high card in a suit and following it with a low card in the same suit.

The lead is a good opportunity for a player to give his partner information about his hand, and the leads listed in the table are standard practice and should be known to all players.

In plain suits

Holding	1st lead	2nd lead
A, K, Q, J	K	J
A, K, Q	K	Q
A, K, x and more	K	A
A, K	A	K
K, Q, J, x	K	J
K, Q, J, x, x	J	K
K, Q, J, x, x and more	J	Q
A, x, x, x, and more	A	4th best of remainder
K, Q, x and more	K	4th best of remainder
A, Q, J	A	Q
A, Q, J, x	A	Q
A, Q, J, x, x and more	A	J
K, J, 10, 9	9	K (if A or Q falls)
Q, J, x	Q	
Q, J, x, x and more	4th best	

In the trump suit

Holding	1st lead	2nd lead
A, K, Q, J	J	Q
A, K, Q	Q	K
A, K, x, x, x, x, x and more	K	A
A, K, x, x, x, x	4th best	

Lacking any of these combinations the fourth highest of the longest suit should be led.

With the hands shown below the mechanics of the game can be illustrated.

South deals and turns up the ♠ 4 to denote trumps.

West leads the ◇ 5, and the play is:

West	North	East	South
◇ 5	◇ J	◇ A	◇ 3

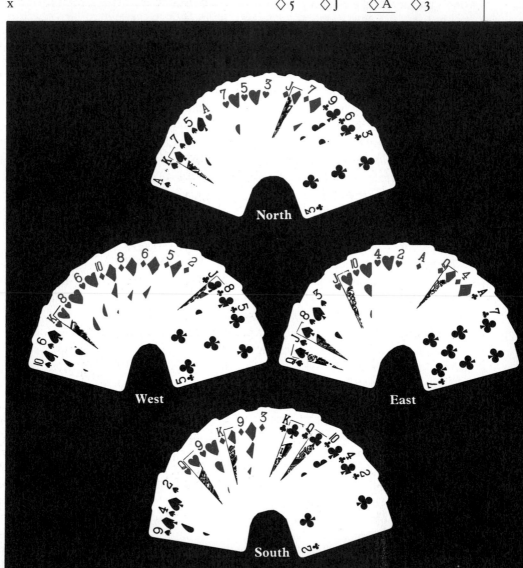

North

West

East

South

West leads the fourth highest of his longest suit, commonly called fourth-best. East wins with the ◇A. It would be finessing against his partner if he played the ◇Q. In the event it makes no difference, because East has no better play than to return his partner's suit, and it is proper to lead the highest from an original holding of three.

◇2   ◇7   ◇Q   ◇K

South, therefore, wins the second trick, instead of the first, with the ◇K.

West	North	East	South
♣5	♣3	♣A	♣K
♣8	♣6	♣7	♣Q

East has no better lead than the ♣7. He knows that South holds the ♣Q, because without it South would not have led the ♣K at the previous trick, but it offers a chance of trumping if West can take the lead early in the play.

◇10	♣5	◇4	◇9
♣6	♣A	♣3	♣2
♣10	♣K	♣8	♣4
♣J	♣9	♡2	♣2

North has no better lead than the ♣9.

◇8	♡3	♣J	♣4
◇6	♣7	♣Q	♣9

East pulls the remaining trumps.

♡K   ♡A   ♡J   ♡Q

The end position is now as below.

West

North

East

South

It is North's lead. North and South have won six tricks, East and West five tricks. North, therefore, leads the ♡5. If East wins with the ♡10 his side will win the odd trick as West will win the last trick with the ♡8. North's only hope is that East will make the mistake of playing the ♡4, because then South will win with the ♡9 and the last trick with the ♣10.

♡6   ♡5   ♡10   ♡9

East makes no mistake.

♡8   ♡7   ♡4   ♣10

East and West, therefore, have won the odd trick and score one point. There is no score for honours as both sides held two.

GAMES FOR FIVE OR MORE PLAYERS

BRAG

BRAG *is almost certainly the ancestor of Poker (see page 177) and itself probably derived from the Spanish game of Primero, the popular card game of Tudor England and, so far as we can trace, the first card game to be played scientifically in that country. It is purely a gambling game.*

NUMBER OF PLAYERS

Any number of players can play, from five to eight being best.

CARDS

The full pack of 52 cards is used. Cards rank from Ace (high) to 2 (low).

THE PLAY

The general principle of the game is quite simple. The players stake on the respective merits of their cards, and the best hand is determined by certain arbitrary rules. Bluffing is an important feature of the game. The ◇A, ♣J and ◇9 are known as braggers, and rank as Jokers or wild cards. There are two versions of the game: Single-Stake Brag and Three-Stake Brag.

SINGLE-STAKE BRAG

In this version of the game the dealer puts up a stake to the agreed limit, and deals three cards face downwards to each player. In turn, beginning with the player on the left of the dealer, each

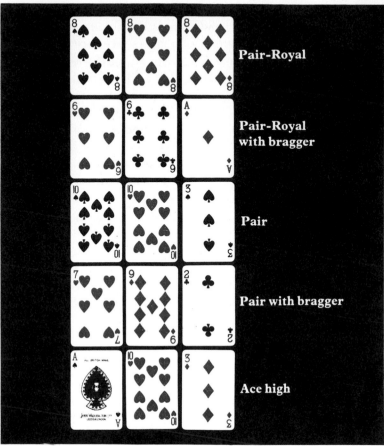

The classes of Brag hands, the highest at the top.

player must either drop out of the game for the round in progress, or put up a stake at least equal to that of the dealer's. If he chooses he may raise the stake, in which event any player coming into the game, or already in the game, must raise his bet to as much as the highest individual stake, or drop out of the game and lose what he has already staked. If no-one meets the dealer's stake he withdraws it, and receives an agreed amount from the other players. The deal then passes to the next player.

Unlike at poker, there is no discarding and drawing more cards. When all those who wish to play have raised their bets to an equal amount, the cards are shown and the player with the best hand collects all the stakes.

Flushes and sequences are of no value. The best hand is a pair-royal; it consists of three cards of equal rank (Aces high, 2s low) and a hand of three natural cards takes precedence over one with braggers. The next best hand is a pair, with a preference for a natural pair over one with a bragger, and if two players have equal pairs the one with the higher third card wins. If no player holds either a pair-royal or a pair, the player with the highest single card wins and if two players hold exactly equal hands the winner is he who was first to stake.

THREE-STAKE BRAG

This game begins by each player putting up three separate stakes; the dealer then deals two cards face down and one card face up to each player.

The first stake is won by the player who is dealt the highest face-upwards card. For this round of the game the braggers take their normal position in the pack, and if two or more players are dealt cards of equal rank, precedence is determined as in the single-stake game.

The hand is next played as in single-stake, and the winner takes the second stake. If no-one bets, the hands are exposed and the highest hand wins.

Finally, the players expose their cards and the third stake is won by the player whose cards most nearly total 31 (over or under), the Aces counting 11, the court cards 10 each and the other cards at their pip values. A player whose hand totals less than 31 may draw a card from the remainder of the pack, but if his total then exceeds 31 he automatically loses the game.

COON CAN

*I*N *the U.S.A. Coon Can is known as Double Rum. It is no bad name for it because it is a variation of Rummy (see page 184) played with two packs of cards shuffled together with two Jokers.*

NUMBER OF PLAYERS

The game may be played by any number of players up to eight; each plays for himself.

CARDS

Two identical packs are used, with two Jokers, making a pack of 106 cards. Ace can rank either high or low, and the Jokers are wild.

Ten cards are dealt face downwards to each player. The rest of the pack (the stock) is placed face downwards in the centre of the table, and the top card of it is turned face upwards and placed alongside it to start the discard file.

THE PLAY

The object of the game is to get rid of all the cards held, by melding them face upwards on the table, either in sets of three or more of the same rank, or in sequences of three or more of the same suit, the Ace either high or low but not round-the-corner. A Joker may be used to represent any card that the holder chooses.

Each player, beginning with the one on the left of the dealer, plays in turn. He is under no obligation to meld, but he must take into his hand either the top card of the stock or the top card of the discard pile, and discard a card to reduce his hand to ten cards. If he chooses to meld he must do so between drawing a card and discarding one, and as well as melding, at the same time he may add cards to melds that he has already made, and to those of his opponents.

A Joker may be moved from one end of a meld to the other, provided the player has the natural card to replace it. If, for example, a sequence is: ♠6, 7 8, Joker, a player who holds a ♠9 may play it in place of the Joker and transfer the Joker to represent the ♠5. Once moved, however, a Joker cannot be moved a second time and a player who holds a ♠5 cannot play it in place of the Joker and place the Joker elsewhere. Nor can a Joker be moved if it is in the interior of a sequence, as in ♠4, 5, 6, Joker, ♠8. The Joker cannot be replaced by a ♠7. When a Joker cannot be moved it is customary to place it crosswise, as a reminder to the other players.

The game is won by the player who is first to meld all his cards. The remaining players pay him the same number of units as the pip value of the unmelded cards left in their hands — a Joker counting 15, an Ace 11, the court cards 10 each, and all other cards their pip values.

It rarely happens that the stock will be exhausted before the game has been won. In this event the game continues and the players draw cards from the discard pile, discarding a different card to that drawn. If this proves insufficient to finish the game, the pip values of the hands are counted and placed into a pool to be scored by the winner of the next hand.

CRAZY EIGHTS

*T*HIS *is a very simple game, not to be confused with the game of Eights described earlier. Crazy Eights is a gambling game.*

NUMBER OF PLAYERS

The game can be played by any number from two to eight, but is best for four or more, each player playing for himself.

CARDS

The full pack of 52 cards is used. The ranking of the cards is immaterial, but cards have a point-scoring value, as described below.

Any player picks up the cards, shuffles, and begins dealing them one to each player face up – the first player to be dealt a Jack becomes first dealer. Subsequently the deal passes clockwise to the left.

Before the deal, each player puts a stake into the centre. The dealer then deals five cards to each player, one at a time to the left, then lays out eight cards face up in the centre of the table, arranged in two rows of four. The remainder of the pack is set aside.

THE PLAY

Beginning with the player on the dealer's left, each player in turn may lay a card from his hand face up on one of the eight cards in the centre. The card must match in rank the card onto which it is played. A card in the centre may be covered as many times as required, i.e. if two players are dealt an 8, and there is an 8 in the centre, each player can play his 8 onto it in turn. A player who cannot go says 'pass'.

Should a player get rid of all his cards, he shouts 'crazy eights' and collects the whole pool of stakes. Frequently the game ends with every player being forced to pass while still holding a card or two. In this case, every player counts the points still held in his hand according to the following scale: Aces 15 points, Kings, Queens, Jacks 10 points, and all other cards their pip value. The pool is then divided between the high player (whose points total is highest) and the low player (whose points total is lowest).

In the illustration, players A, B, C, D, E and F have each contributed two chips to a pool of 12 chips. Player A dealt the hands as shown, and the eight cards in the centre of the table.

Player B plays first and lays his ◇ J on the ♣ J, player C plays his ♠ 8 on ♣ 8 and so on. All players can play to the first round, but player D must pass in the second, players C and A in the third, players B and F in the fourth, and finally player E passes on the fifth round. Player A is left with K, 5, 3 = 18 points; B with K, 7 = 17 points; C with K, 9, 5 = 24 points; D with 7, 5, 3, 3 = 18 points; E with the ♠ 9 only = 9 points; and F with K, 10 = 20 points. So player C collects six chips for high, and player E six chips for low.

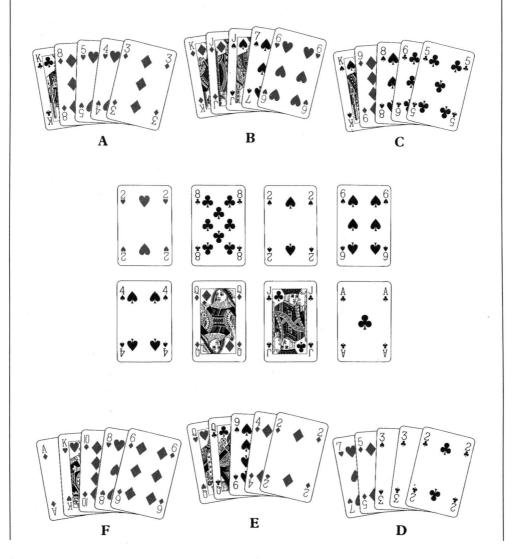

LIFT SMOKE

L *IFT SMOKE is a simple English game. It can be played for stakes by each player putting an amount into a kitty before each deal.*

NUMBER OF PLAYERS

The game is for four to six players, six perhaps being the best. Each player plays for himself.

CARDS

The full pack of 52 cards is used. The cards rank from Ace (high) to 2 (low).

One player picks up the cards and deals them round face up – the first player to be dealt a Jack becomes the first dealer. Thereafter the winner of each game deals for the next.

The dealer deals the cards one at a time in a clockwise direction to each player beginning with the player on his left. Each player receives the same number of cards as there are players in the game, i.e. with six players each player receives six cards. The last card dealt to the dealer is turned face up to establish the trump suit. The cards not dealt are placed in the centre of the table to form a stock.

THE PLAY

When all players have seen the trump suit, the dealer takes his cards into his hand, and the trick-taking phase of the game begins. The player to the left of dealer leads to the first trick, leading any card he likes. Subsequent players must follow suit if able, and if unable may trump or discard. The trick is won by the highest trump, or failing a trump by the highest card in the suit led.

When a trick is won, it is placed face down to one side, and the winner of the trick takes into his hand the top card of the stock. No other player takes a card, so the hands are now unequal. The winner of a trick leads to the next.

Each time a player fails to win a trick, his hand will diminish by one card. When a player is reduced to no cards, he drops out of the game. The last player remaining wins the game and if there is a kitty he takes it.

If the last card is taken from the stock while two or more players still have cards, the winner is the player who takes the next trick.

LOO

*T*HE *modern player may be forgiven if he mistakes the meaning of the name which has been attached to this game. In fact it is a truncation of the now obsolete* lanterloo, *from the French* lanturlu, *a word best translated by our succinct, if vulgar,* fiddlesticks. *There are several variations of the game, of which Three-card Loo, Five-card Loo and Irish Loo are described here.*

NUMBER OF PLAYERS

Loo is suitable for any number of players, though the best number is six or seven.

CARDS

The standard 52-card pack is used, with the cards ranking from Ace (high) to 2 (low), except in Five-card Loo, in which the ♣J is the highest ranking card (see below).

The first player to deal puts into a pool an agreed number of units. It may be any number divisible by three. Three cards are then dealt, one card at a time, to each player, and to an extra hand that is known as 'miss'. The top card of the remainder of the pack is turned up to denote the trump suit.

THE PLAY

The dealer offers the player on his immediate left the choice of refusing to play, playing with the cards dealt to him, or exchanging his cards for miss and playing with those. In turn, each player is offered the same choice, though, of course, once a player has chosen to exchange his hand for miss, a subsequent player is reduced to choosing between playing with the cards dealt to him or not playing the hand. Once a player has made a decision he must stand by it, and if he has chosen not to play he throws his cards face downwards to the centre of the table.

The player who first chooses to play leads to the first trick. Thereafter the player who wins a trick leads to the next. The play is governed by the following rules:

A player must follow suit if he can, and must head the trick if he can.

If a player cannot follow suit he must trump if he can, and if the trick has already been trumped he must overtrump if he can.

If the player on lead holds the Ace of

trumps (or the King if the Ace has been turned up) he must lead it.

If the player on lead holds two or more trumps he must lead one of them, and if there are only two players in the game he must lead the highest.

A player who fails to comply with any of these rules, when able to do so, is deemed to have revoked; the pool is divided among the non-offenders, and the offender pays the full amount back to the pool.

When the hand has been played those who have won tricks divide the pool between them: one-third of the amount in it to the winner of each trick.

Those who have not won a trick are looed, and must put into the pool as many units as there were in it at the beginning of the deal. Unlimited loo, however, can come very expensive, and in practice it is essential for the players to agree upon limiting the losses of looed players.

If no player is looed, the next dealer replenishes the pool as at the beginning of the game.

If every player refuses to play, the dealer takes the entire pool and the next dealer replenishes it.

If only one player chooses to play the dealer must come into the game against him, but if he holds a weak hand, he may protect himself against loss by announcing that he will play for the pool. In this event he is not looed if he fails to win a trick, and, in return for the concession, he leaves in the pool any amount to which he may be entitled by reason of his having won tricks.

FIVE-CARD LOO

This is a variation of the parent game that differs from it in the following five particulars:

Every player is dealt five cards, and as there are five tricks to be won the number of units paid into the pool must be divisible by five.

There is no miss.

A player may exchange cards by drawing them from the stock. He may exchange any number of cards that he chooses, and once he has exchanged a card he must enter the game.

The highest card in the pack is the ♣J. It is known as Pam. It ranks as a trump and takes precedence even over the Ace; if, however, a player leads the Ace of trumps and announces 'Pam be civil' the holder of Pam is debarred from playing it to the trick.

If a player holds five cards of a suit, or four cards of a suit and Pam, he is said to hold a flush and must expose his hand at once. He wins the pool and all the other players, except those who may hold flushes or Pam, are looed. If one or more players hold flushes, one in the trump suit wins over one in a plain suit, and as between two or more in a plain suit, the one with the highest card wins. If two or more in plain suits are exactly equal the pool is divided.

IRISH LOO

This game is a combination of the three-card and five-card games, and is considered by competent players to be the best of the several variations.

Every player is dealt three cards, there is no Pam and no miss, but a player is allowed to exchange cards by drawing from the stock. The game is played in the same way as the parent game, with the added novelty that if clubs are trumps everyone must enter the game. It is known as Club Law and makes it imperative that the penalty for being looed must be limited to a reasonable amount.

Loo, in all its variations, is so bound up by hard and fast rules of play, already mentioned, that there is very little to be said about the play of the cards. At best one can only say that the most successful player is not he who knows how to play, but he who knows when to elect and when to refuse to play.

The most important point to note is that, apart from Pam at Five-card Loo, there are only three certain tricks, namely the Ace, the King-Queen combination and the Queen-Jack-10 combination of the trump suit. Usually the player who holds the Queen, Jack, 9 of trumps will win a trick, but it is by no means certain that he will, and he may be looed if he is in an unfavour-able position at the table. It is the same if a player holds King, 3 of the trump suit. He will certainly win a trick if the suit is led and he is the last to play, but if he is not, he may not win a trick, because if the 4 is played he is compelled to play the King and a later player may win with the Ace. It leaves him only with the remote possibility of winning a trick with the lone 3 of trumps.

Perhaps in practice the picture is not so depressing as it appears in theory, because, even if there are seven players in the game, a large number of cards remain in the stock. Some of the high cards, therefore, may not be active and a combination such as Jack, 10, 9 of trumps, or even Jack, 10 and a card in a plain suit, may win a trick.

In general a player is advised not to be too cautious about electing to play if he holds a weak hand, but he is advised to be careful. In practice he should keep a close watch on the number of units in the pool and weigh up the possible loss against the possible gain. If, for example, there are 15 units in the pool at Five-card Loo and the cost of being looed is 10 units it is not worth while entering the play with a weak hand because, look at it which way you like, the cost of being looed is three times more than the possible gain that will accrue by winning one trick. It is not a good bet.

NAPOLEON

NAPOLEON, *usually called Nap, is one of the simplest of all card games. It is entirely a game for betting.*

NUMBER OF PLAYERS

Any number up to six may play, each playing for himself.

CARDS

The full pack of 52 cards is used, cards ranking from Ace (high) to 2 (low).

Each player is dealt five cards.

THE PLAY

Beginning with the player on the left of the dealer, every player in turn must either pass or declare to win a specified number of tricks in the ascending order: Two, Three, Four and Nap (a declaration to win all five tricks).

The player who has contracted to win most tricks leads to the first trick and the card that he leads determines the trump suit. Play follows the usual routine of trick-taking games: a player must follow suit if he can, otherwise he may discard or trump, and the player who wins a trick leads to the next.

Stakes are paid only on the number of tricks contracted for. Those won above, or lost below, the number contracted for are ignored. The usual method of settlement is by means of a level-money transaction:

Declaration	Declarer wins	Declarer loses
Two	2 units	2 units
Three	3 units	3 units
Four	4 units	4 units
Nap	10 units	5 units

Payment is made to, and received from, all players at the table.

Nap(oleon) is such an elementary game that in some circles interest is added to it by introducing a number of extraordinary declarations:

Misery is a declaration to lose every trick. It ranks between the declaration of Three and Four, and though normally it is played without a trump suit, some play it with a trump suit, determined as in the parent game by the opening lead. It pays and wins three units.

Wellington is a declaration to win all five tricks at double stakes. It cannot be declared, however, except over a declaration of Nap.

Blücher is a declaration to win all

five tricks at triple stakes. It cannot be declared, however, except over a declaration of Wellington.

Peep nap sanctions the player who has declared Nap (or Wellington or Blücher if these declarations are permitted) to exchange the top card of the pack for a card in his own hand.

Purchase nap sanctions each player before declaring to exchange any number of cards in his hand for fresh cards, by paying into a pool one unit for every card exchanged. The pool is carried forward from deal to deal and taken by the first player to win Nap (or Wellington or Blücher if these declarations are permitted).

SEVEN-CARD NAPOLEON

In this variation seven cards are dealt to each player, and a player cannot contract to win fewer than three tricks. There is no Wellington and no Blücher. Misery is optional and, if permitted, ranks between Nap and Six.

Apart from these amendments, the game is played in the same way as the parent game.

Settlement is made as follows:

Declaration	Declarer wins	Declarer loses
Three	3 units	3 units
Four	4 units	4 units
Nap	10 units	5 units
Misery	10 units	5 units
Six	18 units	9 units
Seven	28 units	14 units

Payment is made to, and received from, all players at the table.

PANGUINGUE

*P*ANGUINGUE *is one of the best games of the Rummy type for a large number of players. It arises from the Spanish game of Conquian, and retains the characteristics of using the Spanish 40-card pack and of play rotating to the right. It gained much popularity in the first half of the century on the west coast of the U.S.A. It is played for small stakes.*

NUMBER OF PLAYERS

Any reasonable number may play — perhaps six to eight is best, but the game can accommodate twice this number.

CARDS

Eight of the 40-card packs are used, making a pack of 320 cards. The 40-card pack is formed by removing from a standard pack the 10s, 9s and 8s. It is possible to use fewer packs, but fewer than five should not be used. The cards rank in the order: King, Queen, Jack, 7, 6, 5, 4, 3, 2, Ace. Players may remove the Kings, Queens and Jacks instead of the 10s, 9s and 8s, so that the cards are in their natural sequence and there is no need to remember that 7 and Jack are in sequence.

The 320-card pack is shuffled by many hands and amalgamated. Each player draws a card, and the lowest becomes eldest hand. The second lowest becomes dealer and sits on eldest's left (this is because the dealing and the play rotates to the right, i.e. anti-clockwise).

The final shuffle before the deal is made by the player at the dealer's left. It is unusual for all the cards to be used during one hand, and after the first deal the practice between deals is to shuffle only the cards which have been used together with a batch from the unused cards, these going to the bottom of the total pack. The deal does not rotate – the winner of a hand becomes eldest hand for the next, i.e. the player to the left of the winner deals the next hand.

Without holding the whole pack in his hand, the dealer deals ten cards to each player in bundles of five. The remaining cards are placed face down to form the stock. Here again it is usual to divide the pack in two so that the stock is not unmanageable. The upper part, called the 'head' is used, while the lower part, the 'foot', is put to one side to be used if necessary.

THE PLAY

The top card of the stock is turned face up to begin a discard pile. Beginning with eldest (the player to the dealer's right) and proceeding anti-clockwise, each player in turn announces whether he will stay in the game or drop. A player who drops pays a forfeit of two chips. The chips are placed on that part of the stock called the foot, and the player who drops thus says that he is 'going on top'. His cards are placed face down below the foot, but cross-wise, because they do not become part of the stock and must not be used in the hand.

After all who wish have dropped, those remaining, in turn anti-clockwise, draw a card either from the top of the discard pile or from the top of the stock. The card from the discard pile can be taken only if it can be melded with immediately. A meld, usually called a 'spread', is either of a group or of a sequence, as in the more familiar Rummy, and consists of three cards.

A group consists of three cards of the same rank, but to be valid there are restrictions as to suits. If the rank is King or Ace (called 'non-comoquers') there are no restrictions; any three cards are valid. However, for other ranks, the cards must be either all of the same suit or all of different suits.

A sequence (usually called a 'stringer') consists of three cards of the same suit in sequence (remembering that a sequence continues from 7 to Jack).

A player may lay down any melds on his turn (if taking the card from the top of the discard pile, he must meld with it, as stated). Subsequently, on his turn, he may add to any of his melds, called 'laying off'. A player may lay off on his own melds only – not on his opponents'. A sequence may be added to by laying off additional cards in sequence. A group of the same suit may be added to by laying off cards of the same rank and suit. A group in different suits may be added to by laying off cards of the same rank in *any* suit (this means that such a meld is not restricted to four cards only).

A player may take the top of the discard pile in order to lay off on one of his melds.

Certain melds are called 'conditions', and a player who makes one immediately collects chips from all other players. So far as groups are concerned, certain ranks (7s, 5s and 3s) are called 'valle cards' or value cards. The five classes of condition melds are as follows:

A group of valle cards of different suits (worth one chip from each player).

A group of valle cards in the same suit (worth four chips in spades, two in other suits).

A group of non-valle cards in the same suit (worth two chips in spades, one in other suits).

A sequence of Ace, 2, 3 (worth two chips in spades and one in other suits).

A sequence of King, Queen, Jack (worth two chips in spades and one in other suits).

A player who lays off on a condition collects again from each player its value, except that in the case of three valle cards in the same suit he collects only two chips in spades and one in other suits. A player collects each time he lays off on a condition.

If a player lays off three or more cards on a meld, he may split it into two separate melds, provided that each half is valid. By doing so he may create a condition. For example, if he adds to a sequence of ◇ 5, 4, 3 the ◇ 2, the ◇ 6 and the ◇ A, he may split the sequence of six cards into two sequences: ◇ A, 2, 3 and ◇ 6, 5, 4. This creates a condition (Ace, 2, 3) and the player collects one chip from every other player (or two if it is in spades).

A player may also take a card or cards from a meld to which he has laid off to form a new meld, provided that he leaves a valid meld. This is called 'borrowing'. For example, if he makes a meld of ♡ J, 7, 6 to which he adds ♡ 5, 4, he may later borrow the ♡ 5, 4 to make a new meld with ♡ 3 or another ♡ 6. Or he may borrow the ♡ J to make, for example, a meld of ♡ J, ♣ J, ♠ J. But he could not borrow the ♡ 7, or ♡ 6, or ♡ 5, because to take one of those cards would destroy the sequence, i.e. it would not leave a valid meld.

The object of each player is to meld

all his cards, called 'going out', whereupon he wins the game.

A player's turn consists of taking either the top card of the discard pile or stock, melding or laying off, if he wishes, and, except when going out, discarding. A player who goes out may not discard; thus to go out a player needs 11 cards melded on the table.

If the top card of the discard pile can be laid off on a meld of the player whose turn it is, any other player can demand that he take the card and lay it off. This might be done to disrupt the hand of the player in play, since having laid off the card he is forced to discard.

It follows that a player with nine cards melded and one in his hand still requires to find two cards to lay off. Should he draw a card from stock which he lays off on his melds, he must still discard the card in his hand. This leaves him with ten cards melded and none in his hand, but he has not gone out. He must continue to draw, on his turn, from the discard pile or the stock until he draws a card which he can lay off, and thus go out with 11 cards melded.

If a player is in the situation of having ten cards melded, the previous player must not discard a card which would allow him to go out (unless the previous player has no alternative, i.e. he cannot make a safe discard).

The winner of the game (i.e. the player who goes out) wins one chip from all others remaining in the game (in some schools he collects two chips from any player who has not melded). He also collects from each player chips representing the values of his conditions. (As a player collects for conditions as he melds them, the winner therefore collects twice for his conditions.) The winner also takes the chips of those players who dropped, i.e. those chips stacked on the foot of the stock.

In the unlikely event of the stock (both head and foot) being exhausted before any player has gone out, the discard pile is turned over and becomes the stock, play continuing as usual.

So far as strategy is concerned, the usual principles of good play at all Rummy-type games apply, i.e. a player should try to hold cards giving multiple options of melding rather than isolated pairs or possible sequences with gaps in the middle. As the number and rank of cards held in the hand are immaterial in the settling when an opponent goes out, there is no point in laying down melds prematurely. However, a player should lay down and collect for conditions and get down a first meld if there is a double payment to the winner by players who have failed to meld.

POKER

*P*OKER *is not a difficult game to learn, but by no means is it an easy one to play well because skill at the game is born only of experience coupled with some knowledge of arithmetic. Fundamentally, Poker is a game of calculating chances. It is a gambling game and cannot be played without betting.*

The parent game, described first, is commonly called Straight Poker, but is more correctly Straight Draw Poker.

NUMBER OF PLAYERS

Any reasonable number may play; five, six or seven is considered the ideal number.

CARDS

The full pack of 52 cards is used. The cards rank from Ace (high) to 2 (low).

THE PLAY

Each player is dealt five cards face downwards, and the object of the game is to make the best hand by an exchange of cards, and then bet on it against the other players.

In ascending order the nine classes of poker hands, together with the approximate odds against their being dealt to a player, are:

Highest card: any five odd cards. Evens.

One pair: two cards of the same rank and three odd cards. 15 to 11.

Two pairs: two cards of the same rank, two other cards of the same rank and an odd card. 20 to 1.

Threes: three cards of the same rank and two odd cards. 46 to 1.

Straight: any five cards in sequence, not of the same suit; an Ace may be either high or low. 254 to 1.

Flush: any five cards of the same suit. 508 to 1.

Full house: three cards of the same rank and two other cards of the same rank. 693 to 1.

Fours: four cards of the same rank and an odd card. 4,164 to 1.

Straight flush: a sequence of five cards all of the same suit: an Ace may be either high or low. 64,973 to 1.

Examples of each hand are illustrated overleaf. They are valued on the highest combination, and if the combination of two or more players is equal, by the highest odd card. In the event of

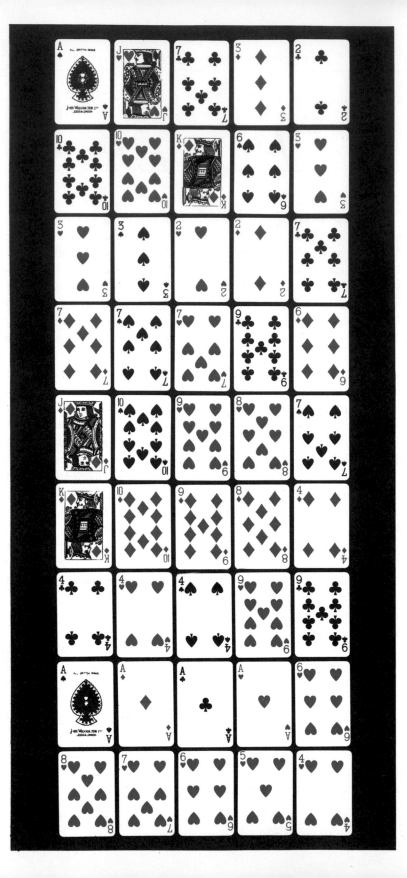

two or more players holding exactly equal hands the stakes are divided.

The player on the left of the dealer begins the game by putting up an agreed amount, known as the ante. For convenience we will assume that it is one chip. The player on his left then puts up a straddle of two chips. Throughout the game every player puts his chips on the table in front of him.

The dealer now deals, face downwards, five cards to each player. After looking at his cards, the player on the left of the straddle has the option of playing or not. If he decides not to play he throws his cards face downwards towards the centre of the table, and takes no further interest in the deal in progress. If he decides to play he puts up four chips. The player on his left now has the choice of throwing in his hand, coming into the game for four chips, or doubling (i.e. coming into the game for eight chips). In the same way, in turn, every player has the choice of throwing in his hand, coming into the game for the same stake as the previous

player, or raising the stakes until the agreed maximum is reached.

When staking reaches the ante and straddle, they can either throw in their hands and sacrifice what they have already put up, or come into the game by raising their stakes to the appropriate amount.

If no player comes into the game, the straddle recovers his two chips and takes the one chip put up by the ante.

Staking continues for some little time, because if a player has come into the game and a subsequent player has doubled, it is open to those who have already staked to increase their stakes, and this progressive staking continues until no-one increases the stakes or the agreed limit is reached.

When all have staked, those left in the game have the chance to improve their hands by exchanging cards. The dealer ignores those who have already thrown in their hands, but gives all the other players in turn as many cards as they wish after they have discarded those cards that they do not wish to retain. A player may discard any number of his cards, but no experienced player would remain in the game to exchange four cards, and only one who has taken leave of his senses will do so to exchange all five cards. Most players will exchange one, two, or three cards.

When cards have been exchanged, the player who was first to come in begins the betting. Either he throws in his hand (sacrificing the stake he has already made to come in), checks (signifies his intention to remain in the game without increasing his stake) or

---

The classes of Poker hand, the highest at the bottom. The numbers of possible ways in which each hand can be made up are as follows:

highest card:	1,302,540
one pair:	1,098,240
two pairs:	123,552
threes:	54,912
straight:	10,200
flush:	5,108
full house:	3,744
fours:	624
straight flush:	40

raises (increases his stake to any amount up to the agreed limit).

If he checks, all the players who follow him have, in their turn, the same choice. If no-one raises those left in the game show their cards and the player with the best hand takes all that has been staked. If a player raises, the subsequent players, in turn, have the option of throwing in their hands, putting up sufficient chips to meet the raise, or raise still further.

In this way the betting continues, until the final bet is either called or not. If the final bet is called, the players left in the game show their cards and the player with the best hand wins all that has been staked: if the final bet is not called, the player whose bet has not been called wins all that has been staked with no need to show his hand.

Poker falls naturally into two parts: the staking and the betting. The staking is the easier part of the game because it is open to a precise arithmetical analysis. We may suppose that a player is dealt:

$$\spadesuit 10, \spadesuit 6, \spadesuit 5, \spadesuit 2, \heartsuit 9$$

Since a pair of 10s is of small value, the player's aim must be to discard the $\heartsuit 9$ hoping to draw a spade to fill the flush.

There are 47 cards from which to draw, and of them only nine are spades. It follows, therefore, that the odds against drawing a spade are 38 to 9, or approximately $4\frac{1}{4}$ to 1. If three players have come into the game with four chips each, making 15 chips on the table with the ante and straddle, it is not worth while playing because it costs four chips to come in so that the table is offering odds of 15 to 4 ($3\frac{3}{4}$ to 1) and the chance of improving is $4\frac{1}{4}$ to 1. If, however, four players have come in it will be just worth while coming into the game, because now there will be 19 chips on the table so that the table is offering odds of $4\frac{3}{4}$ to 1, which is better than the odds against improving.

Poker players should study very carefully the mathematical chances, because the whole theory of staking may be summed up by asking oneself two questions: What are the chances of improving my hand? What odds are the table laying me? Then, if the answer to the first question is greater than to the second the player should come in, if it is not he should throw in his hand.

The betting is the more difficult part of the game because it is largely psychology. At the same time a player has to be gifted with the quality that we call judgement because his betting must be dictated by the manner in which the other players are betting, and how they, on their part, will interpret his betting. Particular note should be taken of the number of cards drawn by each of the other players and deductions drawn from the information gained. The subsequent betting should go a long way towards confirming whether the deductions are correct or not, and whether the player has improved on the draw.

A good poker player is inscrutable and unpredictable, because he varies his game to make the most with his good hands and lose the least with his bad ones. He profits by the advice of Saint Matthew – 'let not thy left hand know what thy right hand doeth' – and he is always imperturbable, because there is no future in gloating over a win and wailing over a loss. If he thinks that he holds the best hand he bets on it boldly: if he thinks that he is beaten he throws in his cards and cuts his losses.

Pot-deals, commonly called pots, are widely played, and are an important feature of all variations of the game. When a pot is played there is no ante and no straddle; instead every player contributes an agreed amount to a pot, or pool, that is independent of the staking and betting. The player on the immediate left of the dealer has first decision whether to open the game by staking or not. If he does not open, the option passes to the player on his left, and so on.

The essence of a pot is that a player is debarred from opening the game, by putting up a stake, unless his hand qualifies him to do so by a pre-arranged standard. If no player opens, the deal passes, and the players sweeten the pot, by adding to it, for the next deal. If the pot is opened, other players may come in even if their hands are below standard, and he who wins the deal also wins the amount in the pot as well as all the stakes put up by the other players. The player who opened the game must show that his hand qualified for opening.

In a *Jackpot* a player must have a pair of Jacks, or better, to qualify for opening.

In a *Progressive jackpot*, if no-one opens the first deal, the second deal is a Queenpot, and if no-one opens it the next is a Kingpot, and so on. Some stop at Acepots, others continue to two pairs before beginning again at a Jackpot if no-one has opened the game.

In a *Freak pot*, sometimes called Deuces wild, all the 2s are wild cards and may be used to represent any cards that the holder chooses. Fives (five cards of the same rank) is now a possible hand, and it is classed above a straight flush, but is beaten if the straight flush is headed by an Ace.

In a *Double pot*, or Legs, any type of pot is chosen, but a player must win it twice before he may take his winnings.

WILD WIDOW

This is a variation of the parent game, but, after four cards have been dealt to each player, a card is turned face upwards in the centre of the table and is left there for the duration of the deal. The dealer then gives each player one more card, and the game is played with the three other cards of the same rank as the exposed card wild.

SPIT IN THE OCEAN

In this variation, only four cards are dealt to each player. A card is then dealt face upwards in the centre of the table. Each player considers this card as the fifth card of his hand. It is a wild card, as also are the other three cards of the same rank.

STUD POKER

In this variation of the parent game the main feature is that some of the cards are dealt face upwards and some face downwards. There are several ways of playing the game.

In *Five-card stud* there is no ante unless agreed on. The dealer gives each player a card face downwards (it is known as the hole card) and then a card face upwards. The deal is then interrupted for a betting interval. After the betting interval the dealer gives each active player another three cards face upwards, and after each there is a betting interval. If two or more players remain in the game after the last betting interval, they turn up their hole cards and the player with the best hand wins.

Each betting interval begins with the player who holds the best combinations of cards exposed, and if two or more players have equal combinations the one nearest to the dealer's left bets first. At the first betting interval the player who opens must make a bet; at subsequent intervals he may check. Any player who drops out of the game must turn his exposed cards face downwards.

Seven-card stud, sometimes called Down the River, or Peek Poker, is played in the same way as five-card stud, except that the dealer first deals to each player two cards face downwards and one card face upwards. There is a betting interval, and, after this, the active players are dealt three cards face upwards and one face downwards, with the deal interrupted for a betting interval after each round of dealing. At the showdown, a player exposes his hole cards and selects five of his seven cards to form his hand.

WHISKY POKER

This variation is so called because it was originally played in the American lumber camps to decide who should pay for the drinks.

Every player contributes an agreed amount to a pool. The dealer deals an extra hand (widow) to the centre of the table, immediately before dealing cards to himself. The player on the left of the dealer, after looking at his cards, may either exchange his hand for the widow, pass (in which case the option of taking the widow passes to his left-hand neighbour) or indicate, by knocking the table, that he will play with the cards dealt to him.

If the player on the left of the dealer (or any subsequent player) takes the widow, he puts his own cards face upwards on the table as a new widow. The player on his left may now either take the whole of the exposed widow in exchange for his own hand, take one or more cards from it in exchange for cards in his hand, or knock. A player, however, cannot draw cards from the widow and knock at the same turn, and the option to exchange the widow or cards with it continues until a player knocks. As soon as a player does so, the remaining players have one turn each to exchange their hands or cards for it. After the player on the right of the knocker has had his turn, the players expose their hands and the best hand wins the pot.

If no-one takes the widow before it is the turn of the dealer, he must either take the widow or turn it face upwards on the table. Even if he decides to knock, without making an exchange, he must still turn up the widow.

of the knocker has drawn and discarded, or dropped out of the game, all players remaining in the game show their cards and settlement is made as follows:

If the knocker has the best hand, all who are in the game pay him twice the ante.

If the knocker and one or more other players have equal hands they divide the winnings except for the amount paid to the knocker by those who dropped out of the game. If the knocker does not have the best hand he pays twice the ante to every player remaining in the game, and the player with the best hand wins the antes.

KNOCK POKER

In this variation, every player puts up an ante. The dealer gives every player five cards, as in the parent game, and the rest of the pack (the stock) is placed face downwards in the centre of the table. The player on the left of the dealer draws the top card of the stock and discards a card from his hand. Thereafter each player in turn draws either the top card of the stock or the top card of the discard pile, and discards a card from his hand.

At any time after drawing a card and before discarding one, a player may knock the table. He then discards a card from his hand. The other players have one more turn each to draw and discard a card, or drop out of the game by paying the knocker the amount of the ante. After the player on the right

HIGH-LOW POKER

Any variation of poker may be played high-low. As a rule the hand is played as a pot. The player plays his hand for either high or low, but does not have to announce which until the last card is dealt. The highest and the lowest hands divide the pot between them. An Ace is always high and cannot be counted as a low card except as part of a sequence in the high hand.

STRIP POKER

In this version of the game the dealer deals five cards, face downwards, to each player. There is no ante and no straddle. After an exchange of cards (as in the parent game) the players expose their cards and the one with the worst poker hand pays the table by removing an article of clothing.

The game, with all its voluptuous prospects, is said to be at its best in mixed company during a heatwave!

RUMMY

*R*UMMY, *or Rum, as the name is frequently truncated to, is one of the most popular of all card games. Derivatives to be found elsewhere in this book include Gin Rummy and Canasta. Coon Can is another game of the type but that predates even Rummy.*

NUMBER OF PLAYERS

Any number up to six may play. More than six should prefer Coon Can (page 164).

CARDS

The full pack of 52 cards is used. They rank from King (high) to Ace (low).

Ten cards are dealt to each player if only two play; seven cards if three or four play; and six cards if five or six play. The rest of the pack (the stock) is placed face downwards in the centre of the table, and the top card of it is turned face upwards and laid alongside it to start the discard pile.

THE PLAY

The object of the game is to make sets of three or more cards of the same rank, or sequences of three or more cards of the same suit (the Ace being low) and declare them by exposing them on the table, after drawing a card from the stock or discard pile and before discarding a card from the hand. At the same time a player may add one or more proper cards to sequences and sets already declared either by himself or the other players.

Each player in turn, beginning with the one on the left of the dealer, must take into his hand either the top card of the stock or the top card of the discard pile, and discard a card from his hand, but if he has drawn the top card of the discard pile he must not discard it in the same turn.

If the stock is exhausted before any player declares all his hand, the discard pile is turned face downwards and becomes the stock.

The player who is first to declare all his cards wins the hand, and the other players pay him ten points each for every court card left in their hands, one point for every Ace, and its pip value for every other card. If a player declares all his cards in one turn he scores rummy and is paid double.

Rummy is a simple game that has acquired a number of improvements.

BOATHOUSE RUMMY

In this version, a player may draw the top card of the stock; or he may draw the top card of the discard pile and then either the top card of the stock or the next card of the discard pile. He may, however, discard only one card.

In a sequence the Ace may be either high, low, or round the corner.

The play does not come to an end until a player can declare his entire hand in one turn.

A losing player pays only for the unmatched cards in his hand, but Aces are paid for at 11 points each.

CONTINENTAL RUMMY

This variation of the parent game is suitable for any number of players up to 12. If two to five play two packs with two Jokers are used; if six to eight play three packs with three Jokers are used; and if nine to 12 play four packs with four Jokers are used.

Each player receives 15 cards. A player may not declare until all 15 of his cards are melded either in five three-card sequences, or in three four-card sequences and one three-card sequence, or in one five-card, one four-card and two three-card sequences. Sets of three or more cards of the same rank are of no value. A Joker may be used as any card. The Ace may be high or low, but not round the corner.

There are many ways of scoring, but generally the winner collects from all the other players one unit from each for winning, and two units from each for every Joker in his hand.

GAMBLER'S RUMMY

This version is so called because it is the variation of the parent game that is most frequently played for high stakes.

Only four players take part and each is dealt seven cards. The Ace is low and, as in the parent game, counts only one point in the settlement. A player is not allowed to declare all his hand in one turn. He must declare it in at least two turns, but he is not debarred from going out second turn even if on his previous turn he played off only one card on another player's declaration.

The stock is gone through only once. When it is exhausted the players must draw the top card of the discard pile, and the game ends when a player refuses it.

KNOCK RUMMY

This version is also called Poker Rum, and is played in the same way as the parent game, but a player does not

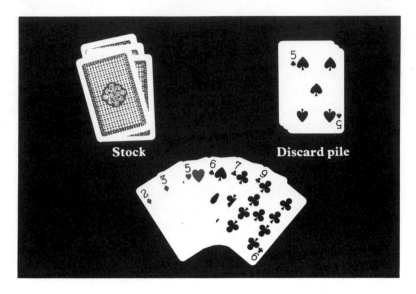

Stock   **Discard pile**

The player should take the ♠5 and discard ♣9, as ♠5 offers alternative chances of melding: either with ♡5 or ♠6.

declare his sequences and sets by exposing them on the table. Instead, after drawing a card, he knocks on the table, and then discards. Play comes to an end. The players separate their matched cards from their unmatched ones, and each announces the count of his unmatched cards, as reckoned in the parent game. The player with the lowest count wins the difference in counts from all the other players. If a player ties with the knocker for the lowest count he wins over the knocker. If the knocker does not have the lowest count he pays a penalty of an extra ten points to the player with the lowest count. If the knocker goes rummy (has all his cards matched when he knocks) and wins, he receives an extra 25 points from all the other players.

SCOTCH WHIST

*S**COTCH WHIST** is sometimes called Catch the Ten because one of the objects of the game is to win the trick that contains the 10 of the trump suit.*

NUMBER OF PLAYERS

Any number from two to eight may play. If two, three, five or seven play, each plays for himself. If four, six or eight play they may either play each for himself, or form into partnerships.

CARDS

Scotch Whist is played with a pack of 36 cards. The 2s, 3s, 4s, and 5s are removed from the standard pack. The cards rank from Ace (high) to 6 (low) with the exception that the Jack of the trump suit is promoted above the Ace.

Every player must begin with the same number of cards: if five or seven players take part the ♠6 is removed from the pack, and if eight take part all four 6s are.

Dealing varies with the number of players taking part in the game. If two play each receives 18 cards that are dealt in three separate hands of six cards each, to be played independently; if three play each receives 12 cards that are dealt in two separate hands of six cards each, to be played independently; if four or more play the cards are dealt in the normal clockwise rotation. In every case the dealer turns up the last card to indicate the trump suit.

THE PLAY

The player on the left of the dealer leads to the first trick. Thereafter the player who wins a trick leads to the next. Play follows the usual routine of trick-taking games: a player must follow suit, if he can, to the suit led and if he cannot he may either trump the trick or discard on it.

The object of the game is to win tricks containing the five top trump cards, and the player, or partnership, that does so scores 11 points for the Jack, four points for the Ace, three points for the King, two points for the Queen, and ten points for the 10. Over and above this, each player, or partnership, counts the number of cards taken in tricks, and scores one point for every card more than the number originally dealt to him, or it.

The game ends when a player, or partnership, has reached an agreed total, usually 41 points.

It stands out that a player must direct his play towards winning tricks that contain the top cards of the trump suit, particularly that which contains the 10, since the Jack can only go to the player to whom it has been dealt, and usually the luck of the deal determines who will win the tricks that contain the Ace, King and Queen.

In a partnership game the player who has been dealt the 10, either singleton or doubleton, would be well advised to lead it. It gives a good score if his partner is able to win with the Jack; if an opponent wins the trick the partnership must hope to recover by aiming to win as many tricks as possible. If the game is being played all against all, the player who has been dealt the 10 should try and get rid of all the cards in his shortest suit, so that he can win the 10 by trumping with it.

SPOIL FIVE

S POIL FIVE, sometimes called Forty-five, is an excellent game of the Euchre family, sometimes regarded as the national card game of Ireland. It calls for a show of skill and is usually played for stakes.

NUMBER OF PLAYERS

Any reasonable number may play, but the game is best for five or six.

CARDS

Spoil Five is played with the full pack of 52 cards, but that it is rarely, if ever, played outside its native Ireland may be ascribed to the eccentric order of the cards. The 5 of the trump suit is always the highest trump, the Jack of the trump suit is the second highest, and the Ace of hearts the third highest. Thereafter, if a black suit is trumps the cards rank in the order Ace, King, Queen, 2, 3, 4, 6, 7, 8, 9, 10 and if a red suit is trumps in the order Ace (if diamonds are trumps), King, Queen, 10, 9, 8, 7, 6, 4, 3, 2. In plain suits, the black suits rank in the order King, Queen, Jack, Ace, 2, 3, 4, 5, 6, 7, 8, 9, 10; the red suits in the order King, Queen, Jack, 10, 9, 8, 7, 6, 5, 4, 3, 2, Ace (except in hearts). It is concisely expressed as 'highest in red; lowest in black', but even with this help it is all rather involved.

Five cards are dealt to each player either in bundles of two then three, or three then two. The next card is exposed to determine the trump suit.

THE PLAY

A pool is formed to which every player contributes an agreed amount, and it is usual to fix a maximum and, after the first deal, only the player whose turn it is to deal contributes to the pool.

The object of the game is to win three tricks, or to prevent another player from winning them.

The player on the left of the dealer leads to the first trick. Thereafter the winner of a trick leads to the next. The rules of play are precise and peculiar to the game:

If the card turned up to denote the trump suit is an Ace, the dealer may rob. He may, that is, exchange the Ace for a card in his hand, but he must do so before the player on his left leads to the first trick.

Any player who has been dealt the Ace of the trump suit may exchange any card in his hand for the turn-up card, but he need not do so until it is his turn to play.

If a trump is led a player must follow suit if he can, but the 5 and Jack of the trump suit and the ♡ A are exempt from following suit to the lead of a lower trump. It is called reneging. It means that the 5 of the trump suit need not be played if the Jack of the trump suit is led, and the Jack of the trump suit need not be played if the ♡ A is led; if, however, the 5 of the trump suit is led no trump can renege.

If a plain suit is led a player may follow suit or trump as he chooses, but he must not discard from another plain suit if he is able to follow suit or trump.

If a player misdeals the deal passes to the next player.

The player who wins three tricks takes the pool; if no-one wins three tricks (a spoil) the deal passes to the next player. When a player has won three tricks the hand ends and the deal passes, unless the player who has won them declares 'Jinx'. This is an undertaking to win the remaining two tricks. Play then continues and if he fails to win the two tricks he loses the pool; on the other hand, if he wins the two tricks not only does he take the pool but the other players each pay him the amount that they originally contributed to the pool.

In the four-handed game illustrated overleaf, South deals and turns up the ◇ 9.

West leads the ◇ J. North may renege the ◇ 5, but it would hardly be good play not to use it to win the second highest trump, so he plays it. East, who holds the ◇ A, robs by exchanging the ♣ 8 for the ◇ 9 and, of course, plays it. West, who started with the hope of a jinx, is now not so sure that he will win even three tricks. His prospects, however, improve when South, perforce, plays the ♡ A.

North leads the ♣ J, East plays the

189

North

West

East

South

East is dealt the ♧8, but exchanges it for the ◇9.

♧5, South the ♧7, and West wins with the ◇2.

West leads the ♤K, North plays the ♤6, and East sees the possibility of himself winning three tricks. He trumps with the ◇A, and South plays the ♤9. With any luck East should be able to win the last two tricks with the ♤J and ♧5.

As it happens, however, East's play has enabled West to win three tricks, because when East leads the ♤J, West wins with the ◇3 and the last trick with the ♤2.

PARTY GAMES

FAN TAN

*F*AN TAN *is also known as Card Dominoes, Parliament and Sevens, and must not be confused with the gambling game that is played in China under the same name. In fact, the well-known Chinese game is not a card game.*

NUMBER OF PLAYERS

Any reasonable number may play, with perhaps four to six being the best.

CARDS

The standard 52-card pack is used, with cards ranking from King (high) to Ace (low).

Players cut for deal, the drawer of the highest card being first dealer. Thereafter the deal passes to the left.

Before each deal an agreed amount is placed by each player into a pool. The cards are dealt one by one, face downwards, until the pack is exhausted.

THE PLAY

Play begins by the player on the left of the dealer placing a 7 face upwards in the centre of the table. If he has no 7 he contributes one unit to the pool, and the player on his left now has to play a 7 to the centre of the table or contribute one unit to the pool, and so on.

As soon as a 7 has been played to the centre of the table, the next player must play either the 6 of the same suit on its left, or the 8 of the same suit on its right, or the 7 of another suit below it. The game continues clockwise round the table, the players building up to the Kings on the right of the 7s and down to the Aces on the left of them.

Any player who is unable to play in his turn contributes one unit to the pool, and if he revokes, by failing to play when he could do so, he forfeits three units to the pool, and five units each to the holders of the 6 and 8 if he fails to play a 7 when he could and should have played it.

The game is won by the player who is first to get rid of all his cards. He receives all that is in the pool and from each of the other players one unit for every card that the player holds.

Skill comes into the game by holding up the opponents. As a general rule a 7, unless it is accompanied by several cards of the same suit, should be kept in hand for as long as possible; and, if a player has a choice of plays, he should prefer the card that will allow him later to play a lower or higher one of the same suit, rather than one that can only help the opponents.

With the situation of the game as in the illustration, the player plays the ♣10 because when the ♣J is played he can follow with the ♣Q. It would be an error of judgement to play the ♡6, because it doesn't help him, but might help the opponents.

The game can, of course, be enjoyed by children (or adults) without the need for a pool.

PLAY OR PAY

The original version of Fan Tan was called Play or Pay and may still be enjoyed. The eldest hand may lead any card (not necessarily a 7). The next player must play the next higher card in the same suit, or, if unable to, pay a chip to a pool. The sequence is built upwards only, and is regarded as continuous, i.e. Ace follows King. Only one suit is played at a time, and only when the first suit is finished is a second begun. The player who lays the last

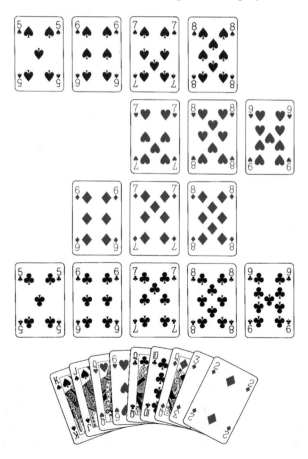

card in the first suit also plays the first card to the next — the suit and the rank are of his choice. The first person to get rid of his cards wins the pool.

The first player to play might choose a suit in which he has two consecutive cards, and lay the higher. By this means he is certain to lay the last card in the suit and thus begin the next. It is clearly an advantage to play first to the final suit, when opposite rules apply, and the player will decide which of his cards provide the biggest gap and lead so that his own cards are played before this gap is filled.

If the hand in the illustration is held by the player to play first, its holder has an excellent chance of winning. He should begin with ♡K, and will play the last card in the heart suit with ♡Q. He then begins spades with ♠8 and

plays the last card with ♠7. He then lays ♣4 and ends the suit with ♣3. Then he plays ◇10 and wins provided each of his opponents holds one of the cards ◇9, 8, 7, 6, 5, 4, 3. An alternative plan would be to play the diamond suit second, and hope that the last suit, whether it be spades or clubs, will begin at such a level that he can play his two consecutive cards before any other player has gone out.

It should be pointed out that if players put in chips for each pass, each player might easily pass 40 times in one deal, so stakes should be geared accordingly. An alternative method of settling would be for each loser to pay the winner at the end of the deal one chip for each card remaining in his hand. Like Fan Tan, the game can, of course, be played for enjoyment only.

NEWMARKET

NEWMARKET is a modern variation of the old game of Pope Joan and is known by a number of other names — Boodle and Stops in England; Chicago, Michigan and Saratoga in America. It is an excellent gambling game that is easy to learn and contains an element of skill that guarantees the better player winning in the long run.

NUMBER OF PLAYERS

From three to eight players may play.

CARDS

The game is played with a full pack of 52 cards, ranking from Ace (high) to 2 (low), and an Ace, King, Queen and Jack (each of a different suit) from another pack. These four extra cards are known as the boodle cards, and are placed, face upwards, in a row in the centre of the table.

THE PLAY

Before the deal each player has to stake an agreed number of chips (usually, but not necessarily, 10) on the boodle cards. He may stake his chips as he pleases, but he must not stake more nor less than the agreed number.

The dealer then deals the cards one at a time to each player in rotation, and to an extra hand or dummy. As the players must each receive the same number of cards, any over-cards are dealt to the dummy hand which remains face downwards on the table throughout the deal.

The player on the left of the dealer makes the first lead. He may lead a card from any suit, but it must be the lowest card that he holds in the suit. The players do not play in rotation round the table. The next play is made by the player who holds next higher cards in the suit, then the next higher card is played by the player who holds it, and so on, until the run is stopped either because a player plays the Ace of the suit, or the next higher card is in the dummy hand. Either way, the player who played the last card leads the lowest card of another suit, and if he has no other suit the lead passes to the player on his left.

When a player plays a card that is identical with one of the boodle cards he collects all the chips from it.

The object of the game, however, is not only to win the chips that have been staked on the boodle cards, but to get rid of all one's cards, because the player who is first to do so receives one chip from each of the other players. If no player gets rid of all his cards, the one who holds the fewest cards wins the hand, and if two players are left with an equal number of fewest cards they divide the winnings.

If when a deal comes to an end the chips on one or more of the boodle cards have not been claimed, because the corresponding cards to the boodle cards are in the dummy hand, they are carried forward to the next deal.

PIP-PIP!

*P*IP-PIP! *can be quite a noisy game, and is an enjoyable one for a party.*

NUMBER OF PLAYERS

Any reasonable number may play up to about 12, but maybe six to eight is best.

CARDS

Two standard packs are required, shuffled together. The cards rank as follows: 2, Ace, King, Queen, Jack, 10, 9, 8, 7, 6, 5, 4, 3, in other words in the usual order except that 2 is promoted to be the top card in each suit.

The players draw cards. He who shows the highest deals first, and the card drawn determines the trump suit. Thereafter the deal passes to the left, and the trump suit is determined by the player to the right of the dealer cutting the pack.

Seven cards are dealt face downwards to each player, and the remainder of the pack is placed face downwards in the centre of the table (the stock).

THE PLAY

The object of the game is to win tricks containing 2s, Aces, Kings, Queens and Jacks, and for winning them a player scores 11 points for each 2, 10 points for each Ace, five points for each King, four points for each Queen and three points for each Jack.

The player on the left of the dealer leads to the first trick. Thereafter the player who wins a trick leads to the next. A player must follow suit if he can; if not he may either discard or trump. If two players play identical cards, the player of the second is deemed to have played the higher card.

Immediately after a player has played to a trick he draws a card from the stock; if he now holds in his hand the King and Queen of the same suit, other than of the trump suit, he may call 'Pip-Pip', and place the two cards face upwards on the table in front of him. For calling 'Pip-Pip' a player scores 50 points and, at the end of the current trick, the trump suit changes to that of the exposed King and Queen.

'Pip-Pip' may be called and 50 points scored if a player is dealt the King and Queen of a suit – other than of the trump suit. The trump suit is then changed before the first trick is played. If two or more players are dealt the King and Queen of a suit — other than of the trump suit — each scores 50 points if he calls 'Pip-Pip'. The trump suit is changed to that of the player who was first to call. 'Pip-Pip' may be called twice in the same suit provided the player has both Kings and both Queens of it. A King or a Queen once paired cannot be paired a second time. It is not compulsory to call 'Pip-Pip' if a player holds the King and Queen of a suit, but if he does not call he cannot score the bonus of 50 points.

Drawing cards from the stock continues until it contains insufficient cards to enable every player to draw one. The remaining cards in the stock are then turned face upwards and the players play the last seven tricks with the cards left in their hands.

The game ends when every player has dealt an equal number of times.

POPE JOAN

*P*OPE JOAN *is a very old card game that at one time was exceptionally popular in Scotland. The* ♢ 9 *is given the name of Pope, and as the Pope was the Antichrist of Scottish reformers, there is reason to think that it was for this reason that the nickname of Curse of Scotland became attached to the card. Pope Joan is a gambling game.*

NUMBER OF PLAYERS

Any number from three to eight may play, with four to six being best.

CARDS

The game is played with a standard pack of 52 cards from which the ♢ 8 is removed.

THE PLAY

Originally a special board, consisting of a circular tray divided into eight compartments, and revolving about a central pillar, was used with counters. To-day these boards are museum pieces, and modern players must make do with eight saucers labelled: *Pope (◇9), Ace, King, Queen, Jack, Matrimony, Intrigue, Game,* placed in the centre of the table.

Each player begins with the same number of counters of an agreed value, and the dealer places six in the saucer labelled Pope (◇9), two each in Matrimony and Intrigue, and one each in Ace, King, Queen, Jack and Game. It is called dressing the board.

Cards are then dealt to the players and to an extra hand (widow) in the centre of the table. The number of cards dealt to each player and the widow depends on the number of players in the game. The players must each hold the same number of cards, so any over-cards go to the widow. The last card is turned face upwards to denote the trump suit, and if it is either the Pope (◇9) or an Ace, King, Queen or Jack, the dealer wins the counters in the corresponding saucer.

The player on the left of the dealer leads to the first trick. He may lead any card he chooses, and at the same time he announces it. Suppose it is the ♣6. Then the player who holds the ♣7 plays it and announces it, the player who holds the ♣8 plays it and announces it, and so on, until the run comes to an end.

The four Kings are stop cards, and in the diamond suit the 7 is as well, because the ◇8 has been removed from the pack. In practice, of course, any card may be a stop card on account of the cards in the widow hand, and because the next higher card may already have been played.

When a run comes to an end, the player of the stop card starts a fresh run by leading any card he likes. In this way the game continues until one of the players has played all his cards. He is then entitled to the counters in the Game saucer, and, in addition, he receives from each player one counter for every card left in his hand. The

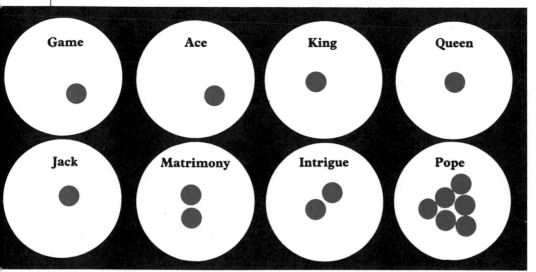

player who is left with the Pope ($\diamond$9), however, is exempt from paying the winner so long as he holds the card in his hand. If he has played it in the course of the game he loses this advantage.

During the course of the game, any player who plays the Ace, King, Queen or Jack of the trump suit, or the Pope ($\diamond$9), wins the counters in the corresponding saucers; if the same player plays the King and Queen of the trump suit he wins the counters in Matrimony, and if the same player plays the Queen and Jack of the trump suit he wins those in Intrigue.

The deal passes round the table clockwise, and any counters that have not been won in a deal are carried forward to the next.

RANTER GO ROUND

RANTER GO ROUND is an old Cornish game with the rather more appropriate alternative name of Cuckoo. It is a game that children enjoy.

NUMBER OF PLAYERS

Ranter Go Round can be played by any reasonable number of players.

CARDS

The full pack of 52 cards is used, cards ranking from Ace (high) to 2 (low).

THE PLAY

Each player begins with an agreed number of units, usually three. The dealer deals one card face downwards to each player. The object of the game is to avoid being left with the lowest card.

The player on the left of the dealer begins the game. He may either retain his card or offer it to his left-hand neighbour with the command 'Change'. There is no choice about it. The player so commanded must exchange cards with his right-hand neighbour unless he holds a King, when he says 'King', and the game is continued by the player on his left.

When an exchange has been made, the player who has been compelled to do so may pass on the card he has received in the same way, and so on, clockwise round the table, until the card is brought to a halt either by a King or by a player receiving a high card in exchange, so that he has nothing to gain by passing it on.

Any player giving an Ace, 2 or 3 in obedience to the command 'Change' must announce the rank of the card.

The dealer is last to play, and if he wishes to exchange his card, he does so by cutting the remainder of the pack and taking the top card of the cut.

If in doing this he draws a King he loses the hand and contributes one unit to the pool. If he does not draw a King, all the players expose their cards and the one with the lowest contributes one unit to the pool. If two or more tie for lowest card, all contribute to the pool.

When a player has contributed all his units to the pool, he retires from the game. The others continue, and the game is won by he who is left with at least one unit in hand.

RED DOG

*A*LTHOUGH *in Red Dog, or High-card Pool, players stake on their cards, it is usually accepted as a party game, rather than a banking game, because the players stake against a pool and not against a banker.*

NUMBER OF PLAYERS

Any number up to ten may play.

CARDS

The full pack of 52 is used, cards ranking from Ace (high) to 2 (low).

THE PLAY

The players contribute to the pool an agreed number of units, and each player is dealt five cards (only four cards if nine or ten players are in the game). Beginning with the player on the left of the dealer, each in turn stakes a minimum of one unit and a maximum that must not exceed the number of units in the pool, that he holds a card that is higher than, and in the same suit as, the top card of the stock when it is his turn to play.

The dealer faces the top card of the stock. If the player can beat it, he shows his card and is paid out of the pool. His remaining cards are not seen.

If he cannot beat it, his stake is added to the pool and his cards are shown to the other players.

If at any time a player's winning bet takes everything in the pool, a new pool is started.

ROCKAWAY

*R*OCKAWAY *or* Go Boom *is a game that may be played by children.*

NUMBER OF PLAYERS

Any reasonable number may play.

CARDS

Two standard packs of 52 cards are shuffled together, making a pack of 104 cards. Cards rank from Ace (high) to 2 (low).

The dealer deals seven cards, face downwards, to each player. The next card (the widow) is placed face upwards in the centre of the table, and the rest of the pack (the stock) is placed face downwards on the table.

THE PLAY

In turn, and beginning with the player on the left of the dealer, each player covers the widow either with a card of the same rank, of the same suit, or with an Ace, drawn from his hand. If he has no card in his hand to comply with the rule he draws a card from the stock and continues to draw one until he draws a card that permits him to cover the widow.

The card that covers the widow then becomes the widow for the next player, and so on, round the table in a clockwise direction.

When the stock is exhausted, the players play out the cards in their hands, and a player who cannot cover the widow misses his turn.

The hand comes to an end when a

player has exhausted the cards in his hand. The remaining players expose their cards, which are scored against them, an Ace counting 15 points, a court card 10 points, and all other cards their pip value.

The deal passes round the table in a clockwise direction, and the game comes to an end when every player has dealt an equal number of times, by

As an Ace counts 15 points against a player who is left with it, E plays ♠A rather than one of his diamonds.

♠10   ♠9   ♠J   ♠8   ?

As E has no spade, no 8 and no Ace in his hand, he must draw from the stock, and continue to do so until he draws a playable card.

arrangement before the game begins.

E dealt the hands illustrated. A, therefore, leads first, and the play is:

A	B	C	D	E
♣6	♣2	♦2	♦K	♠A

It can be seen that E was foolish to play his Ace first round. As no opponent can go out in less than seven rounds, E would have been wise to keep his Ace for six rounds at least. He would not then have found himself in such a bad position on the second round. Usually, an Ace should not be played if another choice is available.

SPINADO

S PINADO is a less complicated version of Pope Joan (see page 196). It is a mild gambling game. No board is necessary and there are only three pools: Matrimony, Intrigue and Game.

NUMBER OF PLAYERS

Any number from two to seven may play, four or five being best.

CARDS

From a standard pack of 52 cards, the four 2s and the ◇8 are removed, leaving a pack of 47 cards. Cards rank from King (high) to Ace (low).

The dealer deals the cards to the players and to an extra hand (widow). As the players must each hold the same number of cards, over-cards go to the widow hand.

THE PLAY

Before dealing the dealer contributes 12 counters to the Matrimony pool, and six each to the Intrigue and Game pools. The other players contribute three counters each to the Game pool.

Matrimony is the King and Queen of Diamonds, Intrigue is the Queen and Jack of Diamonds.

The player on the left of the dealer starts the game by playing any card that he chooses, and the other players continue by playing the next higher cards in succession until a stop is reached. The player who plays the stop card then starts a new run by playing any card that he chooses.

The ◇A is known as Spinado, more usually truncated to Spin, and whoever holds it may play it at any time that he chooses provided that he accompanies it with the proper card, and announces that he is playing Spinado. It constitutes a stop, and he receives three counters from each opponent.

During the game, the player who plays the ◇K receives two counters

from each of the other players, and if he plays the ◇Q as well he wins the Matrimony pool. The player who plays the ◇Q and the ◇J wins the Intrigue pool, and those who play the Kings of spades, hearts and clubs receive one counter from each of the other players.

The game is won by the player who is the first to play all his cards. He takes the counters in the Game pool and is exempt from contributing to the pools in the next deal, unless it is his turn to deal.

A player who is left with Spinado in his hand pays the winner of the game double for each card he is left with.

Spinado, therefore, should not be

Top: matrimony
Centre: intrigue
Bottom: spinado

kept back too long. On the other hand, it is not always advisable to play it with one's first card. If, for example, a 10 is led, and the player who holds Spinado also holds the King and Jack, it is an error of judgement to play Spinado with the Jack, because if the Jack proves to be a stop there was no need for the play of Spinado, and the King is the natural stop if another player follows with the Queen.

It is better to hold up Spinado to be played with some card that is not known to be a stop.

THIRTY-ONE

*T*HIRTY-ONE *may be played by any number of players up to 15. It is a gambling game.*

NUMBER OF PLAYERS

Any reasonable number may play.

CARDS

Thirty-One is played with the full pack of 52 cards, the Aces ranking high, the 2s low.

Three cards are dealt face downwards to each player, and three cards are placed face upwards in the centre of the table. It is known as the widow hand.

The player might be advised to exchange his ◇ 5 with the ♡ 7 and rap, since 25 is not a bad score.

Widow   Hand

THE PLAY

Before each deal the players contribute an agreed amount to a pool.

In turn each player, beginning with the one on the left of the dealer, must exchange one of his cards with a card from the widow. He cannot pass, nor can he exchange more than one card. Counting the Ace as 11, the court cards as 10 each and all the other cards at their pip values, the object of the game is to hold three cards of the same suit which will add up to 31. Next in value is a hand that contains three cards of the same rank. Failing either, the pool is won by the player who holds the highest total in any one suit.

The exchange of cards with the widow hand continues until a player has obtained a 31 hand. When a player holds such a hand he exposes it on the table, claims the pool, and the deal passes. At any stage of the game, however, a player who thinks he has a hand good enough to win, may rap the table. The other players now have the right, in turn, either to stand pat with the cards that they hold, or exchange one more card with the widow. The players then expose their cards and the one with the best hand wins the pool.

BACCARAT

BACCARAT, more correctly Baccarat Banque, is a game of chance that is played in casinos everywhere.

NUMBER OF PLAYERS

The game may be played by any number up to 30 or more.

CARDS

Six packs of cards are shuffled together (in Las Vegas eight packs are used) cut and placed in an open-ended box known as a shoe, designed to release only one card at a time. The court cards rank in value at 10 points each; all other cards at their pip values.

THE PLAY

The banker sits midway down one of the sides of a long, oval table (see illustration), and the players sit in equal numbers on both sides of him. Those for whom there is no room to sit, stand behind them.

The banker, who is also the dealer,

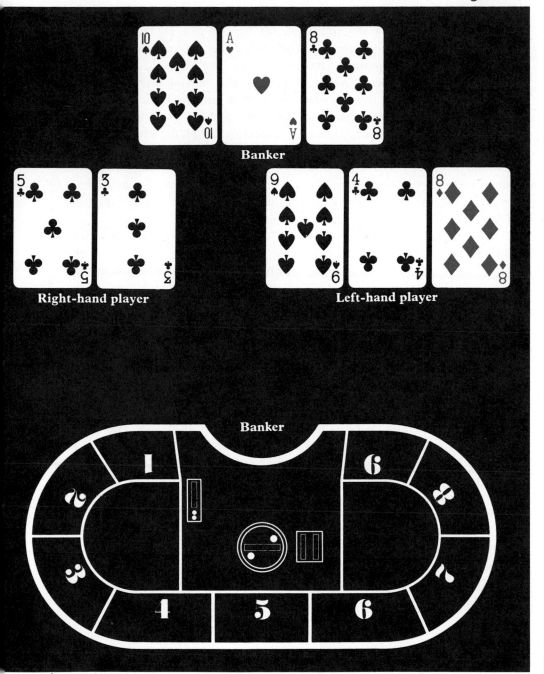

Banker

Right-hand player

Left-hand player

Banker

The layout of the staking table used in baccarat and *chemin de fer*.

puts his stake on the table in front of him, and any player who wishes to bet against the whole of it calls 'Banco'. If two or more call, the one nearest to the banker's left makes the bet. If no-one calls, the players combine their bets to equal the stake put up by the banker.

The banker then gives a card face downwards to the player on his right, a card to the player on his left and a card to himself. He repeats the operation so the three of them have two cards each.

The object of the game is to form in two or three cards a combination counting as nearly as possible to 9. In counting the total, ten is disregarded; if, for example, a player's two cards total 15 it counts as a point of 5.

The banker looks at his two cards and if he has a point of 8 or 9 he shows his cards and wins the hand. If he has not got a point of 8 or 9, he announces that he will give and the player on his right looks at his cards. If he has a point of 8 or 9 he shows his cards and announces his natural. If he has not got a point of 8 or 9 he may ask for one more card which the banker gives to him face upwards. The player on the left of the banker goes through the same performance, and then the banker may, if he chooses, take one more card. Finally, the banker wins or loses to each player according to whose point is nearer to 9; equality neither wins nor loses.

To illustrate (see previous page). The banker holds ♠10 and ♡A, making a point of 1, and he, therefore,

must give. The right-hand player holds ♣5 and ♣3. He faces his cards, announces his natural point of 8, and must win. The left-hand player holds ♠9 and ♣4, making a point of 3. He must draw and the banker gives him ◇8, reducing his point to 1. For the moment, however, the left-hand player does not announce his point. The banker faces his cards, and, as he holds no more than a point of 1, he draws a card. It is the ♣8, which raises his point to 9.

The banker, therefore, wins from the left-hand player, but loses to the right-hand player because though the banker has a point of 9, against the point of 8 held by the right-hand player, a natural beats any point made by the addition of a drawn card.

The rules of play are strict. They should never be deviated from because the player who is holding the cards is playing for all on his side of the table. If he deviates from the rules, and thereby loses the hand, he is liable to make good all losses incurred through his error. A player must not look at his cards until the banker has either announced that he holds a natural or that he will give cards. When a player looks at his cards, if he holds a natural he must expose his cards and declare his natural at once. If a player does not hold a natural, he must draw a card if he holds a point of 4 or less, stand if he holds a point of 6 or 7, and use his discretion to draw or stand only if he holds a point of 5.

BLIND HOOKEY

*B*LIND HOOKEY *is the simplest of all gambling games.*

NUMBER OF PLAYERS

Any number may play.

CARDS

The full pack of 52 cards is used.

After the pack has been shuffled by one player and cut by another to the banker, it is passed to the player on the left of the banker, who removes a few cards (not less than four) from the top of the pack, and places them in a pile face downwards on the table in front of him. He then passes the pack to his left-hand neighbour who does the same thing, and so on until all the players (the banker last) have placed a small pile of cards in front of them.

THE PLAY

Without looking at the cards, all the players (except the banker) stake to an agreed limit and turn their piles face upwards to expose the bottom card.

The banker wins from A, B, C and F and loses to D, E and G. Overall he loses 3 units and, therefore, the bank passes to the next player.

The banker wins from all whose exposed card is lower than or equal with his and loses to all whose card is higher. By agreement, the Ace may be high or low.

Play continues with the same banker if he wins more than he loses, or if he finishes level, but passes to the next player if the banker loses more than he wins.

Another way of playing the game is for the banker to cut the pack into three piles. The players place their stakes on either of two piles, and the third pile is taken by the banker. The three piles are turned face upwards and the players receive from the banker or lose to him according to whether the bottom cards of their piles are higher or lower than the bottom card of his pile.

CHEMIN DE FER

*C*HEMIN DE FER, *nearly always called Chemmy, is the same game as Baccarat (see page 204) modified for social play, because in all games of chance the banker has an advantage to a greater or lesser degree, and his advantage at* Chemin de fer *is nothing like it is at Baccarat because he plays against one hand instead of against two.*

NUMBER OF PLAYERS

Any reasonable number can play.

CARDS

The full pack of 52 cards is used, although two or three packs shuffled together is better. In a casino, a number of packs will be used.

THE PLAY

For all practical purposes the difference between Baccarat and *Chemin de fer* is that at the latter game the bank passes in rotation round the table, the banker holding the bank until he loses a coup, when it is passed to the player on his left; and the banker deals only one hand, not two, to the players, the hand being held by the one who has made the largest bet.

As the banker plays against only one hand, he may not use his judgement whether to draw or stand. The rules for play are precise and strict:

Above: Banker's point is 6. Player has drawn a 6, so banker must draw.
Below: Banker's point is only 4, but as player has drawn a 9 he must stand.

If his point is 8 or 9 he declares a natural.

If his point is 7 he stands whether the player draws any card or stands.

If his point is 6 he draws if the player draws a 6 or a 5, but stands if the player draws any other card or stands.

If he holds a point of 5 he draws if the player draws a 7, 6, 5, 4, 3, or stands, but stands if he draws any other card.

If he holds a point of 3 or 4 he draws if the player draws a 7, 6, 5, 4, 3, 2, or Ace or if he stands, but stands if he draws any other card.

If he holds a point of 0, 1 or 2 he draws whether the player draws any card or stands.

EASY GO

*E*ASY GO *is a very simple game of chance, requiring no skill or concentration.*

NUMBER OF PLAYERS

Any number up to nine may play.

CARDS

The full pack of 52 cards is used.

THE PLAY

The banker deals five cards face upwards to every player, except himself. He now faces a card and any player who holds a card of the same rank pays into a pool two units if it is the same colour and one unit if it is different. In all the banker faces five cards in turn, and for the second card the players pay into the pool three units if the cards are of the same colour and two if they are different; for the third card they contribute five units if the cards are of the same colour and four if they are different; for the fourth card they contribute nine units if the cards are of the same colour and eight if they are different; for the fifth card they contribute 17 units if the cards are of the same colour and 16 if they are different.

There is now a second show of five cards by the banker, but this time the players take out of the pool at the same rate as they paid into it.

After this, anything left in the pool is taken by the banker, but if there is not enough in the pool to meet the requirements of the players he must make it good.

The bank passes clockwise.

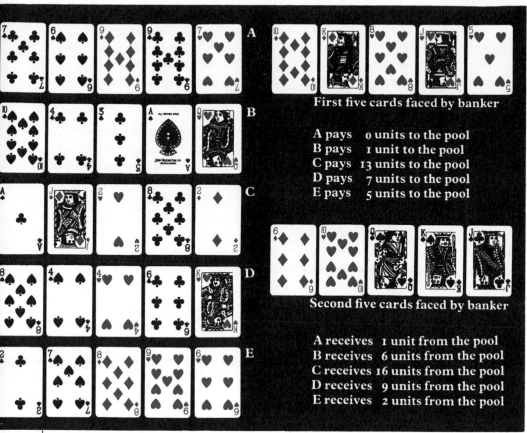

First five cards faced by banker

A pays   0 units to the pool
B pays   1 unit to the pool
C pays 13 units to the pool
D pays   7 units to the pool
E pays   5 units to the pool

Second five cards faced by banker

A receives 1 unit from the pool
B receives 6 units from the pool
C receives 16 units from the pool
D receives 9 units from the pool
E receives 2 units from the pool

Overall result of this game of Easy Go: A wins 1 unit; B wins 5 units; C wins 3 units; D wins 2 units; E loses 3 units; banker loses 8 units.

HOGGENHEIMER

HOGGENHEIMER is known as English Roulette, because the bets and staking bear a similarity to the French gambling game.

NUMBER OF PLAYERS

Any number may play.

CARDS

Hoggenheimer is played with a pack of cards from which the 2s, 3s, 4s, 5s and 6s have been removed, and the Joker (or one of the rejected cards) added.

THE PLAY

After the pack has been shuffled and cut, the banker deals the cards, face downwards, in four rows of eight cards each, and places aside, also face downwards, the 33rd card. Great care must be taken when dealing that no-one sees the face of any of the cards.

The top row is for spades, from Ace to 7; the second row for hearts, from Ace to 7; the third row for diamonds, from Ace to 7; the bottom row for clubs, from Ace to 7.

The players now stake their money. They may stake on a single card being turned up (even chance), or two touching cards being turned up (2 to 1 chance), or all four cards in a column or any group of four touching cards being turned up (4 to 1 chance), or all eight cards in a row being turned up (8 to 1 chance).

Hoggenheimer in progress. Stake 1 is on ♠10 being turned up; Stake 2 on ♠9, ♠8; Stake 3 on all four Queens; Stake 4 on ◇10, ◇9, ♣10, ♣9; Stake 5 on all clubs; Stake 6 on ♡7 and ◇7.

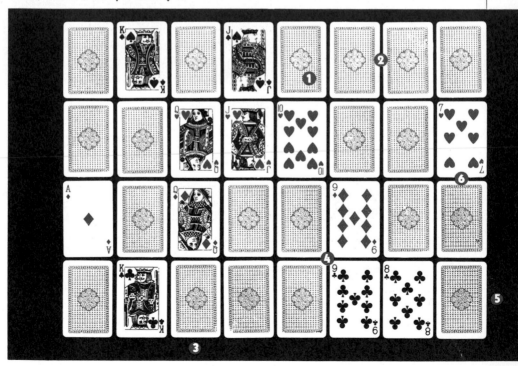

When the players have placed their bets, the banker picks up the 33rd card and shows it. If it is the Joker he wins all the money on the table and there is a redeal. If, as is more likely, it is another card, he places it in its appropriate place in the layout, exposes the card that it replaces and transfers this card to its appropriate place in the layout; and so on until the game is brought to an end when the banker exposes the Joker.

The banker then collects the money on those chances that have not materialized in full, and pays out on those chances that have.

LANSQUENET

L ANSQUENET, of German origin, is a game of pure chance that derives its name from the seventeenth-century German mercenary (landsknecht) *with whom the game is said to have been popular.*

NUMBER OF PLAYERS

Any number may play.

CARDS

The full pack of 52 cards is used.

The banker places the two top cards of the pack (hand cards) face upwards on the table. He then deals a card face upwards to himself, and one face upwards to the players. If either card is of the same rank as one of the hand cards it is put with them and another card dealt in its place.

THE PLAY

The players place their bets, and the banker covers them. He then draws cards from the pack, face upwards, one at a time. If he draws a card of the same rank as the players' card he wins the bets on it; if he draws a card of the same rank as his own card he loses all the bets on the other card; and if he draws a card that matches neither card nor the two hand cards it is placed on the table and the players may bet on it.

When the players' card is matched the banker withdraws both cards and deals another card to the players. Cards that match the hand cards are placed with them. The game ends when the pack is exhausted unless the banker matches his own card first.

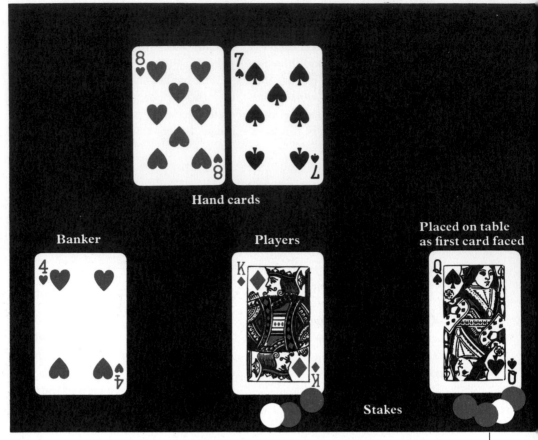

Hand cards

Banker

Players

Placed on table
as first card faced

Stakes

First card drawn from pack: ♤ Q. The card is placed on the table and players may bet on it. Second card drawn: ◇ 8. The card is added to the hand card pile. Third card drawn: ♡ K. The banker wins the two units staked on ◇ K.

MONTE BANK

*I*N *principle Monte Bank is a game of chance that is very similar to Lansquenet.*

NUMBER OF PLAYERS

Any number may play.

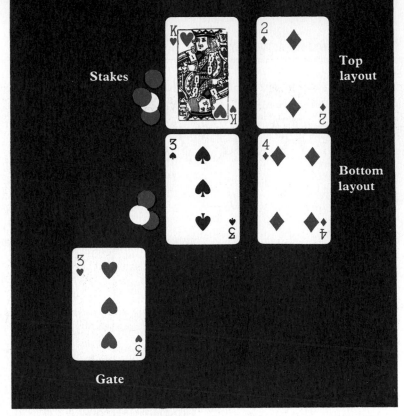

Banker pays four units to players who stake on the top layout and collects the three units on the bottom layout. If the gate had been a diamond, all players would have won; if a club all would have lost.

CARDS

The game is played with a pack of cards from which the 8s, 9s and 10s have been removed.

After the cards have been shuffled and the pack cut by one of the players, the banker draws the two cards from the bottom of the pack and places them face upwards on the table (the bottom layout), and then the two cards from the top of the pack and places them face upwards on the table (the top layout).

THE PLAY

The players place their bets up to an agreed maximum on whichever layout they choose. The banker then turns the pack face upwards and if the exposed bottom card (known as the gate) is of the same suit as any of the four cards in the layouts, he pays all bets on that layout, and collects all bets on a layout that shows no cards of the same suit as the gate.

The layouts and gate are then discarded, and the game is continued with new layouts and gate. The bank passes after five coups.

RACING

*R*ACING *is a simple gambling game.*

NUMBER OF PLAYERS

Any number may play.

CARDS

Racing is played with the standard pack of 52 cards.

THE PLAY

The four Aces are placed in a row on the table. The remainder of the pack is shuffled and cut, and the banker draws the top seven cards from the pack and lays them in a vertical column immediately below the Aces, so that the layout takes the form of a T (see illustration).

The banker deals the remaining cards one at a time, and each time that the card of a suit is dealt the Ace of the same suit is moved one card forward, the winner being the Ace that is first to pass the seventh card.

Players place their stakes on whichever Ace they choose. The race ends when an Ace passes the seventh card.

SLIPPERY SAM

SLIPPERY SAM, or Shoot, as it is sometimes called, is probably the only banking game which favours the player rather than the banker, because the player has the advantage of seeing his cards before he bets and, therefore, can calculate whether the odds are in his favour or against him. Provided he bets with intelligence he should come out a winner.

NUMBER OF PLAYERS

Any number up to ten may play, with six to eight the best.

CARDS

The full pack of 52 is used, the cards ranking from Ace (high) to 2 (low).

Racing layout. The banker might offer evens on a suit if there are no cards in the layout, 2–1 if there is one card (as with clubs and hearts here), 3–1 if there are two cards (diamonds here), 5–1 if there are three cards (spades here) and 10–1 if there are four cards. If there are five or more cards of a suit in the layout, it is impossible for that suit to win, and there must be a redeal.

THE PLAY

The banker places an agreed sum in a pool and then deals three cards, one at a time, face downwards, to each player. The remainder of the pack (the stock) he places face downwards on the table in front of him and topples it over to make it easier to slide off the top card.

The player on the left of the dealer, after looking at his cards, bets that at least one of them will be in the same suit as, and higher than, the top card of the stock. He may bet all that is in the pool or any part of it, but he may not bet less than an agreed minimum. When he has made his bet, the banker slides the top card off the stock and exposes it. If the player has won his bet he exposes his card and takes his winnings out of the pool. If he has lost his bet he pays the amount that he betted into the pool and does not expose his card. The four bets are then thrown into a discard pile, and the opportunity to bet passes to the next player.

Meanwhile: a player must not look at his cards until it is his turn to bet; if the pool is exhausted the bank immediately passes to the next player, otherwise the banker holds the bank for three full deals round the table, and then he may either pass the bank to the player on his left or hold the bank for one more, but only one more, deal round the table.

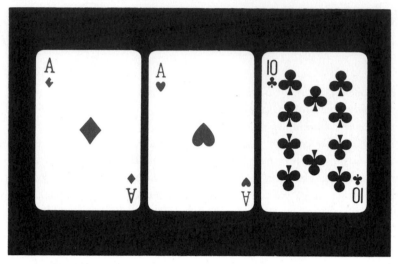

Since the player wins if a red card or a club lower than the 10 is exposed, and loses only if a spade or the Ace, King, Queen or Jack of clubs is exposed, he has 32 chances of winning and 17 of losing: he should stake heavily.

TRENTE ET QUARANTE

*T*RENTE ET QUARANTE, or Rouge et Noir, is a game of pure chance and, like Baccarat (see page 204) is essentially a casino game. It is played on a long table, each end marked as in the accompanying diagram. The banker sits midway down one of the sides, the players sit, and some stand behind them, at each end.

NUMBER OF PLAYERS

Any number of players may play.

CARDS

Six full packs of 52 are used, shuffled together.

THE PLAY

The six packs of cards are shuffled together, cut, and – with the Ace counting as one, the court cards 10 each, and other cards their pip values – the banker deals a row of cards until the total exceeds 30. He then deals a second row immediately below it in a similar manner. The top row is *noir* (black) the lower *rouge* (red) and whichever row adds up to the lesser total wins. Apart from these two chances the players can bet on whether the first card dealt will be the same colour as the winning row (*couleur*) or the opposite colour (*inverse*). All four are even chances, but if both rows add up to 31 it is a *refait* (drawn game) and the player may either halve his stake with the bank, or allow the whole of it to be put in prison. He has the right to choose between the red and black prisons, and if his stake wins on the next deal he withdraws it.

All other identical totals end in the deal being declared void, and leave the player at liberty to withdraw his stake or leave it on the table to win or lose the next deal.

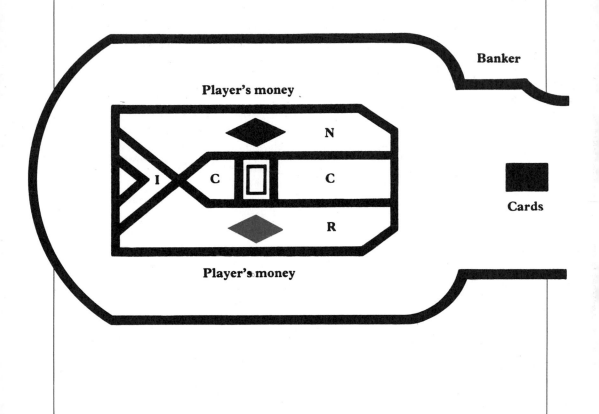

VINGT-ET-UN

*V*INGT-ET-UN, or Twenty-one, is a leading game in the casinos of America where it is known as Black Jack. Although it is a game of chance, in which the odds on winning are heavily in favour of the banker, in Great Britain it is far more of a social pastime and, under the name of Pontoon (almost certainly an easy corruption of punting) it was exceptionally popular in the trenches during the First World War.

NUMBER OF PLAYERS

Any number up to ten may play (or more if two packs of cards are used).

CARDS

The full pack of 52 cards is used (but see above).

THE PLAY

The banker deals one card face downwards to each player and to himself, and the players, after looking at their cards, stake any amount up to the agreed maximum.

The object of the game is to obtain a total of 21, or as near to it as possible, but without exceeding it. For this purpose an Ace counts 11 or 1 (at the option of the holder) a court card 10, and any other card its pip value.

When the players have made their bets, the banker looks at his card, and has the right to double. In this event the players must double their bets.

The banker then deals another card, face downwards, to all the players and to himself. If a player holds a pair he may announce his intention to split. He stakes the same amount as his original bet on both cards, and the banker deals a second card to each. The player plays both hands separately. The banker may not split pairs.

If the banker holds a natural (an Ace and a court card or a 10) he turns the two cards face upwards and receives from the players double what they have staked, except that if a player also holds a natural he loses only his original stake. The hands are thrown in, and the banker deals another hand.

If the banker does not hold a natural, but a player does, the banker pays him double his stake, and, after the deal has been completed, the bank passes to him. The bank, however, does not pass on a split natural. If two or more players hold naturals, the one nearest to the banker's left takes the bank.

When all naturals (if any) have been declared and settled, the banker asks each player in turn (beginning with the one on his left) whether he wants more cards or not. The player has three options. He may *Stand*; that is he elects to take no more cards. He may *Buy*;

Banker pays B (double), C, D and F. Banker wins from A and E. Banker loses 9 units on deal.

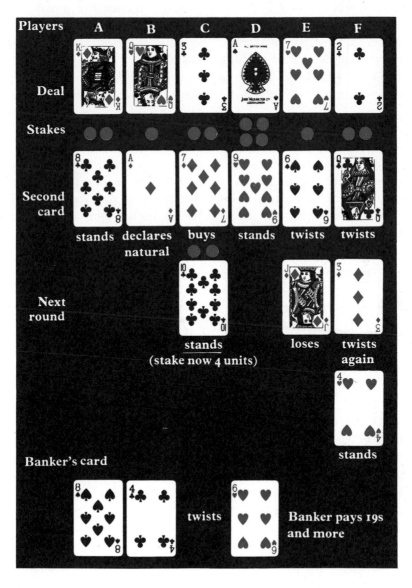

that is he increases his stake for the advantage of receiving a card face downwards. He may *Twist*; that is he does not increase his stake and receives a card face upwards. The rules to be observed are:

A player may not stand if he holds a count of 15 or less.

A player may not buy for more than his original stake.

If a player has twisted a third card he may not buy a fourth or fifth, though a player who has bought a third card may twist subsequent cards.

A player may not increase, though he may decrease, the amount for which he bought a previous card.

If a player has received four cards he may not buy a fifth if the total of his four cards is 11 or less.

Five cards is the most that a player may hold, and if they total 21 or less the banker pays him double, unless the banker also holds five cards that total 21 or less when the banker wins.

The player who makes a total of 21 with three 7s, receives triple his stake from the banker. The banker does not have this privilege.

When the total of a player's cards exceeds 21 he turns his cards face upwards and the banker wins all that he has staked.

When all the players have received cards, the banker turns his two cards face upwards and deals himself as few or as many cards as he chooses. If when doing so he exceeds a total of 21 he pays the players their stakes. At any time, however, he may elect to stand and agree to pay those players who have a higher total and receive from those who have a lower or equal total.

PATIENCE GAMES

BELEAGUERED CASTLE

SINGLE-PACK

Beleaguered Castle, also called Laying Siege and Sham Battle, has a pleasing tableau although it must be admitted that it can be a frustrating game.

The four Aces are removed from the pack and placed in a column in the centre of the table to form the foundations. The remainder of the pack is shuffled and a column of four cards is dealt to the left of the Aces, followed by a column to the right of the Aces. Succeeding columns are dealt on these successively, each column overlapping the last until the whole pack is dealt

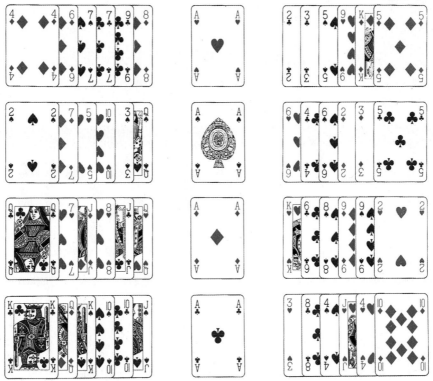

and the tableau resembles that in the illustration. The cards to the left of the Aces are called the left wing and those to the right the right wing.

The object is to build on the foundations suit sequences up to the Kings. The cards available for play are those at the far end of each row, i.e. those whose faces are fully exposed. They can be built directly onto the foundations or packed onto another available card in descending order of rank, irrespective of suit, e.g. a 6 can be packed on any 7. When one of the rows is emptied, it can be filled by any available card. There are thus always

eight available cards for play.

In the illustration, the ♡2 and ♤2 can be played to the foundations; the ♢4 to ♢5; ♧5 to ♢6; ♢3 to ♢4; ♢2 to foundation; ♢3, 4, 5 to foundation; ♤6 to ♢7; ♧4 to ♧5; ♧Q to ♧K; ♡6 to ♡7; ♢K to the space created in the rows; ♡9 to ♢10; ♤5 to ♤6; ♧3 to ♧4; ♧2 to foundation, thus clearing another row and allowing the club foundation to be built on. But the game is soon doomed to failure, there being too many high cards burying low ones. The game is a quick one and the player will soon be optimistically re-dealing, which is the way with patience games.

BISLEY

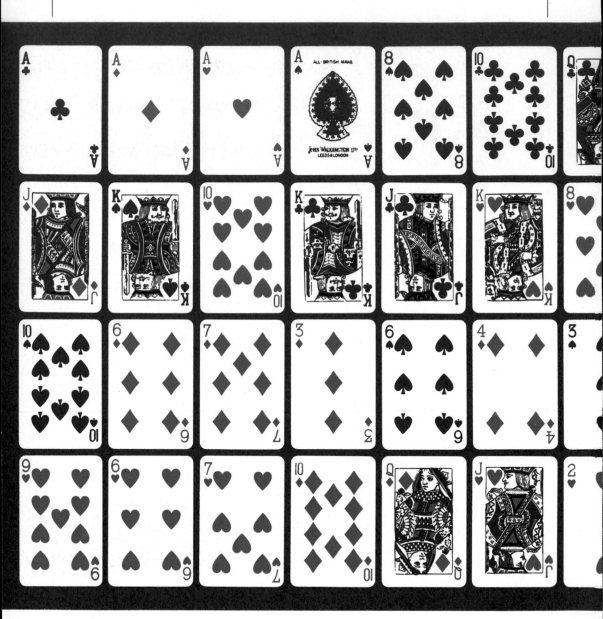

SINGLE-PACK

Remove the four Aces from the pack and place them face upwards in a row on the table. Deal nine cards in a row to the right of them, and the rest of the pack in three rows of 13 cards each, below them (see illustration). When the four Kings become available they are placed above their respective Aces.

The Aces are built on upwards and the Kings downwards in suit-

sequences. It does not matter where the two sequences meet.

Only the bottom card of a column is available for play. It may be built either on its Ace or King foundation, packed on the bottom card of another column, or itself be packed on. Packing may be either upwards or downwards in suit sequence, and the player may change this at his convenience. A space left vacant in the layout, by the removal of a card, is not filled.

In the layout illustrated, the ◇ K is played above the ◇ A, the ♤ 2 is built on the ♤ A, and the ♡ 2 on the ♡ A. This exposes the ♤ 3 which is built on the ♤ 2. The ◇ Q is built on the ◇ K. The ◇ 9 is packed on the ◇ 10, and the ◇ 8 on the ◇ 9. Now the ♧ 8 is packed on the ♧ 9, exposing the ♧ 2 which is built on the ♧ A. And so on.

CALCULATION

SINGLE-PACK

Calculation, or Broken Intervals, is a one-pack patience that is well-named, because it is necessary to calculate at the turn of every card, and it offers more scope for skilful play than any other patience.

Any Ace, any 2, any 3 and any 4 are placed in a row on the table to form four foundations. The object of the game is to build, regardless of suits, the remaining 48 cards on them, as follows:

On the Ace in the order Ace, 2, 3, 4, 5, 6, 7, 8, 9, 10, Jack, Queen, King.

On the 2 in the order 2, 4, 6, 8, 10, Queen, Ace, 3, 5, 7, 9, Jack, King.

On the 3 in the order 3, 6, 9, Queen, 2, 5, 8, Jack, Ace, 4, 7, 10, King.

On the 4 in the order 4, 8, Queen, 3, 7, Jack, 2, 6, 10, Ace, 5, 9, King.

The cards are dealt from the pack one at a time, and every card must either be built on a foundation or played to any one of a waste heap below each foundation. The pack is dealt only once, but play from a waste heap may continue after it has been exhausted. Only the top card of a waste heap may be played; it may be built on a foundation and may not be played to another waste heap.

The cards in the pack are now dealt one at a time. Suppose a 10 is dealt, as it cannot be built on a foundation it is best played to waste heap B. Next a 6 is dealt; it is built on the 3-foundation. Next comes an 8, and, of course, is built on the 4-foundation. The next card is a King. It must be played to a waste heap, but as a King is the last card to be built on a foundation it would be wrong to play it to waste

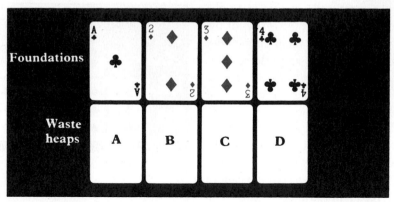

| Foundations | | | | |
| Waste heaps | A | B | C | D |

heap B and so cover the 10. It should be played to another waste heap, and experienced players would now reserve this for Kings. Play continues in this way until all 48 cards have been dealt.

If the play is carefully thought out, by building on the waste heaps descending sequences of two to four or more cards, towards the end of a game excellent progress will be made.

DEMON

SINGLE-PACK

Demon is probably the best known of all the many one-pack patiences. It is sometimes known as Fascination, sometimes as Thirteen, and, in America, as Canfield, because it was reputedly invented by Richard A. Canfield, a well-known gambler of the late 19th century, whose practice it was to sell the pack for $52 and pay $5 for every card in the foundation row when the game came to an end. It was not altogether as profitable as it may seem,

because for every player he had to employ a croupier to keep an eye on him during the play.

Thirteen cards are dealt face downwards in a pile and the top card is faced. The pile is known as the heel, and four cards are dealt face upwards in a row to the right of it. The next card of the pack is dealt face upwards and placed above the first card of the row. It indicates the foundations.

The ◇ 10 is the first of the four foundations, and the ◇ 3 is the top card of the heel. As they become available, the other three 10s are played to the right of the ◇ 10, and the object of the game is to build on them round-the-corner suit sequences up to the 9s. The four cards to the right of the heel are packed in descending sequences of alternate colours. As a start, therefore, the ◇ J is built on its foundation card; the ♣4 is packed on the ♡5 and the ◇3 on the ♣4. The card in the heel below the ◇3 is turned and, if it cannot be built on a foundation or packed on a card in the layout, is played to the space left vacant by the ◇ J. The next card in the heel is then exposed.

The bottom card of the four columns may be built on a foundation, but a sequence may be moved from one column to another only as a whole, and then only if the sequence can be packed on the next higher card of a different colour.

The stock is dealt to a waste pile in batches of three cards at a time, but if there are fewer than three cards at the

end of the stock they are dealt singly. The stock is dealt and redealt until the game is won, or lost because no further move can be made.

When all the cards in a column have been played, the space that is left must be filled at once with the top card of the heel and the next card of the heel exposed. A space must not be filled from the cards in hand, and when the heel is exhausted, spaces are filled from the waste heap, and the player need no longer fill a space at once, but leave it vacant until a suitable card is available.

GOLF

SINGLE-PACK

Golf is a patience game, but addicts of the real game of golf might like to play it against an opponent, as described later.

Seven cards are dealt face up in a row, and second, third, fourth and fifth

rows are dealt, each overlapping the previous row, until 35 cards are dealt in a tableau as shown in the illustration. This tableau is known as the 'links'.

The remainder of the cards are held in the hand and dealt one at a time to a talon or waste heap. Any of the cards exposed in the bottom row of the links are available to play onto the top card of the talon in either ascending or descending order, irrespective of suit. As many cards as possible may be played onto the talon at a turn, and the sequence may go up and down at will. However, the sequence does not go 'round-the-corner', i.e. Aces cannot be played onto Kings and vice-versa.

When a card has been removed from the bottom row, the card below it becomes available for play, i.e. a card fully exposed is available.

The object is to clear as many cards from the links as possible by the time the cards in the hand have run out. The number of cards remaining in the links

is the score for the hole. Eighteen such holes are played to establish a player's score for the round. Sometimes the links will be cleared before all the cards in hand are exhausted, in which case the cards in hand represent a minus score for the hole, and can be deducted from a player's total. The object when played purely as a patience game is to beat par: 72 'strokes'.

In the layout in the illustration the ◇7 is turned over as the first card from hand onto the waste heap. Cards from the links can be played onto the ◇7 as follows: ♠8, ◇9, ◇10, ♡J, ♡Q, ♣J, ♣10. A good start. The next card is turned over and so on.

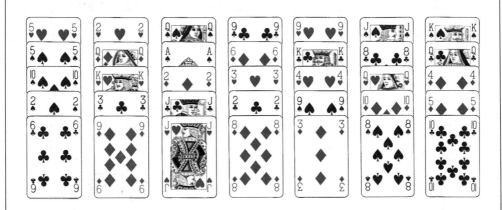

COMPETITIVE GOLF

Golf Patience can be played as a competitive game by two or more players. Each player has his own pack, and each deals 35 cards into a links as related. Each player plays a hole simultaneously so that each records a score for each of the 18 holes, the lowest being the winner.

Two players can play 'match-play', in which instead of recording the score for each hole, each hole is either won, lost or halved, so that at any stage a player is 'two-up', 'three down', etc, as in the real game. Four can play as a 'four-ball', i.e. in two partnerships, each player using his own pack and only the lower score of each pair counting.

It is well known that patience players face a great temptation to cheat from time to time. Of course, players taking part in Competitive Golf must be as scrupulous over the rules as their counterparts out on the course.

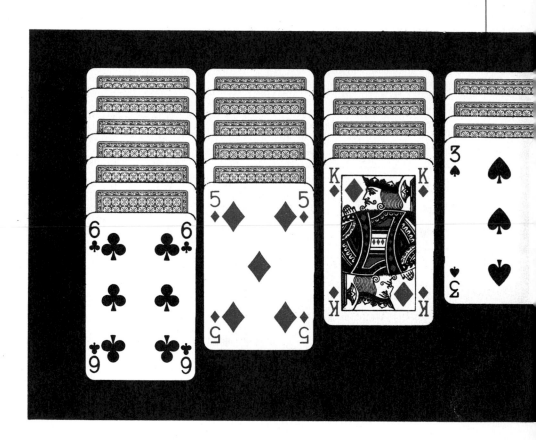

KLONDIKE

SINGLE-PACK

The Demon (see page 227) and the Klondike are probably the two best-known and most popular of the one-pack patience games. In England the name of Canfield is sometimes attached to the Klondike. This name, however, is a misnomer, and to be corrected, because Canfield is the name that in America is given to the patience that in England is called the Demon.

Twenty-eight cards are dealt face downwards in slightly overlapping rows of seven cards, six cards, five cards, four cards, three cards, two cards and one card. The bottom card of each row is turned face upwards (see illustration).

As they become available, Aces are played as foundations to a row above the layout; the object of the game is to

build on the Aces ascending suit sequences to the Kings.

An exposed card at the bottom of a column is available to be built on a foundation, or it may be packed in a descending sequence of alternate colour. A sequence may be moved from one column to another, but only as a whole and when the highest card of the sequence may be placed on the next higher card of another colour. When an exposed card is played, the face-downwards card immediately above it is turned face upwards; when a whole column is moved, the space must be filled by a King which may or may not have a sequence attached to it.

The stock is dealt one card at a time to a waste heap, of which the top card is available for building on a foundation or packing on a column in the layout. Only one deal is allowed.

An Ace must be played to the foundation row as soon as it becomes available, but all other cards may be left in position if the player prefers to wait on the prospect of finding a better move later in the game.

In the layout shown the ◇5 is packed on the ♣6, and the card under the ◇5 is turned face upwards. The ♣J is packed on the ♡Q, and the ◇K moved to fill the space vacated by the ♣J. The card under the ◇K is now turned face upwards. And so on.

JOKER KLONDIKE

Klondike has been the subject of several variations. One of the best is Joker Klondike. It is played in the same way as the parent game, but with the Joker added to the pack. Whenever the Joker becomes available for play it must be built on a foundation as the next card in sequence. Other cards, if in correct sequence, are built on it, but when the natural card that it replaces becomes available it is substituted for the Joker which is built on another foundation.

A player may choose on which foundation he will build the Joker. If it becomes available for play before a foundation has been started it must remain in its position until an Ace turns up and a foundation started.

LA BELLE LUCIE

SINGLE-PACK

La Belle Lucie, or the Fan, is one of the classical one-pack patiences; it has a very pleasing layout. The entire pack is spread on the table in 17 fans of three cards each and one of a single card, as illustrated.

As the Aces become available they are placed above the layout as foundations, to be built on in ascending suit sequences to the Kings. Only the end

card of each fan and the single card are available for play. They may be built on a foundation, packed on the end card of another fan in descending suit sequence, or themselves be packed on in descending suit sequences. A space made by playing off a complete fan is not filled.

When all possible moves have been made, all the cards except those played to the foundations are picked up, shuffled, and redealt in fans of three. If one or two cards are left over they make separate fans. Two redeals are allowed.

In the layout illustrated the ♡A and ♣A are played to the foundation row. The ♡2 is built on the ♡A, and the ♣7 is packed on the ♣8. This releases the ♣2 that is built on the ♣A. The ◇J is packed on the ◇Q, the ♡J on the ♡Q, and the ♠A followed by the ♠2 go to the foundation row. And so on.

LITTLE SPIDER

SINGLE-PACK

The red Aces and the two black Kings (or the two black Aces and the two red Kings) are placed in a row on the table to serve as foundations. The remaining 48 cards are dealt, face upwards, in two rows of four cards each, one above the foundation cards, the other below them.

The object of the game is to build ascending suit sequences on the Aces to Kings, and descending suit sequences on the Kings to Aces.

During the deal a card may be built from the upper row on any of the four foundation cards, but from the lower row only on the foundation card directly above it.

After every batch of eight cards has been dealt, the top cards of all eight piles are playable and may be built on any foundation cards or packed on any other pile in the layout. The piles are packed in ascending or descending, continuous sequences (an Ace ranks below a 2 and above a King) regardless of suit. A space made by removing an entire pile is not filled.

In the layout illustrated, the ♣Q may be built on the ♣K and the ♡2 on the ♡A. The ♣10 may be packed on the ♠J, and the ♣5 on the ♠6. And so on.

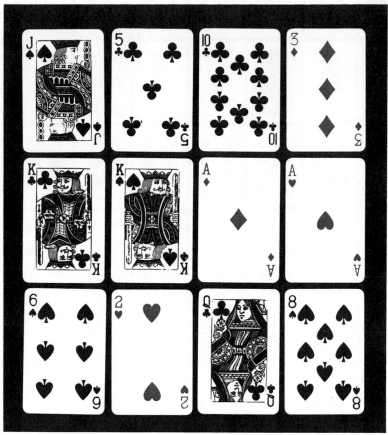

MAZE

SINGLE-PACK

Maze is an excellent patience because some skill is necessary if it is to be successful.

The 52 cards of the pack are dealt face upwards in two rows of eight cards each, and four of nine cards each.

The four Kings are then discarded. This leaves four spaces, or six in all, because as well as the spaces left by the discard of the Kings, the spaces at the end of the first and second rows are taken into the layout for the play (see illustration).

The object of the game is to arrange

the 48 cards in four ascending suit sequences, from Aces to Queens, beginning with an Ace at the extreme left of the top row and ending with a Queen at the extreme right of the bottom row. The sequences follow on, from the end of one row to the beginning of the next, as in reading. Only one card may be moved at a time.

The rules for moving a card into a space are:

The card must be in suit sequence one higher than the card on the left of the space or one lower than the card on the right of the space, and it is to be assumed that not only are the rows continuous but that the bottom row is continuous with the top row.

When a space occurs on the right of a Queen it may be filled with any Ace, as an alternative to the card one lower in suit sequence than the card on the right of the space.

Suppose the layout is as in the illustration. After the four Kings have been discarded, the space left vacant by the ♡K may be filled by any Ace, or with the ♤9 (by reason of the ♤10 on the right of the space) or the ♤8 (by reason of the ♤7 at the end of the bottom row). The space at the extreme right of the top row may be filled either with the ♡2 or ♡4, that at the extreme right of the second row either with the ♡10 or ♤10. The space left vacant by the ◇K may be filled either with the ♧Q or ♤5.

To begin the game play the ♤A to the top left corner of the layout, and the ♡10 to its vacant place. Play the ◇5 to the left of the ◇6 in the top row, and the ◇J to the left of the ◇Q in the bottom row. Play the ♤10 to the extreme right of the second row, and the ♤2 followed by the ♤3 to the right of the ♤A in the top row. Play the ♤5 to the left of the ♤6, the ♧J to the left of the ♧Q and the ♤4 to the left of the ♤5. The ♡5 is played to the left of the ♡6, the ♡9 to the left of the ♡10 and the ♤9 to the left of the ♤10. Now the ◇5 in the top row may be played to the right of the ◇4 and the ♤4 to the right of the ♤3 in the top row. With the ♤A, ♤2, ♤3 and ♤4 in position, the game progresses well.

MISS MILLIGAN

DOUBLE-PACK

This is a classic patience, the enduring popularity of which must be due, in part, to its amazing ability to turn out from apparently hopeless positions.

Use two packs shuffled together, and deal out eight cards side by side, face up. Take out any Aces to start the building – the object of the game is to build all eight Aces in sequence and in suit up to their Kings. Having taken the Aces out, pack the remaining cards in descending sequence, red on black

(or black on red) wherever they fit. You may also build any 2s which fit onto their Aces, and 3s on the 2s etc. Kings may be moved into spaces.

When no further building or packing can be done, deal out another eight cards on top of the piles (or into the spaces where piles have been emptied), then pause for another session of building and packing. Any card or properly packed sequence which fits may be moved from the top of one pile and packed onto the top of another pile. Aces are taken out as they appear,

Miss Milligan in progress.

and building onto these Aces is allowed during the packing.

The illustration shows a position reached after three deals and some packing. From this position we can pack the sequence from ◇J down to ♤6 onto the ♤Q, then build the ♤2 onto the ♤A, and the ♤3 onto the ♤2. No more packing can be done, so eight more cards are then dealt out.

Continue to alternate phases of packing and dealing until all the cards have been dealt out. You will probably have reached a pretty hopeless looking position, with all the cards you really need buried under something else, but at this point we introduce a new rule.

The rule is called 'waiving' and the process of waiving is simply to pick up the top card from one of the piles and

hold it in your hand, continuing the play as if it didn't exist until you find somewhere to build or pack it. You may only waive one card at a time, but this is often enough to bring the patience out. Some people allow a whole sequence to be waived at once so long as it is properly packed.

A technique which is particularly useful in Miss Milligan is the transfer of parts of sequences. Suppose, for example, that you have an awkward sequence with a black Jack at the top of it blocking one of the piles, and that there is another black Jack exposed elsewhere. Then you can transfer the bottom part of the sequence, from the red 10 downward, to the other Jack, then waive the offending Jack and start work on the rest of the pile.

PAGANINI

DOUBLE-PACK

Paganini is a double-pack patience game, similar in principle to but more interesting than, the single-pack game known as Spaces. It was composed by Mr Charles Jewell.

The entire pack is dealt face up-wards on the table in eight rows of 13 cards each, as shown in the illustration overleaf.

The object of the game is to arrange the cards so that each row consists of one suit beginning with an Ace (on the left) and ending with a King (on the right). No row is singled out for any particular suit; the player makes his own decision but, having made it, must not alter it.

Play begins by moving one of the Aces to the extreme left of a row. It will be appreciated, therefore, that as the game proceeds the whole of the layout is moved one space to the left so to speak. When a card is moved it leaves a space in the layout which is filled with the next higher card of the same suit as the card on the left of the space. Filling a space leaves another space in the layout. In turn this is filled in the same way, and so on, until a run is brought to an end by removing a card from the right-hand side of a King, because no

card is available to be played to the space on the right of a King.

The game calls for a show of skill. To begin, a player has to decide which of the eight Aces he will move first and to the extreme left of which of the eight rows he will move it to. Then, when-ever a card is moved in the layout, there is, at all events early in the play, a choice of two cards to fill the available space. It will be seen, therefore, that when all eight Aces have been moved to the extreme left of the layout, each move will offer the choice of filling one of eight spaces with either of two cards.

The layout in the illustration is not as difficult as it may appear. Indeed, with a little care the game should be won.

After a general survey of the possi-bilities in the game, the ♡A in the bottom row should be moved to the extreme left of the row; the ♡Q in the fifth row is moved to the space left vacant by the ♡A; and the ♣9 in the bottom row is moved into the space left vacant by the ♡Q. The space left vacant by the ♣9 may be filled either with the ♡2 in the second row or the one in the seventh row. Consideration shows that it should be filled with the one in the second row, because the ♣6

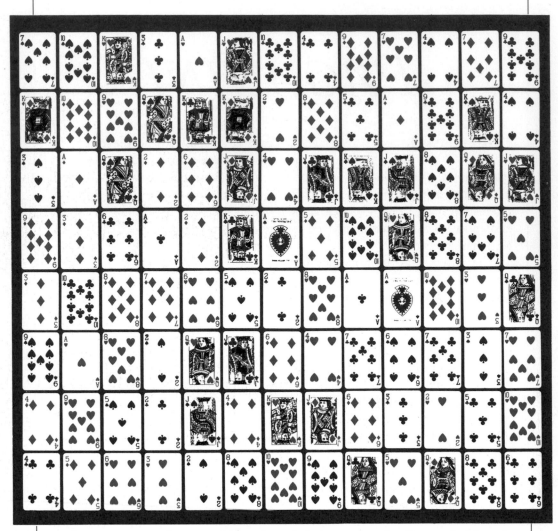

in the top row can be moved into the vacant space, the ♣A in the fifth row can be moved to the extreme left of the top row, the ♣6 in the top row can be moved to the space in the second row left vacant by the ♡2, and either the ♣2 in the second row or that in the fourth row can be moved into the space (alongside the ♣A) left vacant by the ♣6. And so on.

ROYAL PARADE

DOUBLE-PACK

Royal Parade is a popular two-pack patience with the alternative names of Financier, Hussars and Three Up.

Twenty-four cards are dealt in three rows of eight cards each (see illustration). Aces take no part in the game and are discarded. The cards in the layout must be arranged so that the top row consists of eight 2s, the middle row of eight 3s, and the bottom row of eight 4s, and these cards must be built on in suit sequences at intervals of three cards, namely:

2	3	4
5	6	7
8	9	10
J	Q	K

In the layout illustrated the ◇A, in the top row, and the ♣A, in the

bottom row, are discarded; the ♠4, in the middle row, is moved to the space in the bottom row left vacant by the discard of the ♣A, and the ♠7, in the top row, built on it. Either the ♡3 or ♣3, both in the top row, may be moved to fill the space in the middle row left vacant by the ♠4, and clearly the ♡3 should be chosen because the ♡6 in the bottom row may be built on it. And so on.

When all moves have been made, eight cards are dealt to waste heaps below the layout. Aces, as they are dealt, are discarded; other cards are used to build on the foundations or to fill spaces in the layout. Play continues in this way, making moves after each deal of eight cards to the waste heaps, until the pack is exhausted. Only the top cards of the waste heaps may be moved to the layout.

SAINT HELENA

DOUBLE-PACK

Saint Helena, or Napoleon's Favourite, is a two-pack patience in which the packs are not shuffled together but used one after the other. Although the game gives a player some scope for ingenuity and the exercise of his memory, it is such a simple game that one rather doubts that it received its name because it was Napoleon's chief amusement during his last years.

An Ace and a King of each suit are arranged in two rows, the Kings above the Aces. Twelve cards are then dealt, clockwise, beginning above the left-hand King, as shown in the diagram on the opposite page.

The Kings are built on in descending suit sequences to the Aces, and the Aces in ascending suit sequences to the Kings; with the restriction that cards dealt to spaces 1, 2, 3, 4 may be built only on the Kings, cards dealt to spaces 7, 8, 9, 10 only to the Aces, and cards dealt to spaces 5, 6, 11, 12 to either.

When all moves have been made the spaces are filled from the pack, and when no further moves are to be made, another 12 cards are dealt to cover the cards in position.

When the pack has been exhausted, the restriction of play is lifted, and cards may be built on any foundation from any one of the 12 surrounding waste heaps. Also, the top card of each

waste heap may now be packed on either in ascending or descending suit sequence.

Three deals in all are allowed. The waste heaps are picked up in reverse order 12 ... 1, and turned face downwards, so that the bottom card of the 12th waste heap becomes the top card of the re-made stock. No shuffling is allowed.

SPIDER

DOUBLE-PACK

There are several variations of Spider. The one described in this article is deservedly considered the best, and, indeed, among the best of all patiences, because it frequently calls for deep analysis. According to *Redbook Magazine* it was the favourite patience of the late President Franklin D. Roosevelt.

Forty cards are dealt to the table in four overlapping rows of ten cards each: the first, second and third rows face downwards, the fourth row face upwards, as in the illustration overleaf.

Foundation cards are not played to the centre. The game is to build within the layout descending suit sequences

on the eight Kings to the Aces. A completed sequence is discarded, so that the game is won when the table is cleared of all cards.

The cards at the bottom of the columns may be packed in descending sequences irrespective of suit and colour, and when a card is moved from one column to another the face-downwards card immediately above it is turned face upwards and becomes available for play.

In the diagram any of the three sixes may be packed on the ♠7 and the ♢9

may be packed on either of the tens. Two cards will thus be exposed.

When all the cards have been moved from a column, the space may be filled by any exposed card or sequence.

After all possible moves have been made, and spaces filled, ten cards are dealt from the stock, face upwards, one to the bottom of each column, overlapping the cards in position.

Play is continued in this way until the stock is exhausted. The last deal from the stock will, of course, be of only four cards.

SULTAN

DOUBLE-PACK

Sultan, sometimes, but rarely, known as Emperor of Germany, is a two-pack patience that calls for some skill if it is to be successful.

The eight Kings and one ♡ A are removed from the pack and arranged on the table as shown in the illustration

overleaf. With the exception of the central ♡ K they serve as foundations to be built up in suit sequences to the Queens, the Aces ranking between the Kings and the 2s.

On each side of the foundations deal a column of four cards, as shown in the illustration. It is known as the divan, and the cards dealt to it are available to

be built on the foundations. When one is played, the space is filled either from the stock or from the waste heap, but need not be filled immediately.

The pack is turned one card at a time to a waste heap, and may be dealt three times.

Management of the divan is of great importance. The general rule is not to fill a space with a card that is unlikely to be wanted during the immediate deal. If, for example, a foundation is built up to a 7, and both 8s are already buried, the 9s and higher cards should be played to the waste heap, because if used to fill a space in the divan they would be wasted.

TERRACE

DOUBLE-PACK

Also known as Signora and Queen of Italy, this is an excellent patience which calls for considerable foresight. Its special feature is that all the blocking cards (the problems you will have to dodge round) are laid out in a line at the beginning.

Shuffle two packs together. Deal out 11 cards in an overlapping line, the 'terrace', so that you can see what they all are. Leave space below them for the eight bases on which you will be building. Below that deal out four cards side by side, then stop and think.

At this stage you must choose one of the four cards. That card and the other seven of the same rank will form the bases for all the building, though you have to wait for the others to appear. The choice will depend on the cards in the terrace.

Having chosen your base card, put it in the building area, fill the gap it occupied from the pack, and deal out another five cards to make a row of nine. These form the working area, where packing is allowed. Continue packing these cards, taking out base cards for building and filling in the gaps until you get stuck, then turn over cards from the pack to start forming a waste pile. When you get to the end of the pack, there is no redeal – if the cards are not all built onto the bases by then you have failed.

Cards are built up on the bases in sequence, alternating red and black cards and increasing, turning the corner from King to Ace to 2 when you reach it. The exposed cards in the working area, the top card of the waste pile and the top card of the terrace are available for building.

Within the working area, packing is done in descending sequence, alternating red and black cards, turning the

Terrace soon after the waste pile has been started.

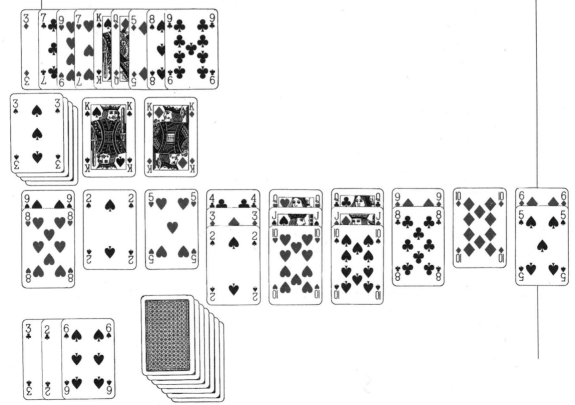

corner from 2 to Ace to King as necessary. Only one card at a time may be moved – sequences in the working area can only be moved by building – and gaps which appear may only be filled with the top card of the waste pile. Cards from the terrace may not be used for packing – they must be built directly. The only cards available for packing are single cards in the working area and the top card of the waste pile.

The illustration shows a game shortly after the waste pile has been started. Kings were chosen as base cards, and three of them have been found. One of these has been built up to a black 3, getting rid of the first two cards of the terrace in the process. In order to get rid of the next card, the ♧9, it will be necessary to find a red 4, a black 5, and so on up to a red 8 (the 5, the 6 and the 8 are already waiting in the working area, so this won't be too

difficult). Note that it is illegal to pack the ♡8 and ♤9 onto the ♡10 in the working area, since only one card may be moved at a time.

The art of getting this patience to turn out is to work out in advance where the terrace cards are going, and not to do any building which does not contribute directly to this aim. For much of the time you will be turning cards from the pack to the waste pile, waiting for some particular card to come up so that you can move the top card off the terrace. While doing this, though, you can prepare a 'reception committee' for the next cards in line down the terrace. It hardly matters how big the waste pile becomes – it has an almost magical way of disappearing once the terrace has been got rid of. With care this patience can be turned out successfully about half the number of attempts.

THREE BLIND MICE

SINGLE-PACK

This is a simple patience which more or less operates itself. This one does not turn out very often (about one time in ten) and has a way of getting stuck very near the end which you may find

amusing or aggravating depending on temperament.

Use a single 52-card pack and deal out ten piles of five cards, overlapping so that you can see all the faces, as shown in the illustration. All the cards in the seven piles on the left should be

Three Blind Mice starting position.

face up, but the bottom three cards in each of the three piles on the right should be face down. Keep the two odd cards on one side and play them wherever possible.

The object is to build each of the four suits in descending sequence (Queen on King, 8 on 9, etc.) from King down to Ace. This is done directly by building cards onto each other in suit. For this purpose the card being built onto must be on top of its pile, but the card doing the building can be anywhere except further down the same pile, so long as it is face up. If there are other cards on top of the one being built, they are carried with it.

When one of the 'blind' cards is exposed it is turned over and can join in the play.

Kings may be played into the spaces which arise when one of the ten piles becomes empty.

The illustration shows the start of a game. From here we can put the ♠Q directly on to the ♠K, but the ◇5 has to wait until the ◇6 is exposed.

The building might start with the ♣7 being played on the ♣8, keeping the ♣3 and ♡A on top of it. This exposes the ♡3, so we can continue by putting the ♡2 (and ◇7) on the ♡3. Now one of the blind cards is exposed and can be turned over.

WINDMILL

DOUBLE-PACK

The game known as Windmill or Propeller gets its name from the layout. Any King is placed face upwards on the table, and two cards are dealt above it, two below it, and two on each side of it, to form a cross (see illustration). The first four Aces that are dealt, whether to the layout or as the stock is turned, are played to the angles of the cross.

The object of the game is to build on the central King a descending, round-the-corner, sequence of 52 cards, regardless of suit and colour, and ascending suit sequences, regardless of suit and colour, on the four Aces to the Kings.

In the layout shown, the ♢A is played to an angle of the cross, the ♢Q is built on the ♤K, and the ♡J on the ♢Q. At any time a card may be taken from an Ace foundation and played to the King foundation, but only one card may be taken from each Ace-foundation during the building of any one sequence on the King foundation.

The stock is turned to a waste heap, and a space in the layout must be filled

from the waste heap, or from the stock if there is no waste heap.

There is no second deal, but when the stock is exhausted, the waste heap may be taken up and the first card dealt. If it can be played to a foundation, the next card is dealt, and so on. The game, however, comes to an end when a card can no longer be played to a foundation.

GLOSSARY

All pastimes have a vocabulary their own. That of card playing is probably the most extensive, because there are so many different games and most are of obscure origin. This list, therefore, is by no means complete and comprehensive; rather it includes only the words and expressions that are used in this book and, due to limitation of space, those that are self-explanatory and those that most readers may be expected to know are omitted.

ABOVE THE LINE. In games of the Bridge family, bonus scores and penalty scores are recorded above a horizontal line across the scoresheet. cf BELOW THE LINE.

ABUNDANCE (ABONDANCE). In games of the Solo Whist family, a declaration to win nine tricks.

ALONE. In Euchre, the right of the player who has named the trump suit to play without his partner.

ANTE. A compulsory bet made before the deal.

ASSIST. In Euchre, a declaration made by the dealer's partner to accept the suit of the turn-up card as the trump suit.

BANCO. A bet equal to the amount staked by the banker.

BASTO. The ♣A in Ombre.

BEG. In games of the All Fours family, a rejection by the non-dealer of the suit of the turn-up card as the trump suit.

BELLA. In Klaberjass, an announcement made by the player who holds the King and Queen of the trump suit, after he has played the second one, allowing him to score 20 points.

BELOW THE LINE. In games of the Bridge family, scores for tricks bid and won are recorded below a horizontal line across the scoresheet. cf ABOVE THE LINE.

BETE. In Pinocle, failure to make the contract. cf DOUBLE BETE and SINGLE BETE.

BEZIQUE. In games of the Bezique family, the ♠Q (or ♣Q if spades or diamonds are trumps) and ◇J (or ♡J if spades or diamonds are trumps).

BLACK MARIA. In games of the Black Maria family,,the ♠Q.

BLITZ. In Gin Rummy, winning a game against an opponent who has failed to score.

BOODLE CARDS. In games of the New-market family, the Ace, King, Queen and Jack, each of a different suit, from another pack, placed in a layout and on which bets are staked.

BOOK. In games of the Bridge and Whist families, the first six tricks won by a side, that do not count in the scoring.

BOTTOM LAYOUT. In Monte Bank, the two cards from the bottom of the pack placed by the banker face upwards on the table. cf TOP LAYOUT.

BOWER. In Euchre, the Jack of a suit. cf LEFT BOWER and RIGHT BOWER.

BOX. In Gin Rummy, the score for winning a hand.

BRAGGERS. In Brag, the ◇A ♣J and ◇9,

that serve as wild cards.

BRISQUE. In games of the Bezique family, any Ace or 10.

BUILD. (1) In Casino, the play of a card to a card in the layout to make up a total that may be taken with another card in the hand. (2) In games of Patience, the play of a card of the same suit on the next one above or below it in rank.

BUY. Increasing a bet for the advantage of drawing a card face downwards.

BURY A CARD. In Pinocle, discarding face downwards a card from hand.

CACHETTE. In Quinto, the widow-hand.

CALYPSO. In Calypso, a complete suit, from Ace to 2, in a player's trump suit.

CANASTA. In games of the Canasta family, a meld of seven or more cards. cf MIXED CANASTA and NATURAL CANASTA.

CAPOT. In Piquet, the winning by one player of all 12 tricks.

CARDS. In Piquet, the score for winning the majority of tricks.

CARTE BLANCHE. A hand that contains no court card.

CASH. Leading and winning a trick with an established card.

CASINO. cf GREAT CASINO and LITTLE CASINO.

CENTRE. In games of Patience, that part of the table to which the foundation cards are played.

CHECK. In Poker, a nominal bet that reserves the right to call or raise if another player bets.

CODILLE. In Ombre, one opponent winning more tricks than ombre.

COMBINE. In Casino, picking up cards from the layout of the total pip value of a card in hand.

COMET. In games of the Comet family, a wild card, usually a 9.

COMMON MARRIAGE. In games of the Bezique family, the meld of the King and Queen of the same plain suit. cf ROYAL MARRIAGE.

CONDITIONS. In Panguingue, certain melds by making which a player immediately collects chips from all other players.

CONTRA. A call which doubles the score for a hand in Skat.

COUP. A winning play or bet.

COURT CARD. Any King, Queen or Jack.

CRIB. In Cribbage, an extra hand formed by the discards of the players.

CUT THROAT. A version of what is usually a partnership game in which each player plays for himself.

DIS. In Pinocle, the 9 of the trump suit.

DISCARD. The play of a card that is not of the suit led nor a trump.

DOUBLE BETE. In Pinocle, the penalty suffered by the bidder whose score for melds and cards taken in tricks fails to equal his contract. cf SINGLE BETE.

DOUBLETON. An original holding of two cards of a suit.

DUMMY. In games of the Bridge family, the partner of the declarer, and the hands he exposes on the table.

ELDER HAND. In Piquet and other games for two players, the non-dealer. cf YOUNGER HAND.

ELDEST HAND. The player who sits next to the dealer and whose privilege it is to play first. In most games, this is the player to dealer's left, but in a few games, such as Panguingue, where play rotates anti-clockwise, it is the player to dealer's right.

EUCHRE. In Euchre, failure to win at least three tricks.

FACE CARD. Same as COURT CARD *q.v.*

FIFTEEN. In Cribbage, the play of a card which, with those already played, adds up to fifteen.

FINESSE. An attempt to win a trick with a card that is not the best held nor in sequence with it.

FLUSH. A hand with all cards of the same suit.

FOLLOW SUIT. To play a card of the same suit as that of the led card.

FOOT. In Panguingue, the lower half of the stock set aside for use if the HEAD *q.v.* is exhausted.

FOREHAND. In Skat and Schafkopf, the player to the dealer's left. cf MIDDLEHAND.

FOUNDATION. In games of Patience, a card played to the centre on which a complete suit or sequence must be built.

GATE. In Monte Bank, the bottom card of the pack.

GIFT. In games of the All Fours family, the point scored by the dealer if he begs and the dealer decides to play.

GIN. In Gin Rummy, a hand in which all the cards are melded.

GO. In Cribbage, the announcement that a player cannot play without exceeding 31.

GO DOWN or GO OUT. Same as KNOCK (1) *q.v.*

GOULASH. In Towie, a redeal of the four hands unshuffled and with each hand arranged in suits.

GRAND. In Skat, a contract in which the four Jacks in effect form a trump suit of their own.

GRAND SLAM. In games of the Bridge and Whist families, the winning of all 13 tricks. cf SMALL SLAM.

GREAT CASINO. In Casino, the ◇ 10. cf LITTLE CASINO.

HAND CARDS. In Lansquenet, the two top cards of the pack exposed face upwards on the table.

HEAD. In Panguingue, the top half of the stock. cf FOOT.

HEEL. Same as TALON *q.v.*

HIGH. In games of the All Fours family, the score for being dealt the highest trump in play. cf LOW.

HIS HEELS. In Cribbage, a Jack turned up as the start.

HIS NOB. In Cribbage, the Jack, either in hand or crib, of the same suit as the start.

HOLE CARD. In Stud Poker, the first card dealt, face downwards, to a player.

HONOURS. (1) In games of the Bridge family, the Ace, King, Queen, Jack and 10 of a suit. (2) In Whist, the Ace, King, Queen and Jack of a suit.

HUITIÈME. In Piquet, a sequence of eight cards.

IN HAND. In Skat, a contract in which the declarer does not look at the skat.

INTRIGUE. In Pope Joan, the Queen and Jack of the trump suit played by the same player.

JACK. In games of the All Fours family, the score for winning the Jack of the trump suit.

JACKPOT. In Poker, a deal in which a player must hold at least a pair of Jacks to open.

JASZ. In Klaberjass, the Jack of the trump suit.

JINX. In Spoil Five, an undertaking, by the player who has won three tricks, to win the remaining two.

JOKER. An extra card supplied with the standard 52-card pack used in some games as a wild card.

KITTY. Same as POOL *q.v.*

KNOCK. (1) In games of the Rummy family, signification by a player that all his cards are melded. (2) In Poker, signification by a player that no further bet will be made by him.

LAYING OFF. (1) In Gin Rummy, the playing of cards to opponent's melds. (2) In Panguingue the playing of cards to one's own melds.

LAYOUT. Cards laid out on the table in a prescribed pattern either for the purpose of placing bets or to be moved in accordance with the rules of the game.

LEAST. In Schafkopf, the hand played when no player has offered to be Player, so each plays for himself.

LEFT BOWER. In Euchre, the Jack of the same colour as the Jack of the trump suit. cf RIGHT BOWER.

LEFT PEDRO. In Cinch, the 5 of the same colour as the 5 of the trump suit. cf RIGHT PEDRO.

LITTLE CASINO. In Casino, the ♠2. cf GREAT CASINO.

LOO. In Loo, failure to win a trick.

LOW. In games of the All Fours family, the score made by the player who is dealt the lowest trump in play. cf HIGH.

LURCH. In Cribbage, winning a game before the opponent has gone half-way round the scoring board.

MAKER. The player who names the trump suit.

MANILLE. In Ombre, the ♡7 or ◇7 if either suit is trumps, the ♠2 or ♣2 if either suit is trumps.

MARCH. In Euchre, winning all five tricks by one side or one player.

MARRIAGE. cf COMMON MARRIAGE and ROYAL MARRIAGE.

MATADORES. In Ombre, the collective name for the three top trumps — SPADILLE, MANILLE and BASTO.

MATRIMONY. In Pope Joan, the King and Queen of the trump suit played by the same player.

MELD. A matched set of three or more of a kind or a sequence of three or more of the same suit in consecutive order of rank.

MENEL. In Klaberjass, the 9 of trumps.

MIDDLEHAND. In Skat and Schafkopf, the player to Dealer's right i.e. the player between FOREHAND *q.v.* and dealer.

MISÈRE. In Solo Whist, a contract not to win a trick.

MISERY. Same as MISÈRE *q.v.*

MISS. In Loo, the widow-hand.

MIXED CANASTA. In Canasta, a meld of seven or more cards of which one, two or three cards are wild. cf NATURAL CANASTA.

MUGGINS. In Cribbage, an announcement that enables a player to take points that his opponent has overlooked.

NAP. A declaration in Nap(oleon) to win all five tricks.

NATURAL CANASTA. In Canasta, a meld of seven or more cards of which none is a wild card. cf MIXED CANASTA.

NON-COMOQUER. In Panguingue, a group of Kings or Aces.

NULL. In Skat, a contract to take no tricks.

NULLO. Same as MISÈRE *q.v.*

OMBRE. In Ombre, the player who plays against the other two players in partnership against him.

ORDER UP. In Euchre, the declaration of an opponent of the dealer accepting the suit of the turn-up card as the trump suit.

PAIR. (1) In Casino, the play of a card and taking up as a trick all the other cards of the same rank in the layout. (2) In Cribbage, playing a card of the same rank as the previous one played.

PAIR-ROYAL. (1) In Brag, three cards of equal rank. (2) In Cribbage, playing a third card of the same rank as a pair.

PAM. In Loo, the ♣J.

PARTIE. In Piquet, a game.

PEDRO. cf LEFT PEDRO and RIGHT PEDRO.

PEG. In Cribbage, a marker used for scoring on a board.

PINOCLE. In Pinocle, the ♠Q and ◇J.

PITCH. In Auction Pitch, the opening lead that determines the trump suit.

PIQUE. In Piquet, the winning of 30 points in hand and play before an opponent scores. cf REPIQUE.

PLAIN SUIT. A suit other than the trump suit.

PLAYER. In Calabrasella and Schafkopf, the player who elects to play on his own against the other two players.

POINT. In Piquet, the number of cards held in the longest suit.

POLIGNAC. In Polignac, the ♠ J.

POOL. The collective amount of players' stakes and fines.

POPE. In Pope Joan, the ◇ 9.

POT. In Poker, a game in which all the players put up an ante.

PROPOSE. In Ecarté, a request by the non-dealer that cards may be exchanged for others from the stock.

PUESTA. In Ombre, ombre and one or both of his opponents winning the same number of tricks.

PUNTO. In Ombre, the Ace of whichever red suit is trumps.

QUART. In Piquet, a sequence of four cards.

QUATORZE. In Piquet, any four cards of the same rank higher than the 9.

QUINT. (1) In Piquet, a sequence of five cards. (2) In Quinto, the 5 of every suit, and every pair of cards in a suit that totals five.

QUINT ROYAL. In Quinto, the Joker.

RAISE. In Poker, increasing a bet by putting up more than is necessary to equal the previous player.

RECONTRA. In Skat, a call which after a call of Contra *q.v.* redoubles the score for a hand.

REFAIT. In *Trente et Quarante,* a drawn game.

REFUSE. (1) In games of the All Fours family, the rejection by the dealer of a proposal by the non-dealer to make another suit trumps. (2) In Ecarté, the rejection by the dealer of the non-dealer's proposal that cards may be exchanged for others from the stock.

REPIQUE. In Piquet, the winning of 30 points in hand alone before opponent scores. cf PIQUE.

REVOKE. Failure to follow suit when able to or to play a card in accordance with the laws of the game.

RIGHT BOWER. In Euchre, the Jack of the trump suit. cf LEFT BOWER.

RIGHT PEDRO. In Cinch, the 5 of the trump suit. cf LEFT PEDRO.

ROB THE PACK. In Cinch, the privilege accorded to the dealer of selecting cards from the stock.

ROUND. A division of dealing, betting or playing in which each player participates once.

ROUND THE CORNER. A sequence of cards in which the highest is considered adjacent to the lowest.

ROYAL MARRIAGE. In games of the Bezique family, the meld of the King and Queen of the trump suit. cf COMMON MARRIAGE.

RUBBER. Three successive games between the same sides or players: winning two of the three games.

RUBICON. Failure of the loser of a game to reach a specified minimum total of points.

RUFF. Playing a trump card on the lead of a card of a side suit.

RUMMY. In games of the Rummy family, the declaration by a player of all his cards in one turn.

RUN. Same as SEQUENCE *q.v.*

RUN THE CARDS. In games of the All Fours family, to deal more cards and a fresh turn up after a beg has been accepted.

SACARDO. In Ombre, ombre winning more tricks than either of his opponents individually.

SCHMEISS. In Klaberjass, an offer to play with the turn-up card as the trump suit or throw in the hand, as the opponent prefers.

SCHNEIDER. In Skat or Schafkopf, to take 90 or more card points in tricks.

SCHWARTZ. In Skat or Schafkopf, to take all the tricks.

SEPTIÈME. In Piquet, a sequence of seven cards.

SEQUENCE. Two or more cards of adjacent rank.

SIDE SUIT. Same as PLAIN SUIT *q.v.*

SINGLE BETE. In Pinocle, the concession of defeat and payment of a forfeit, without playing. cf DOUBLE BETE.

SINGLETON. An original holding of only one card of a suit.

SINK. In Piquet, omitting to announce a scoring combination.

SIXIÈME. In Piquet, a sequence of six cards.

SKAT. In Skat, the two cards remaining after a deal i.e. the WIDOW *q.v.*

SLAM. cf GRAND SLAM and SMALL SLAM.

SMALL SLAM. In games of the Bridge and Whist families, winning 12 tricks. cf GRAND SLAM.

SMUDGE. In Auction Pitch, a bid to win all four tricks.

SOLO. In games of the Solo Whist family, a bid to win five tricks.

SPADILLE. In Ombre, the ♠A.

SPINADO. In Spinado, the ♦A.

SPOIL. In Spoil Five, when no player wins three tricks.

SPREAD. In Panguingue, a meld.

STAND. (1) In games of the All Fours family, to accept the suit of the turn up card as the trump suit. (2) In *Vingt-et-Un*, to elect to take no further cards.

START. In Cribbage, the top card of the cut turned face upwards by the dealer.

STOCK. The undealt part of the pack which may be used later in the deal.

STRADDLE. In Poker, a compulsory bet of twice the ante.

STRINGER. In Panguingue, a sequence.

SWEEP. In Casino, taking in all the cards in the layout.

TABLANETTE. In Tablanette, an announcement that a player is able to take all the cards on the table.

TAKE-IT. In Klaberjass, to accept as the trump suit the suit of the turn up card.

TALON. In Piquet and some games of Patience, cards laid aside in one or more packets for later use in the same deal.

TOP LAYOUT. In Monte Bank, the two top cards of the pack placed by the banker face upwards on the table. cf BOTTOM LAYOUT.

TRAIL. In Casino, the play of a card to the layout by a player who can neither pass, combine, build nor call.

TRIO. In Piquet, three cards of the same suit higher than the 9.

TURN UP. A card faced after the deal to determine, or propose, the trump suit.

TWIST. In *Vingt-et-Un*, a request to be dealt a card face upwards.

UP CARDS. (1) In Gin Rummy, the card turned up after each player has been dealt ten cards. (2) In Stud Poker, a card dealt face upwards.

VALLE CARD. In Panguingue, the 7s, 5s and 3s, the melding of which wins chips.

VOID. Having no cards of a specified suit.

VOLE. In Ecarté, winning all five tricks.

VULNERABLE. In games of the Bridge family, being subject to bigger penalties and bonuses after winning a game.

WAIVE. The privilege, in some games of patience, to lift a card and play the one under it.

WIDOW. Extra cards dealt to the table usually at the same time as the hands are dealt to the players.

WILD CARD. A card that the rules of the game permit the holder to specify as representing any card.

YOUNGER HAND. In Piquet and other games for two players, the dealer. cf ELDER HAND.